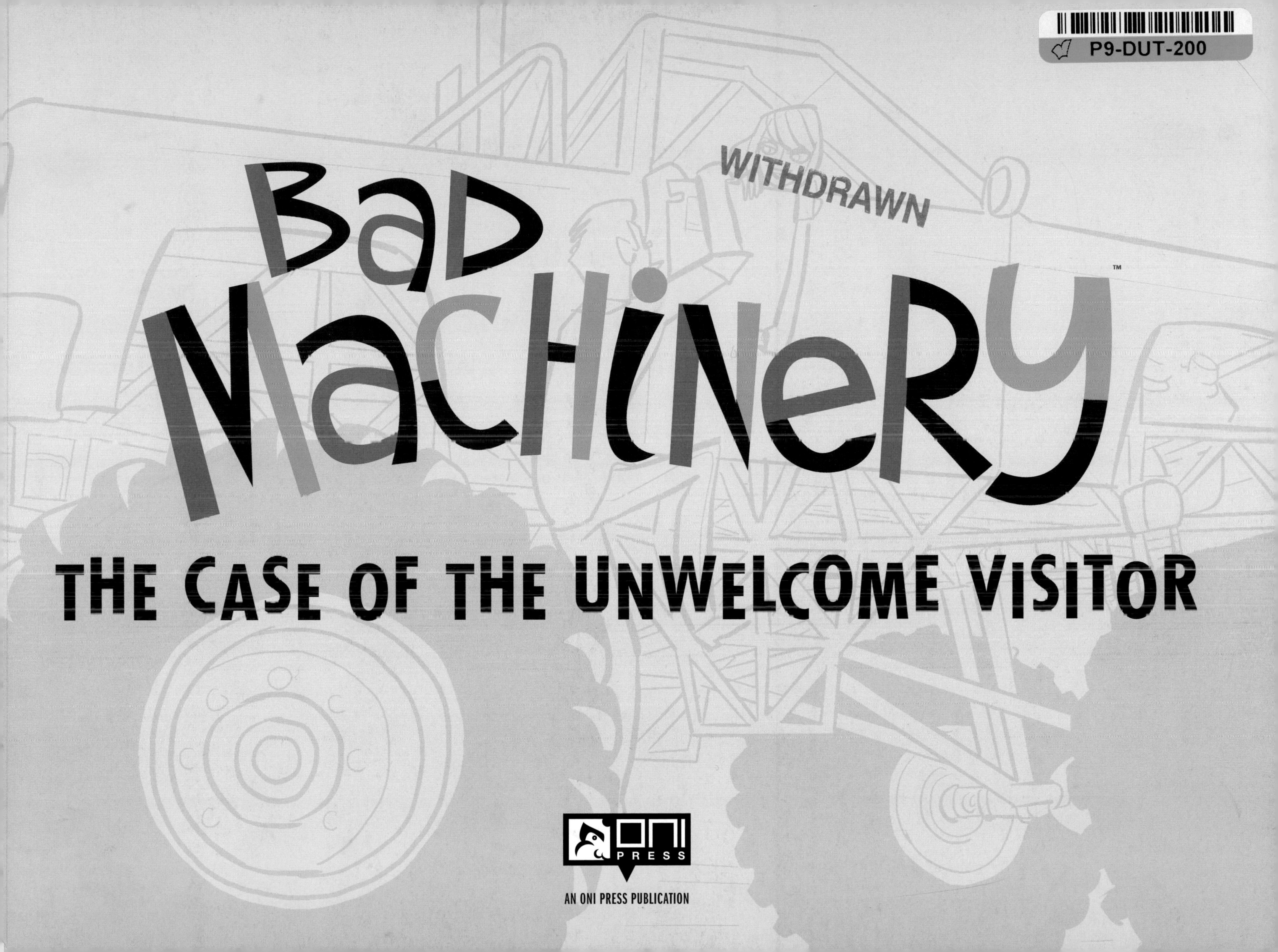

Bad Machinery™

The Case of the Unwelcome Visitor

ONI PRESS

AN ONI PRESS PUBLICATION

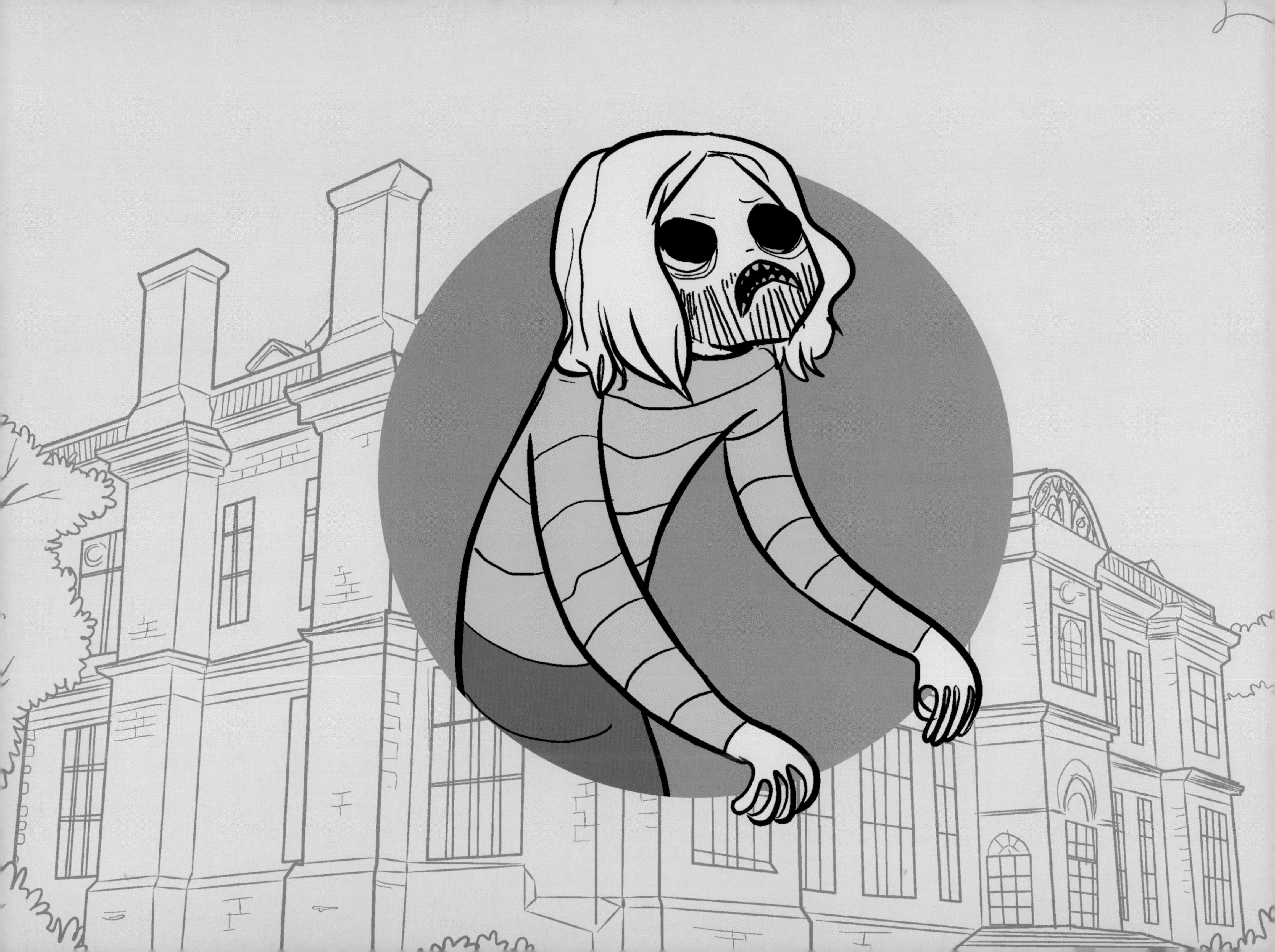

Bad Machinery™

THE CASE OF THE UNWELCOME VISITOR

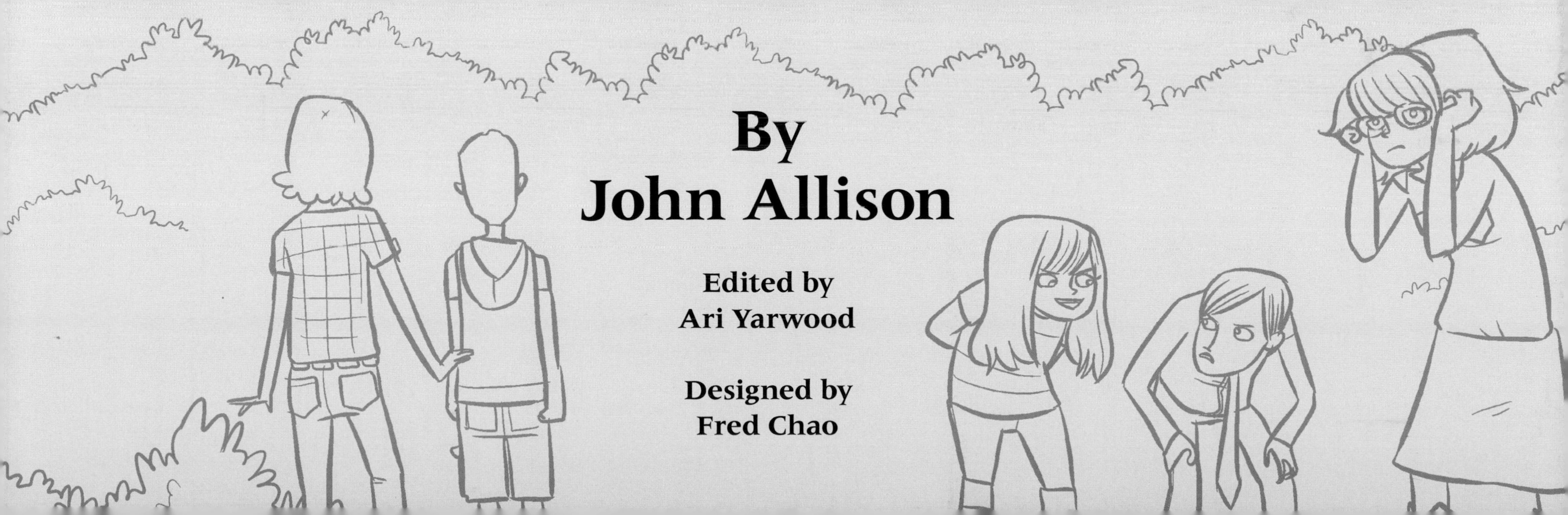

**By
John Allison**

**Edited by
Ari Yarwood**

**Designed by
Fred Chao**

Published by Oni Press, Inc.
publisher, Joe Nozemack
editor in chief, James Lucas Jones
v.p. of marketing & sales, Andrew McIntire
publicity coordinator, Rachel Reed
director of design & production, Troy Look
graphic designer, Hilary Thompson
digital art technician, Jared Jones
managing editor, Ari Yarwood
senior editor, Charlie Chu
editor, Robin Herrera
editorial assistant, Bess Pallares
director of logistics, Brad Rooks
logistics associate, Jung Lee

onipress.com
facebook.com/onipress
twitter.com/onipress
onipress.tumblr.com
instagram.com/onipress

First Edition: November 2016

ISBN 978-1-62010-351-7
eISBN 978-1-62010-352-4

Bad Machinery Volume Six: The Case of the Unwelcome Visitor, November 2016.
Published by Oni Press, Inc. 1305 SE Martin Luther King Jr. Blvd., Suite A, Portland,
OR 97214. Bad Machinery is ™ & © 2016 John Allison. All rights reserved. Oni Press
logo and icon ™ & © 2016 Oni Press, Inc. All rights reserved. Oni Press logo and icon
artwork created by Keith A. Wood. The events, institutions, and characters presented
in this book are fictional. Any resemblance to actual persons, living or dead, is purely
coincidental. No portion of this publication may be reproduced, by any means, without
the express written permission of the copyright holders.

Printed in Singapore.

Library of Congress Control Number: 2012953355

1 2 3 4 5 6 7 8 9 10

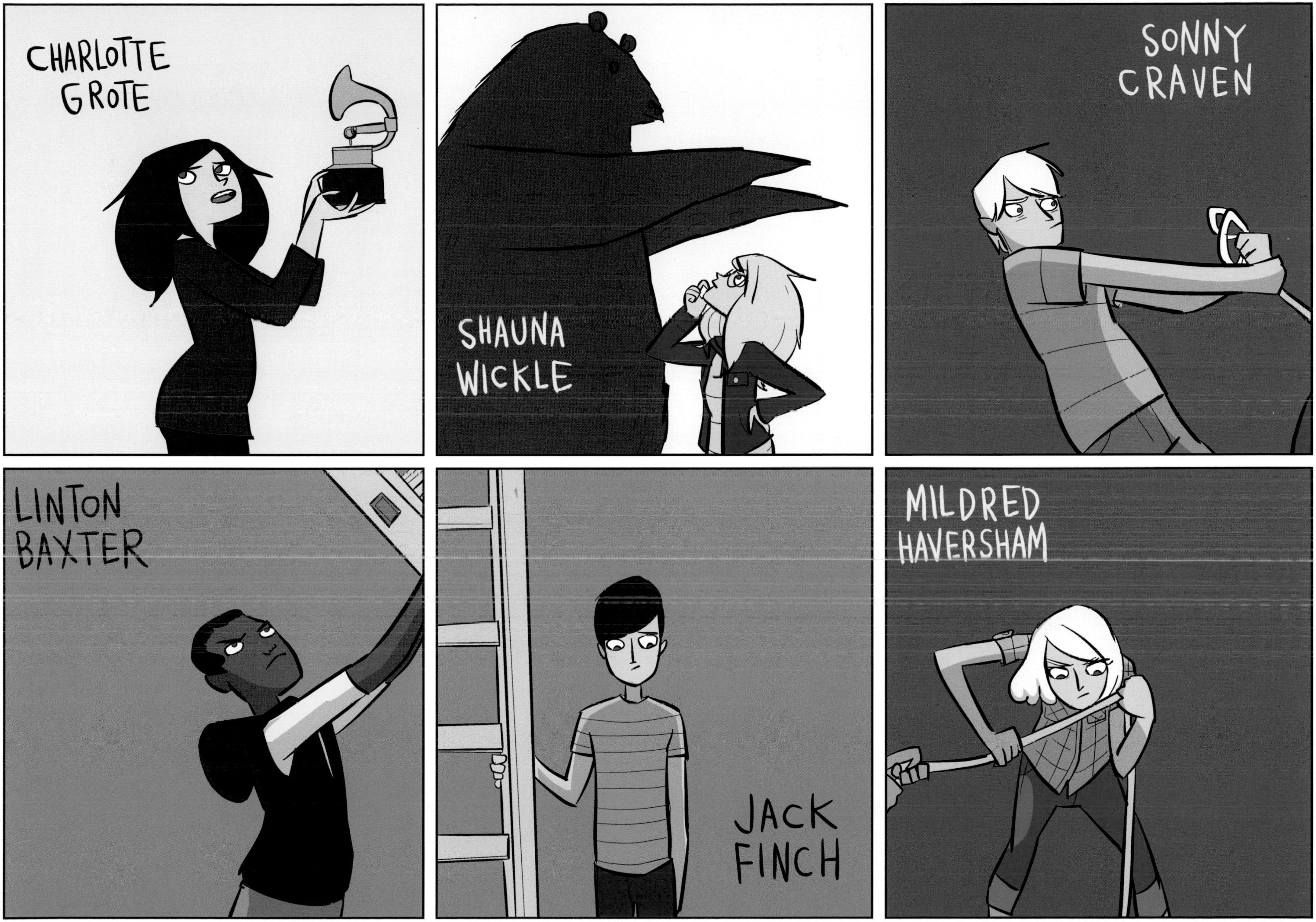
CHARLOTTE GROTE
SHAUNA WICKLE
SONNY CRAVEN
LINTON BAXTER
JACK FINCH
MILDRED HAVERSHAM

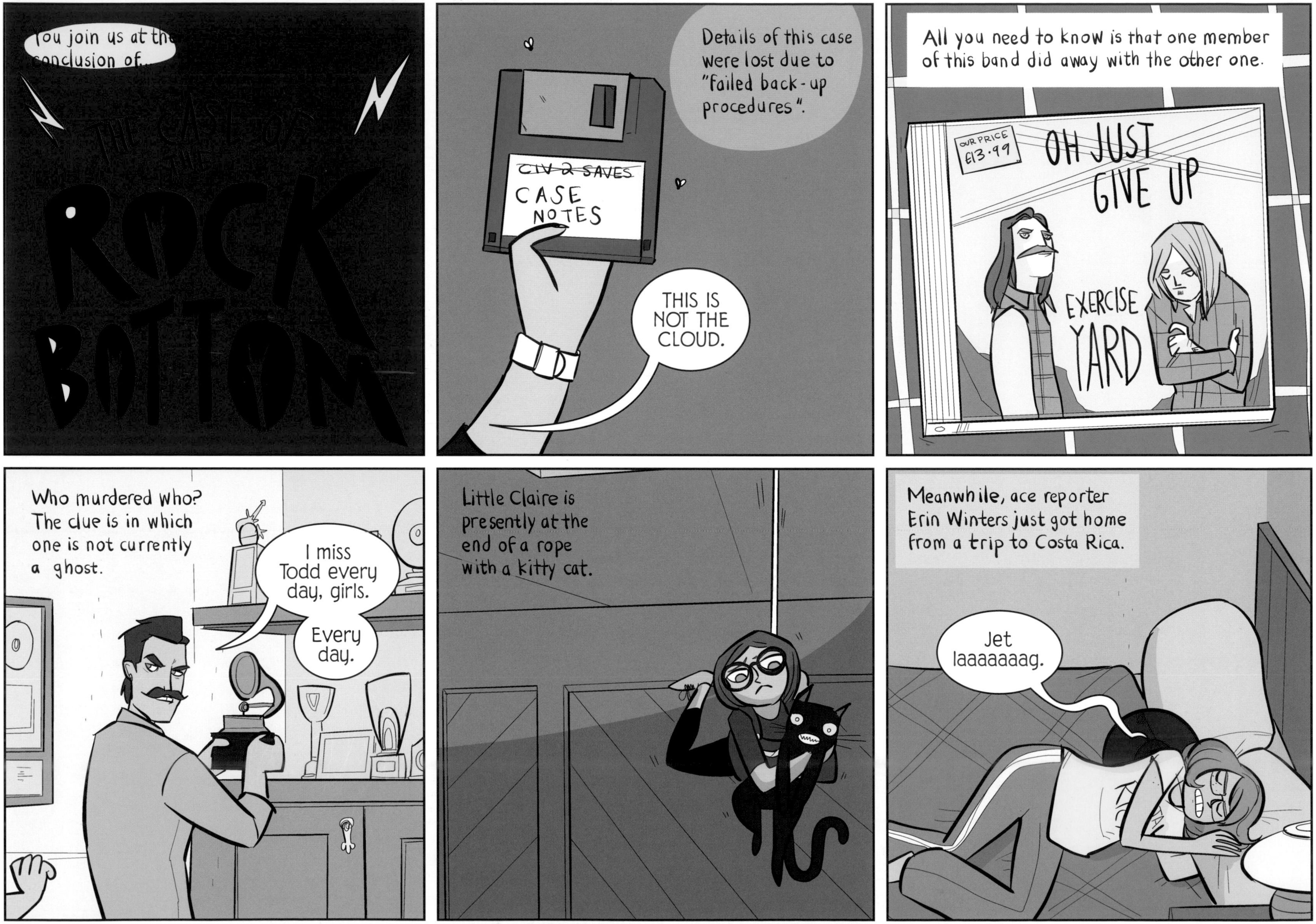
You join us at the conclusion of...
THE CASE OF THE ROCK BOTTOM
Details of this case were lost due to "failed back-up procedures".
CIV 2 SAVES
CASE NOTES
THIS IS NOT THE CLOUD.
All you need to know is that one member of this band did away with the other one.
OUR PRICE £13·99
OH JUST GIVE UP
EXERCISE YARD
Who murdered who? The clue is in which one is not currently a ghost.
I miss Todd every day, girls.
Every day.
Little Claire is presently at the end of a rope with a kitty cat.
Meanwhile, ace reporter Erin Winters just got home from a trip to Costa Rica.
Jet laaaaaaag.

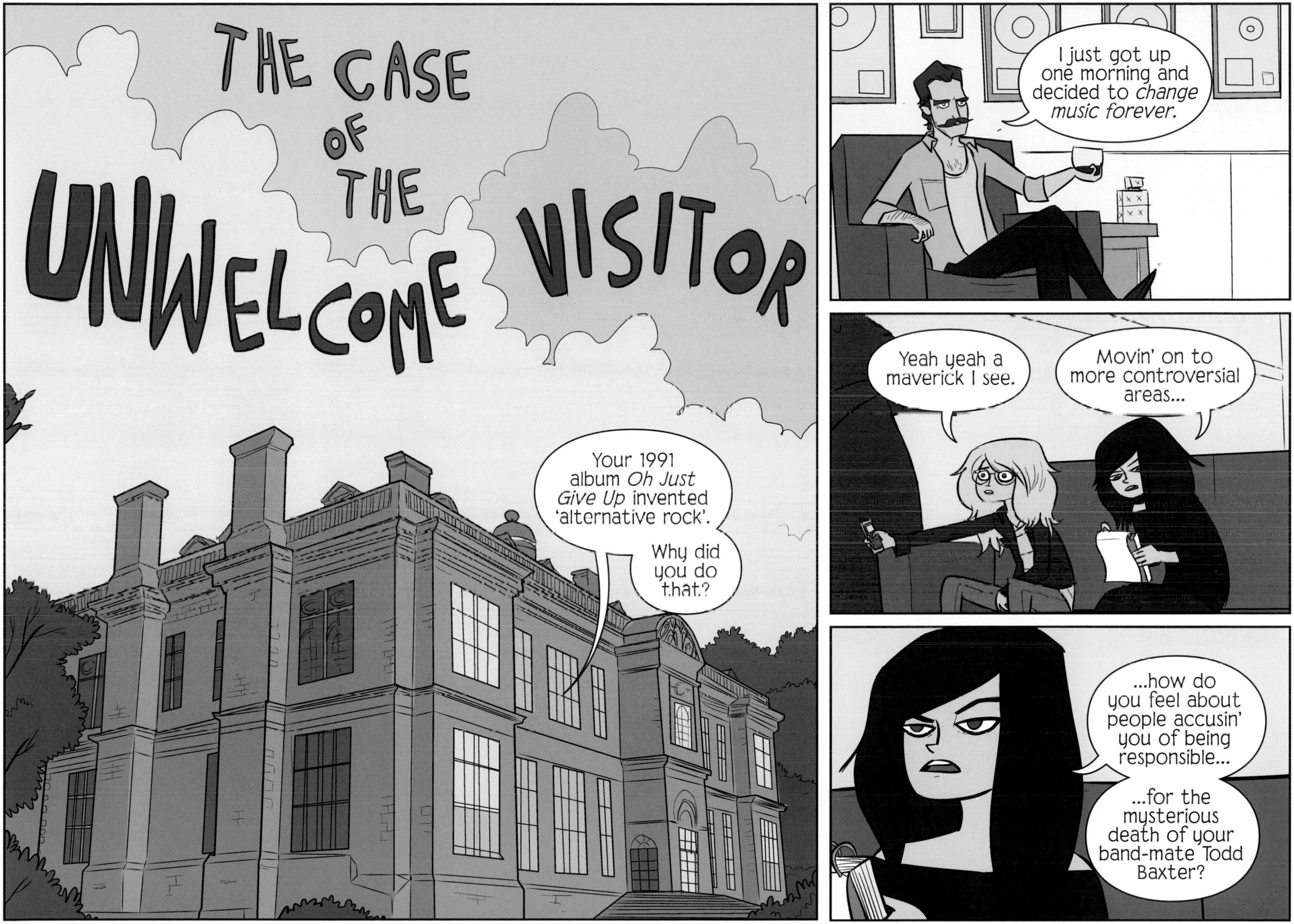
THE CASE OF THE UNWELCOME VISITOR
Your 1991 album *Oh Just Give Up* invented 'alternative rock'.
Why did you do that?
I just got up one morning and decided to *change music forever.*
Yeah yeah a maverick I see.
Movin' on to more controversial areas...
...how do you feel about people accusin' you of being responsible...
...for the mysterious death of your band-mate Todd Baxter?

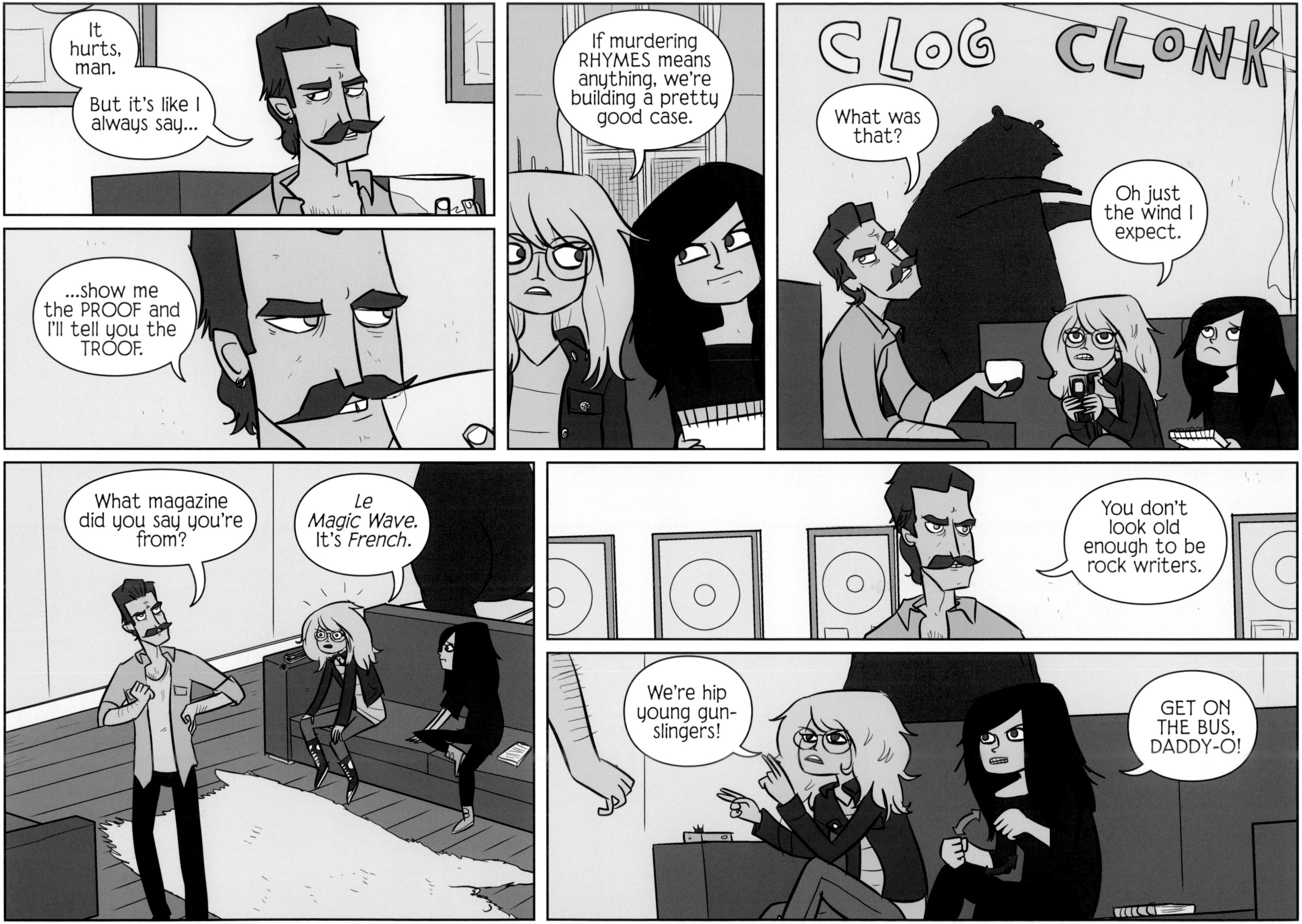
It hurts, man.
But it's like I always say...
...show me the PROOF and I'll tell you the TROOF.
If murdering RHYMES means anything, we're building a pretty good case.
CLOG CLONK
What was that?
Oh just the wind I expect.
What magazine did you say you're from?
Le Magic Wave. It's *French.*
You don't look old enough to be rock writers.
We're hip young gun-slingers!
GET ON THE BUS, DADDY-O!

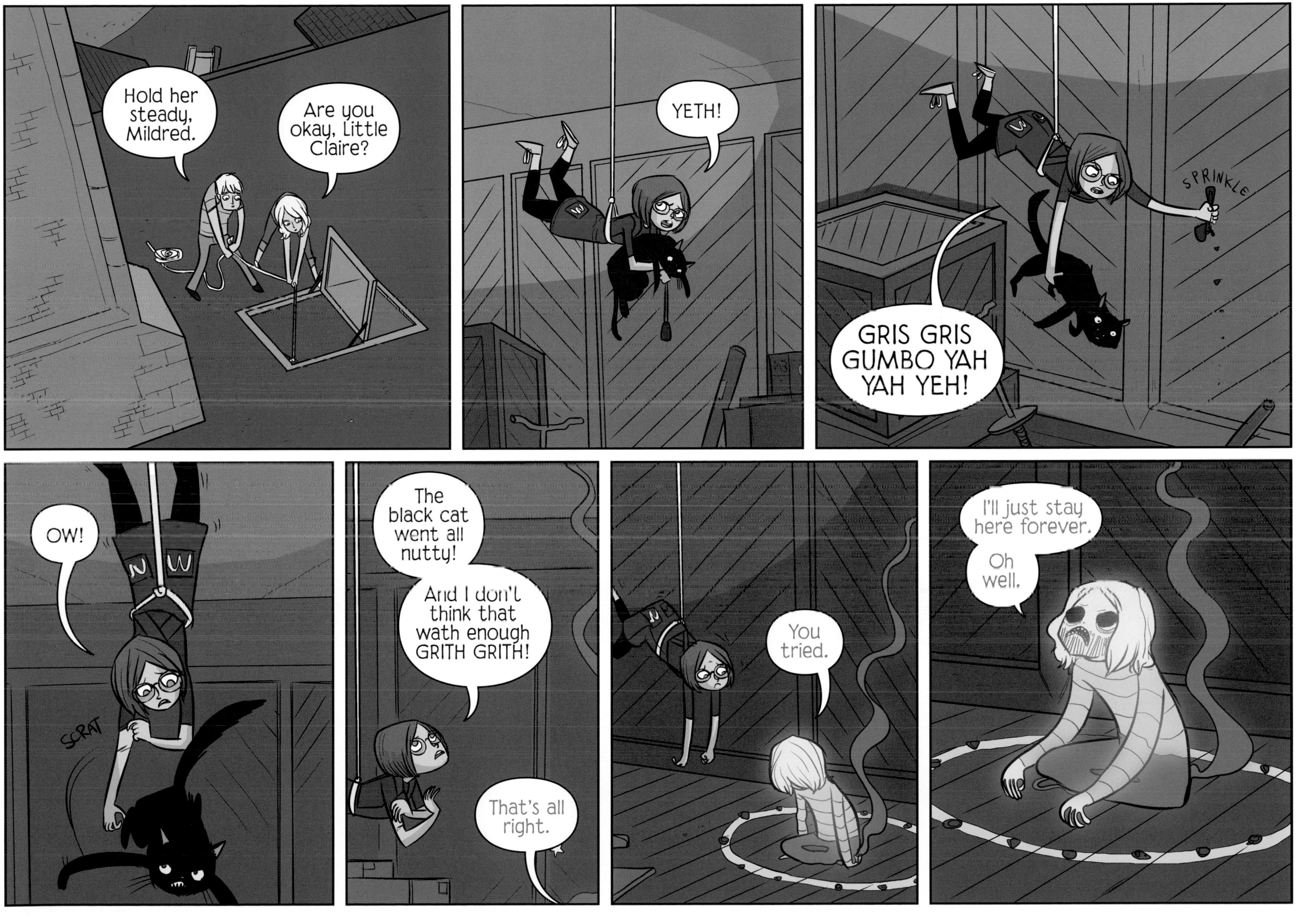
Hold her steady, Mildred.
Are you okay, Little Claire?
YETH!
SPRINKLE
GRIS GRIS GUMBO YAH YAH YEH!
OW!
SCRAT
The black cat went all nutty!
And I don't think that wath enough GRITH GRITH!
That's all right.
You tried.
I'll just stay here forever.
Oh well.

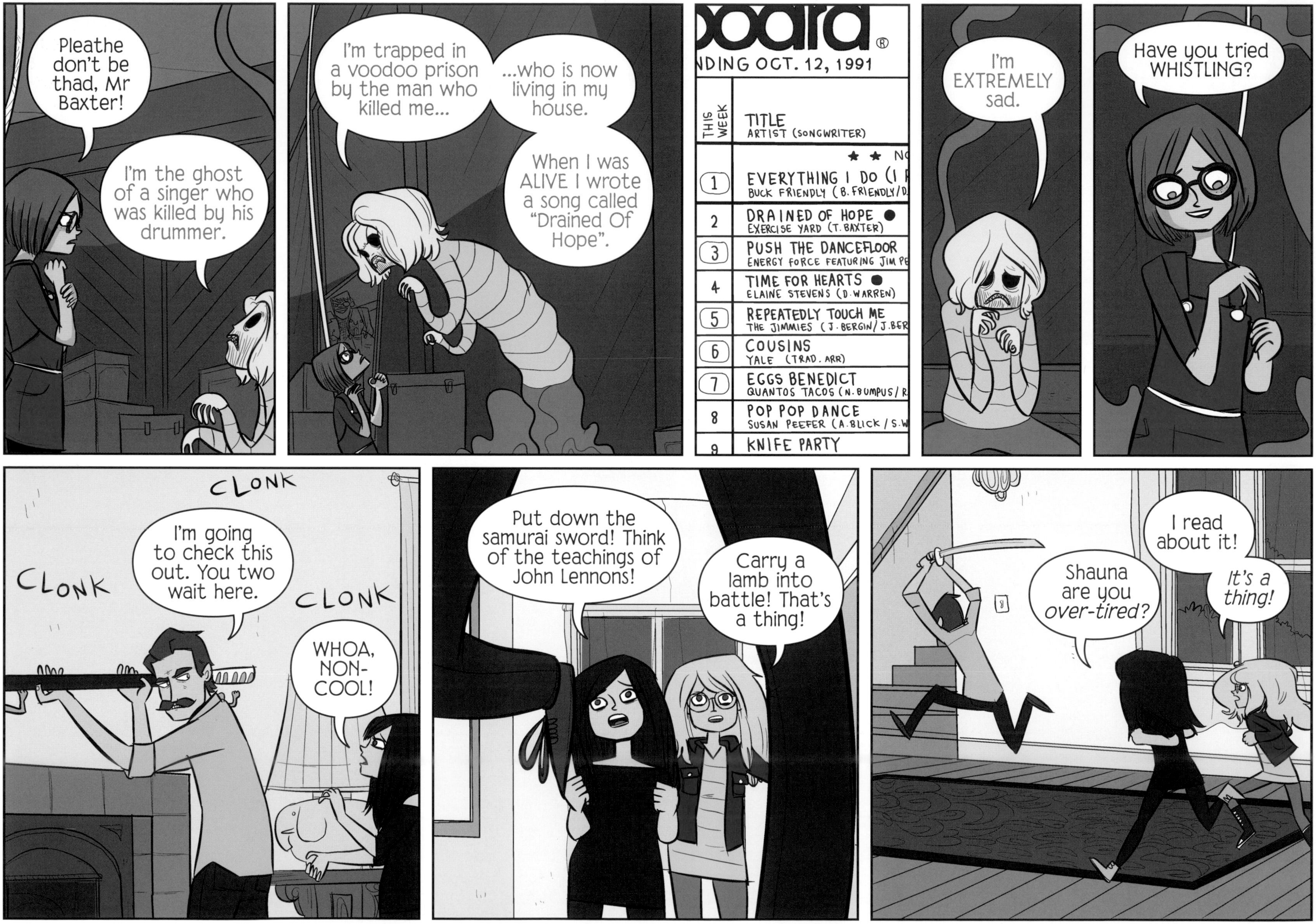
Pleathe don't be thad, Mr Baxter!
I'm the ghost of a singer who was killed by his drummer.
I'm trapped in a voodoo prison by the man who killed me...
...who is now living in my house.
When I was ALIVE I wrote a song called "Drained Of Hope".
NDING OCT. 12, 1991
THIS WEEK
TITLE
ARTIST (SONGWRITER)
1 EVERYTHING I DO (I
BUCK FRIENDLY (B. FRIENDLY/D.
2 DRAINED OF HOPE
EXERCISE YARD (T. BAXTER)
3 PUSH THE DANCEFLOOR
ENERGY FORCE FEATURING JIM PE
4 TIME FOR HEARTS
ELAINE STEVENS (D. WARREN)
5 REPEATEDLY TOUCH ME
THE JIMMIES (J. BERGIN/ J. BER
6 COUSINS
YALE (TRAD. ARR)
7 EGGS BENEDICT
QUANTOS TACOS (N. BUMPUS/ R
8 POP POP DANCE
SUSAN PEEFER (A. BLICK / S. W
KNIFE PARTY
I'm EXTREMELY sad.
Have you tried WHISTLING?
CLONK
I'm going to check this out. You two wait here.
CLONK
CLONK
WHOA, NON-COOL!
Put down the samurai sword! Think of the teachings of John Lennons!
Carry a lamb into battle! That's a thing!
Shauna are you over-tired?
I read about it!
It's a thing!

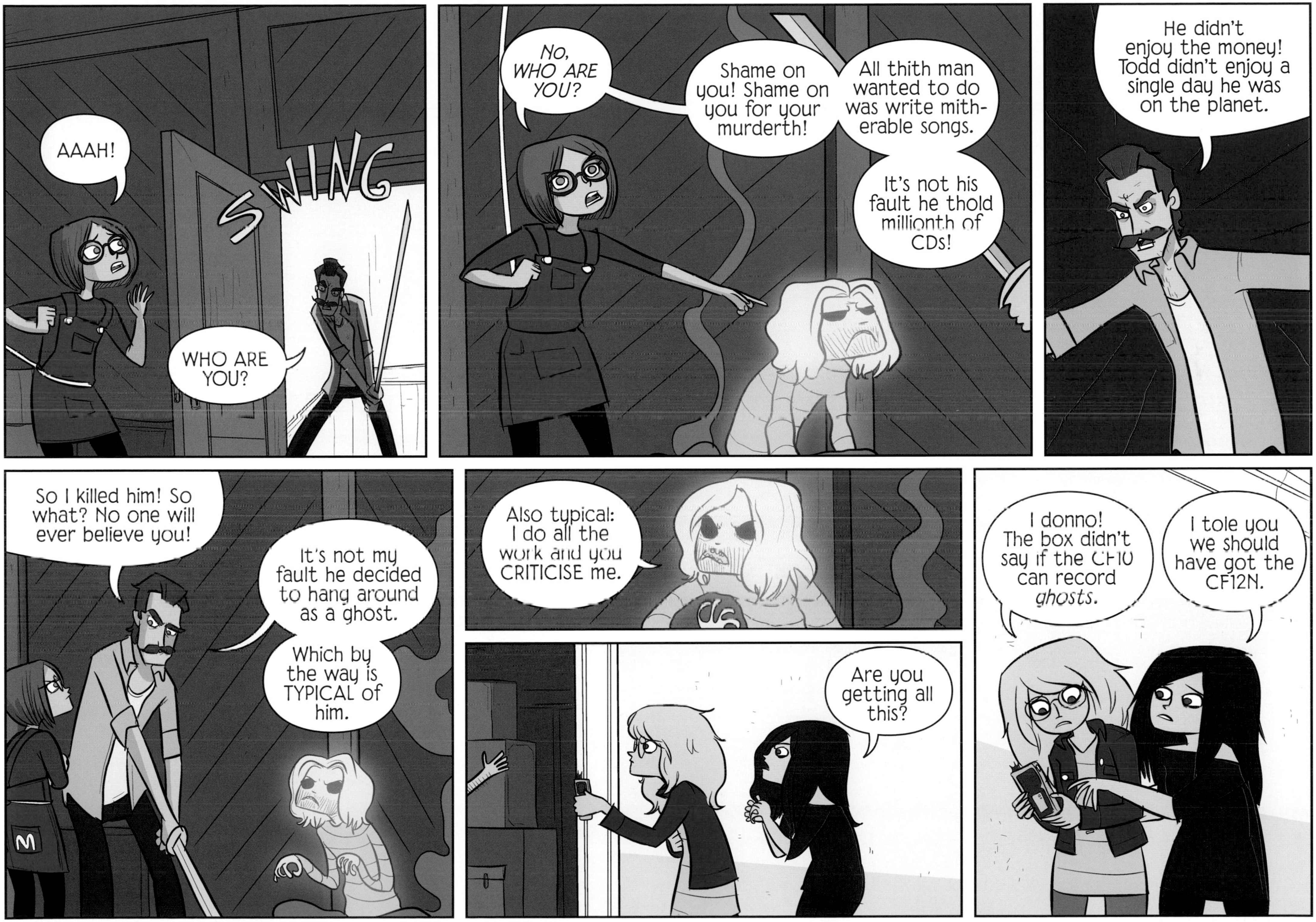
AAAH!
SWING
WHO ARE YOU?
No, WHO ARE YOU?
Shame on you! Shame on you for your murderth!
All thith man wanted to do was write mith-erable songs.
It's not his fault he thold millionth of CDs!
He didn't enjoy the money! Todd didn't enjoy a single day he was on the planet.
So I killed him! So what? No one will ever believe you!
It's not my fault he decided to hang around as a ghost.
Which by the way is TYPICAL of him.
Also typical: I do all the work and you CRITICISE me.
Are you getting all this?
I donno! The box didn't say if the CF10 can record *ghosts*.
I tole you we should have got the CF12N.

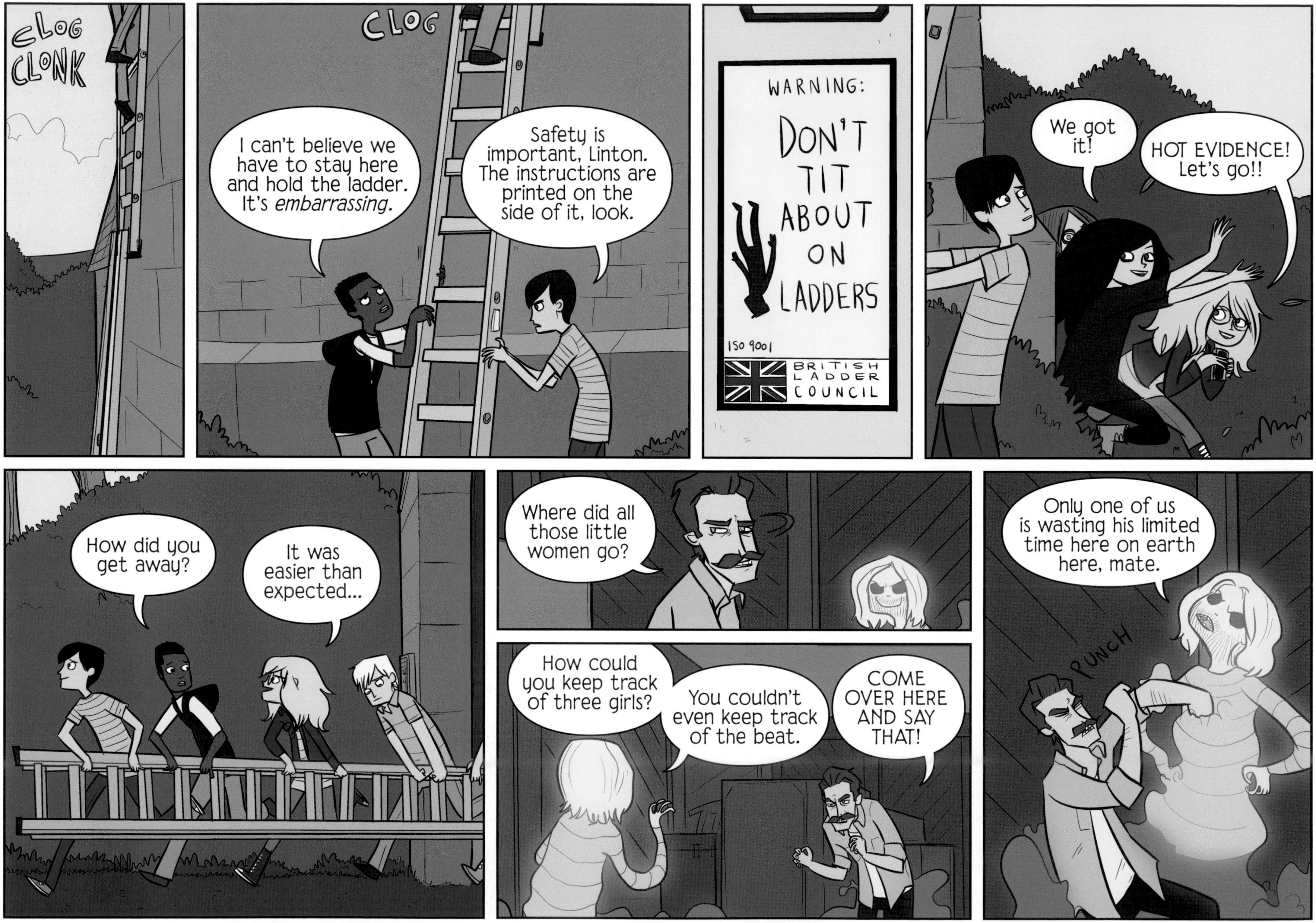
CLOG
CLONK
CLOG
I can't believe we have to stay here and hold the ladder. It's *embarrassing*.
Safety is important, Linton. The instructions are printed on the side of it, look.
WARNING:
DON'T TIT ABOUT ON LADDERS
ISO 9001
BRITISH LADDER COUNCIL
We got it!
HOT EVIDENCE! Let's go!!
How did you get away?
It was easier than expected...
Where did all those little women go?
How could you keep track of three girls?
You couldn't even keep track of the beat.
COME OVER HERE AND SAY THAT!
Only one of us is wasting his limited time here on earth here, mate.
PUNCH

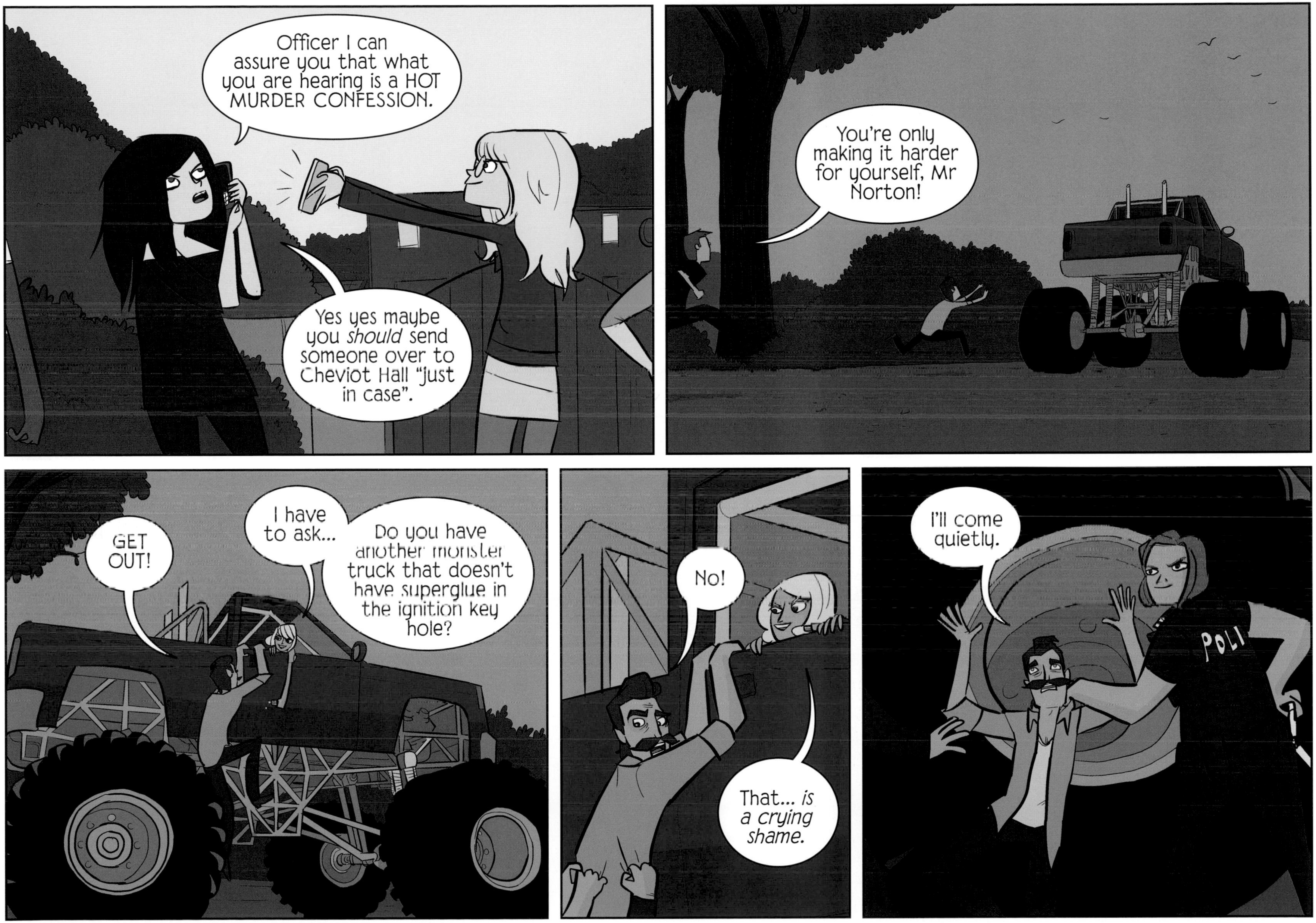

Officer I can assure you that what you are hearing is a HOT MURDER CONFESSION.
Yes yes maybe you *should* send someone over to Cheviot Hall "just in case".
You're only making it harder for yourself, Mr Norton!
GET OUT!
I have to ask...
Do you have another monster truck that doesn't have superglue in the ignition key hole?
No!
That... *is a crying shame.*
I'll come quietly.
POLI

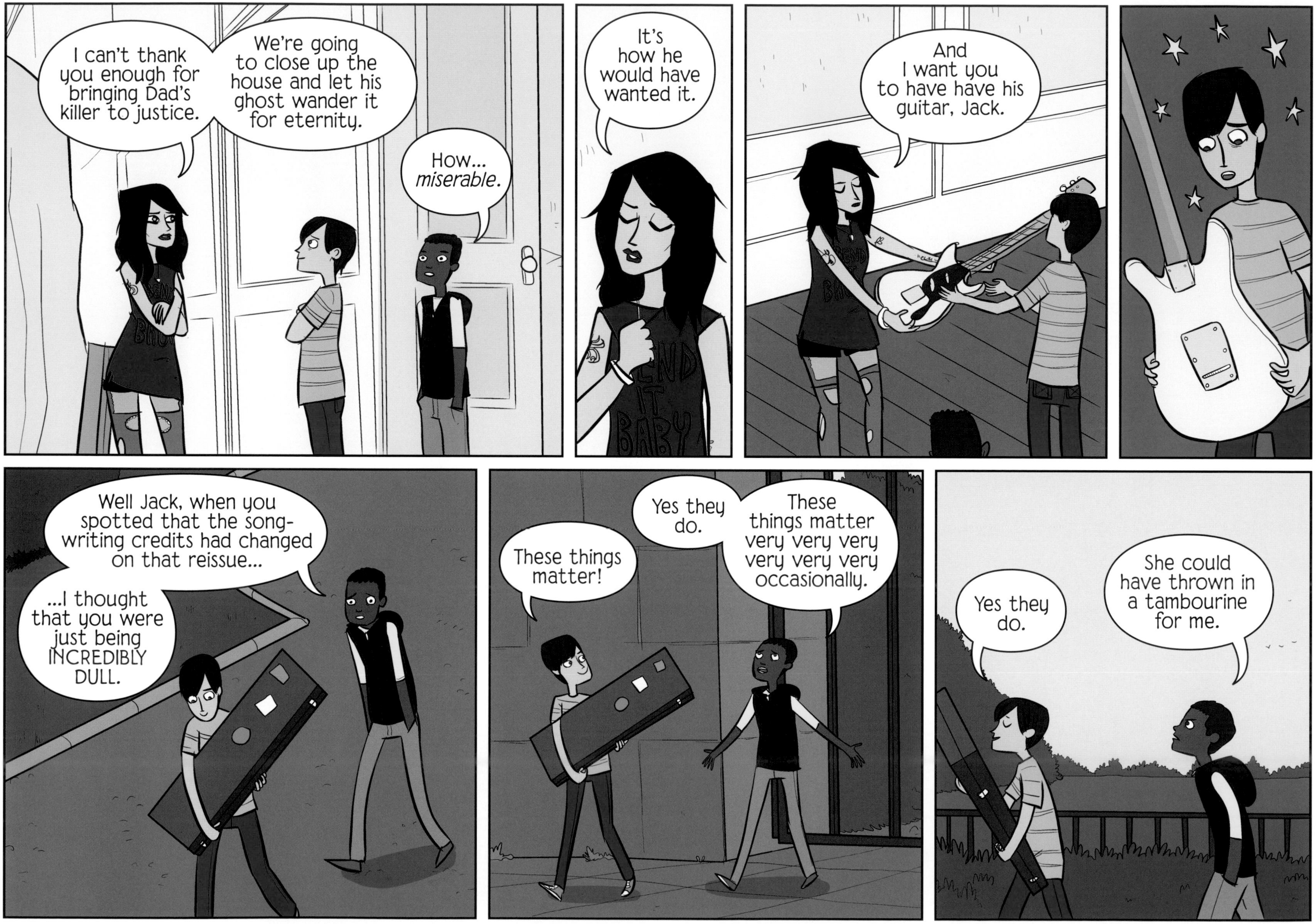
I can't thank you enough for bringing Dad's killer to justice.
We're going to close up the house and let his ghost wander it for eternity.
How... *miserable.*
It's how he would have wanted it.
And I want you to have have his guitar, Jack.
Well Jack, when you spotted that the song-writing credits had changed on that reissue...
...I thought that you were just being INCREDIBLY DULL.
These things matter!
Yes they do.
These things matter very very very very very very occasionally.
Yes they do.
She could have thrown in a tambourine for me.

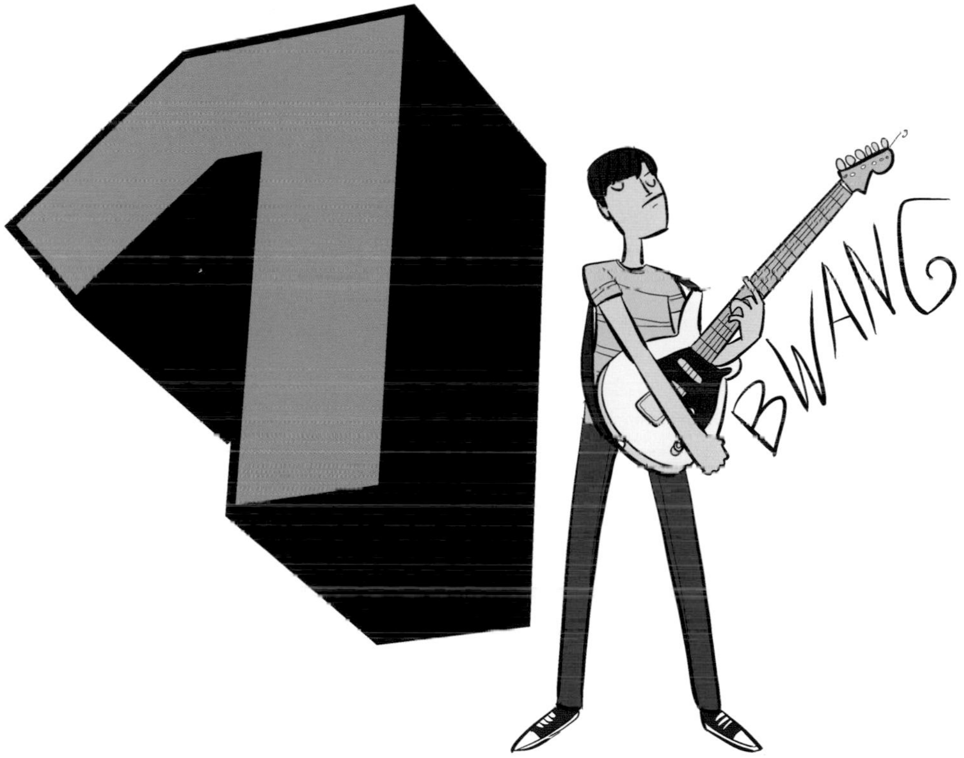
BWANG

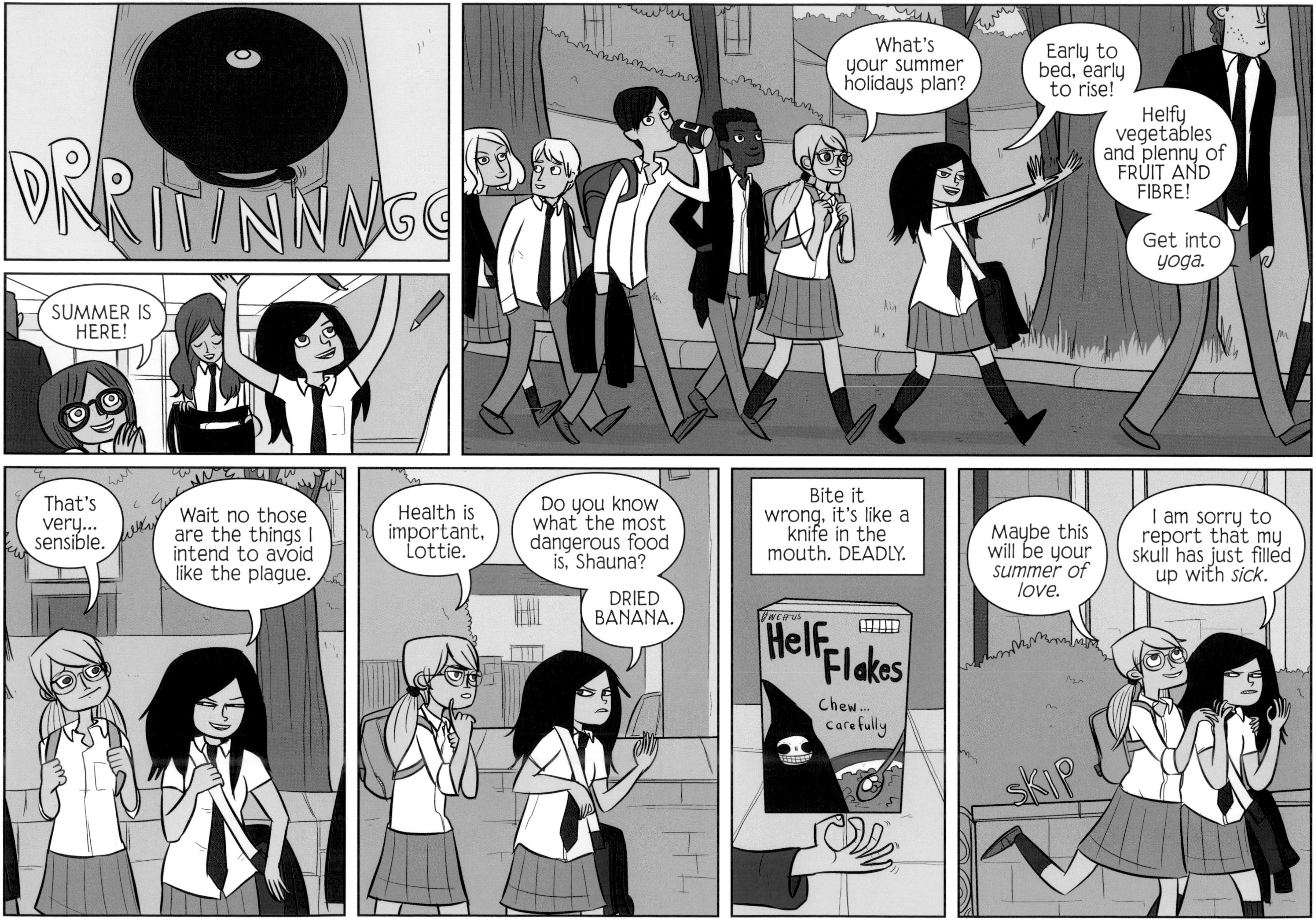
DRRIIINNNGG
SUMMER IS HERE!
What's your summer holidays plan?
Early to bed, early to rise!
Helfy vegetables and plenny of FRUIT AND FIBRE!
Get into *yoga.*
That's very... sensible.
Wait no those are the things I intend to avoid like the plague.
Health is important, Lottie.
Do you know what the most dangerous food is, Shauna?
DRIED BANANA.
Bite it wrong, it's like a knife in the mouth. DEADLY.
Helf Flakes
Chew... carefully
Maybe this will be your *summer of love.*
I am sorry to report that my skull has just filled up with *sick.*
SKIP

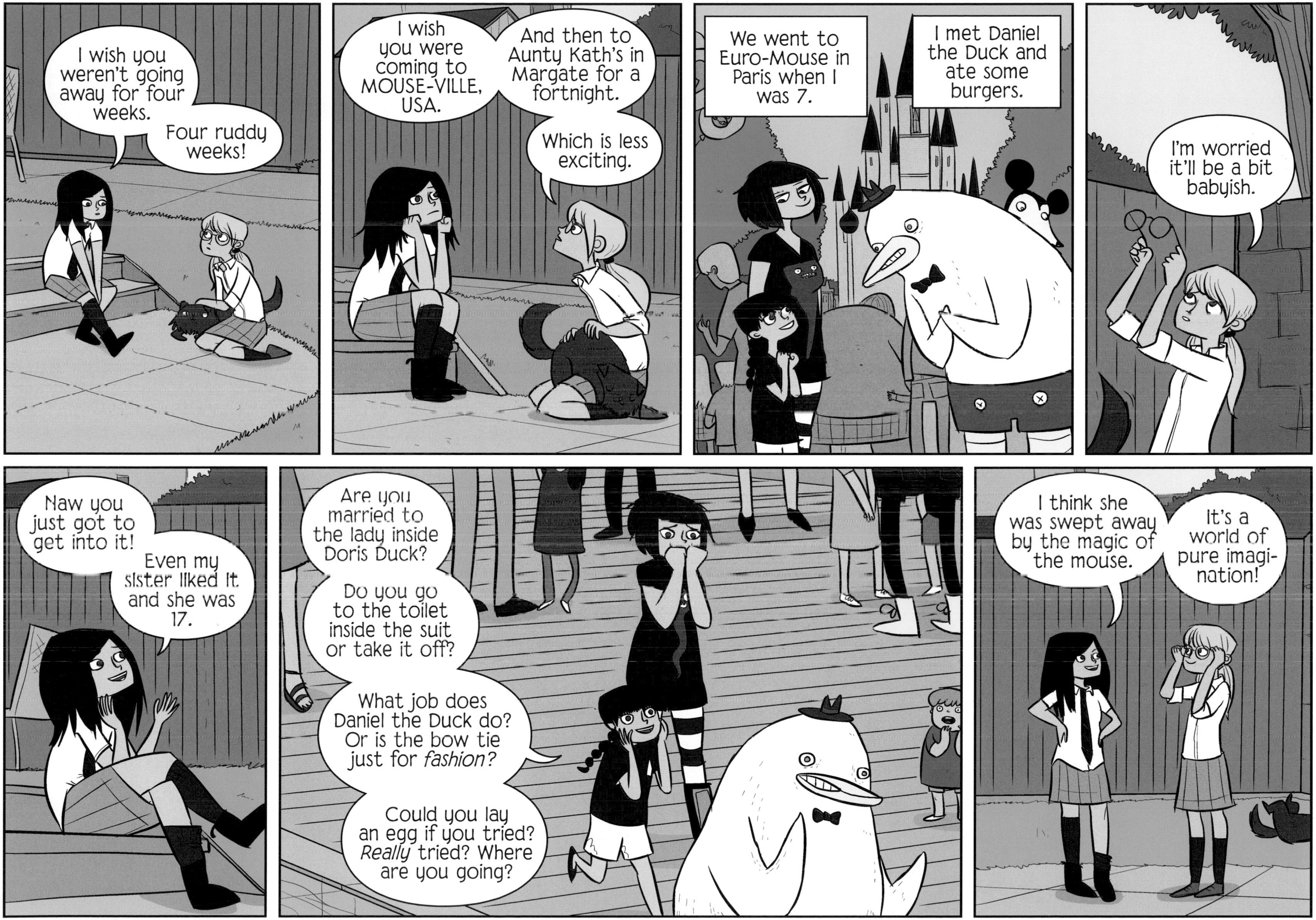
I wish you weren't going away for four weeks.
Four ruddy weeks!
I wish you were coming to MOUSE-VILLE, USA.
And then to Aunty Kath's in Margate for a fortnight.
Which is less exciting.
We went to Euro-Mouse in Paris when I was 7.
I met Daniel the Duck and ate some burgers.
I'm worried it'll be a bit babyish.
Naw you just got to get into it!
Even my sister liked it and she was 17.
Are you married to the lady inside Doris Duck?
Do you go to the toilet inside the suit or take it off?
What job does Daniel the Duck do? Or is the bow tie just for *fashion?*
Could you lay an egg if you tried? *Really* tried? Where are you going?
I think she was swept away by the magic of the mouse.
It's a world of pure imagi-nation!

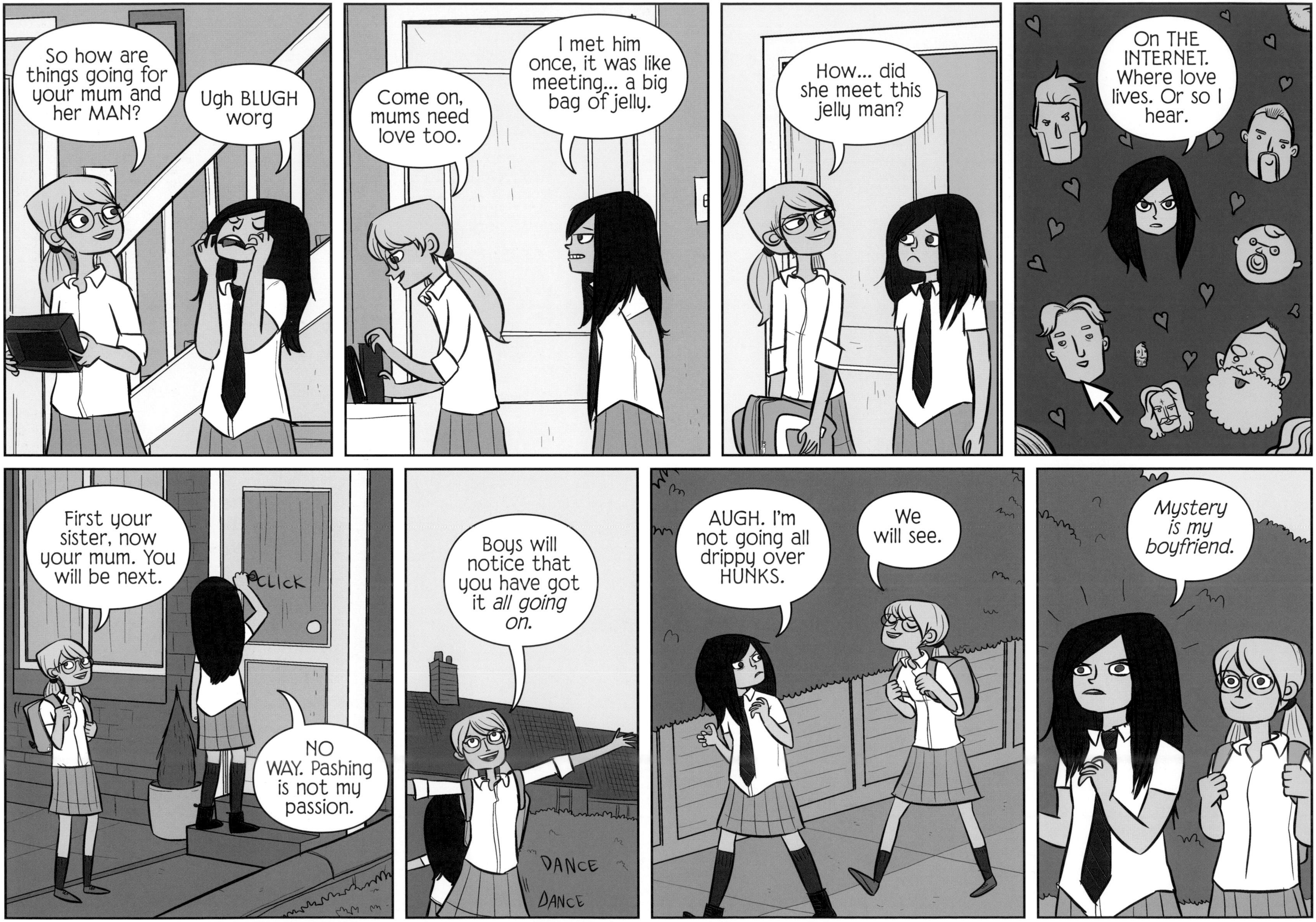
So how are things going for your mum and her MAN?
Ugh BLUGH worg
Come on, mums need love too.
I met him once, it was like meeting... a big bag of jelly.
How... did she meet this jelly man?
On THE INTERNET. Where love lives. Or so I hear.
First your sister, now your mum. You will be next.
CLICK
NO WAY. Pashing is not my passion.
Boys will notice that you have got it *all going on.*
DANCE
DANCE
AUGH. I'm not going all drippy over HUNKS.
We will see.
Mystery is my boyfriend.

The Case of the Unwelcome Visitor

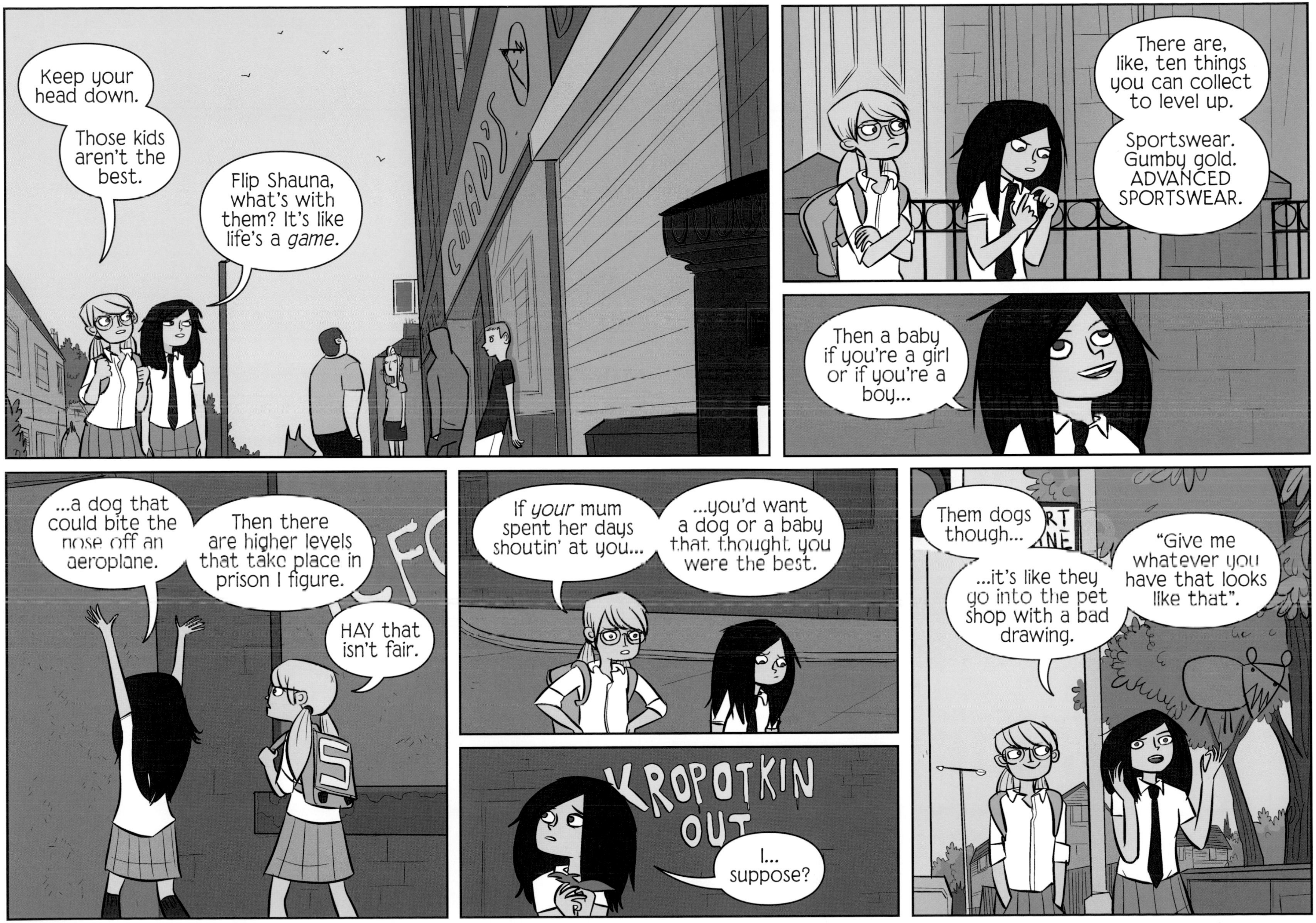

Keep your head down.
Those kids aren't the best.
Flip Shauna, what's with them? It's like life's a *game*.
There are, like, ten things you can collect to level up.
Sportswear. Gumby gold. ADVANCED SPORTSWEAR.
Then a baby if you're a girl or if you're a boy...
...a dog that could bite the nose off an aeroplane.
Then there are higher levels that take place in prison I figure.
HAY that isn't fair.
If *your* mum spent her days shoutin' at you...
...you'd want a dog or a baby that thought you were the best.
KROPOTKIN OUT
I... suppose?
Them dogs though...
...it's like they go into the pet shop with a bad drawing.
"Give me whatever you have that looks like that".

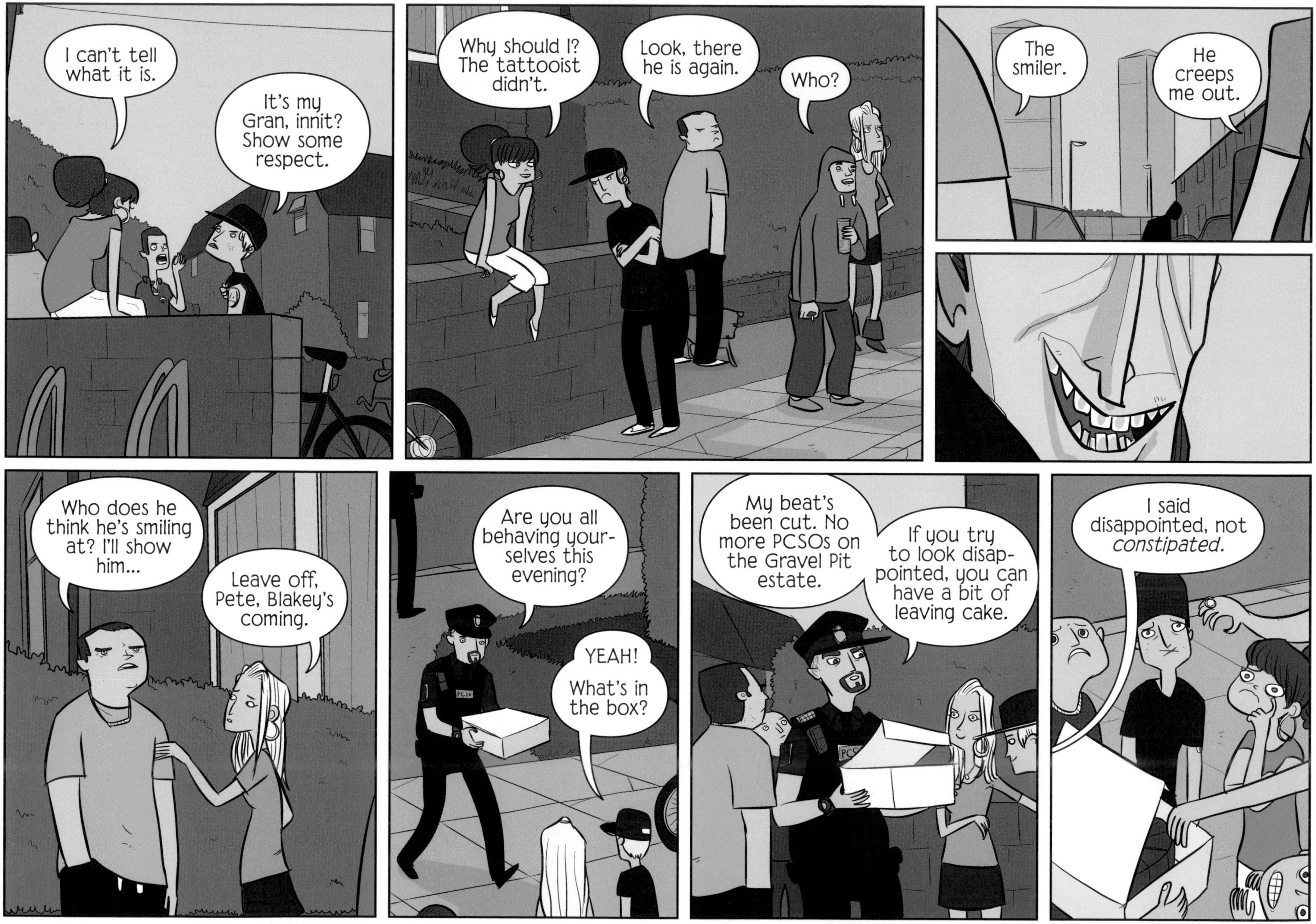
I can't tell what it is.
It's my Gran, innit? Show some respect.
Why should I? The tattooist didn't.
Look, there he is again.
Who?
The smiler.
He creeps me out.
Who does he think he's smiling at? I'll show him...
Leave off, Pete, Blakey's coming.
Are you all behaving yourselves this evening?
YEAH!
What's in the box?
My beat's been cut. No more PCSOs on the Gravel Pit estate.
If you try to look disappointed, you can have a bit of leaving cake.
I said disappointed, not *constipated.*

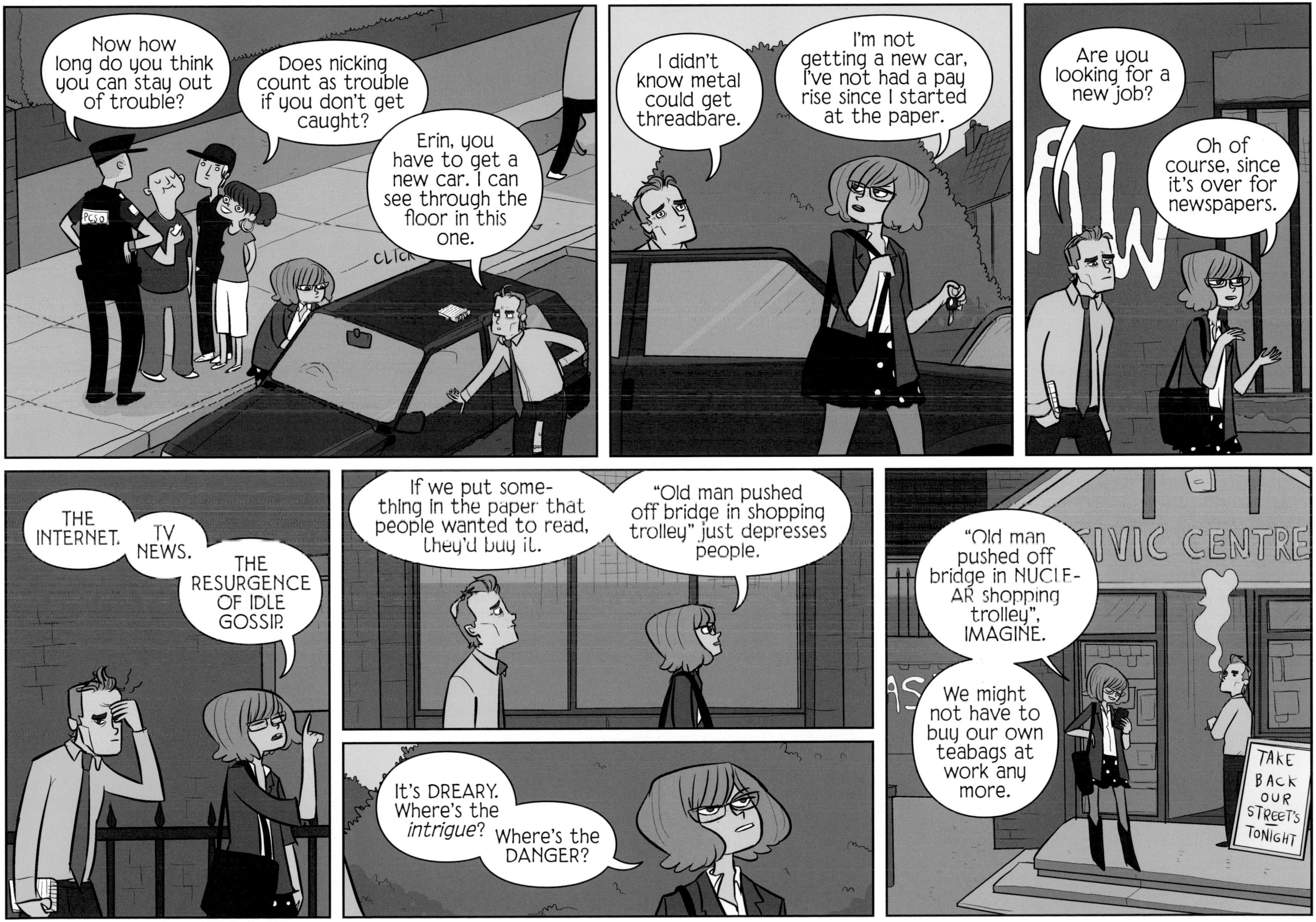

Now how long do you think you can stay out of trouble?
Does nicking count as trouble if you don't get caught?
PCSO
CLICK
Erin, you have to get a new car. I can see through the floor in this one.
I didn't know metal could get threadbare.
I'm not getting a new car, I've not had a pay rise since I started at the paper.
Are you looking for a new job?
Oh of course, since it's over for newspapers.
THE INTERNET.
TV NEWS.
THE RESURGENCE OF IDLE GOSSIP.
If we put something in the paper that people wanted to read, they'd buy it.
"Old man pushed off bridge in shopping trolley" just depresses people.
It's DREARY. Where's the *intrigue*?
Where's the DANGER?
CIVIC CENTRE
"Old man pushed off bridge in NUCLE-AR shopping trolley", IMAGINE.
We might not have to buy our own teabags at work any more.
TAKE BACK OUR STREET'S TONIGHT

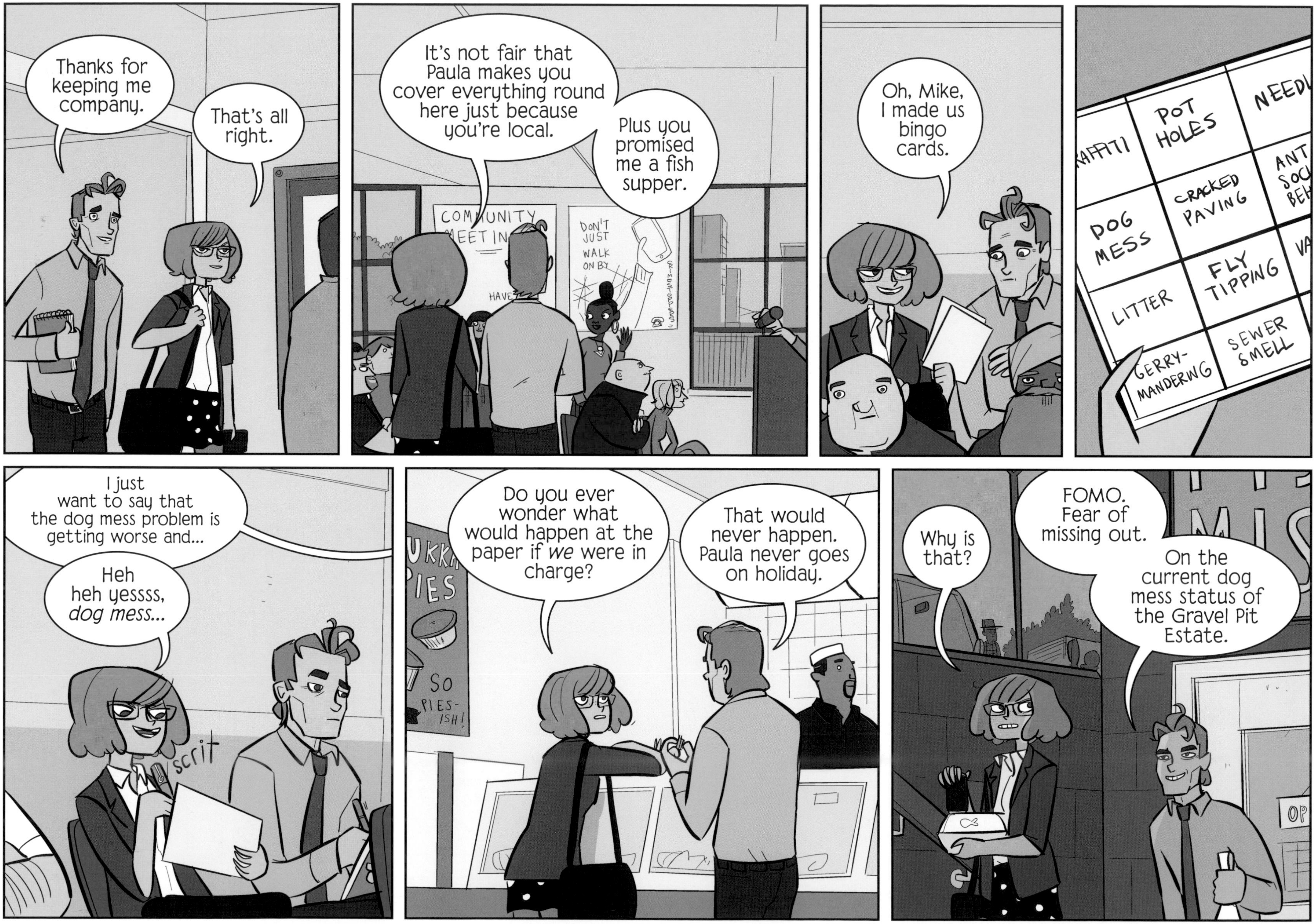
Thanks for keeping me company.
That's all right.
It's not fair that Paula makes you cover everything round here just because you're local.
Plus you promised me a fish supper.
COMMUNITY MEETIN
DON'T JUST WALK ON BY
Oh, Mike, I made us bingo cards.
POT HOLES
DOG MESS
CRACKED PAVING
LITTER
FLY TIPPING
SEWER SMELL
I just want to say that the dog mess problem is getting worse and...
Heh heh yessss, *dog mess...*
scrit
Do you ever wonder what would happen at the paper if *we* were in charge?
That would never happen. Paula never goes on holiday.
PIES
SO PIES-ISH!
Why is that?
FOMO. Fear of missing out.
On the current dog mess status of the Gravel Pit Estate.

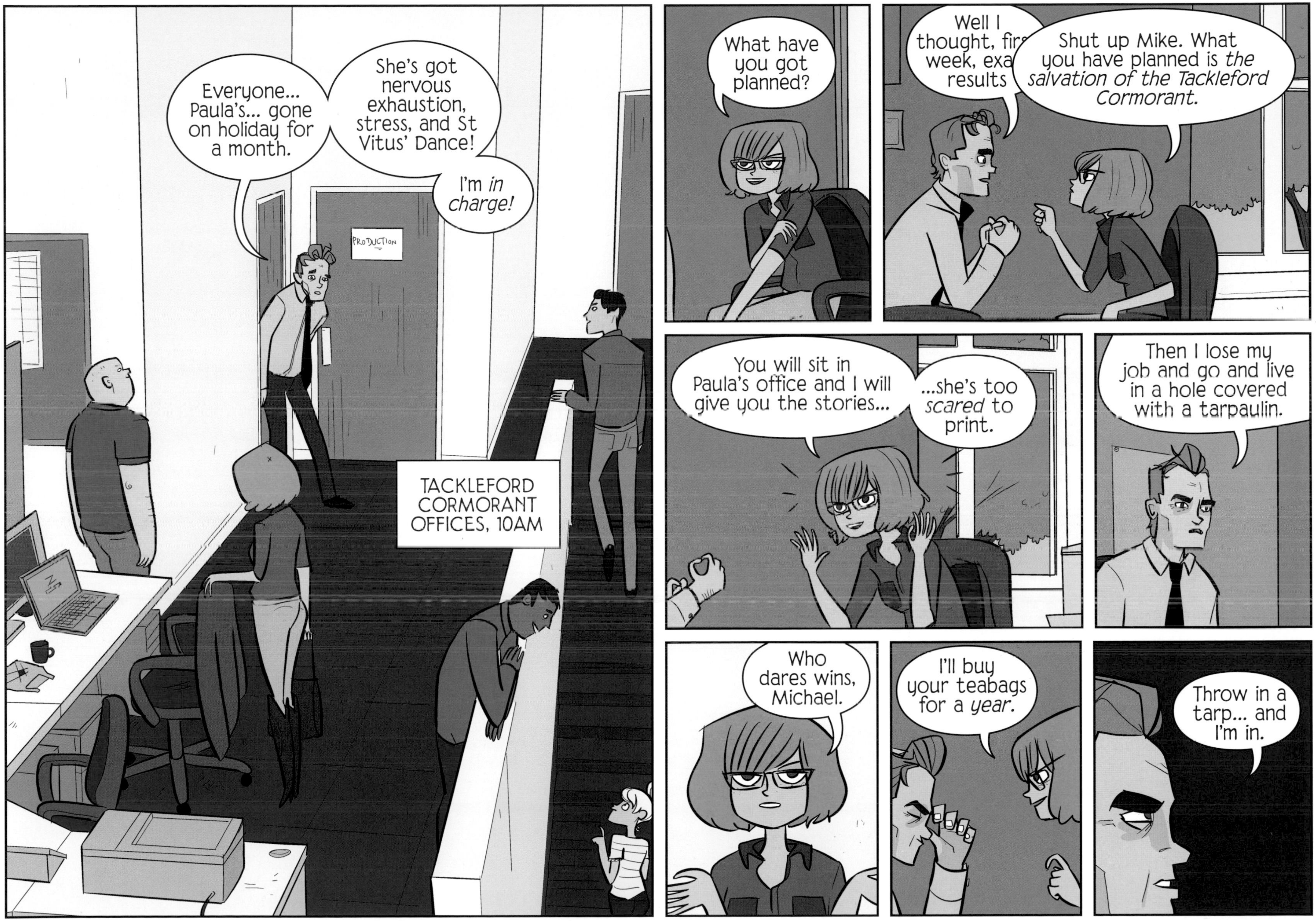
Everyone... Paula's... gone on holiday for a month.
She's got nervous exhaustion, stress, and St Vitus' Dance!
I'm *in charge!*
PRODUCTION
TACKLEFORD CORMORANT OFFICES, 10AM
What have you got planned?
Well I thought, firs week, exa results
Shut up Mike. What you have planned is *the salvation of the Tackleford Cormorant.*
You will sit in Paula's office and I will give you the stories...
...she's too *scared* to print.
Then I lose my job and go and live in a hole covered with a tarpaulin.
Who dares wins, Michael.
I'll buy your teabags for a *year.*
Throw in a tarp... and I'm in.

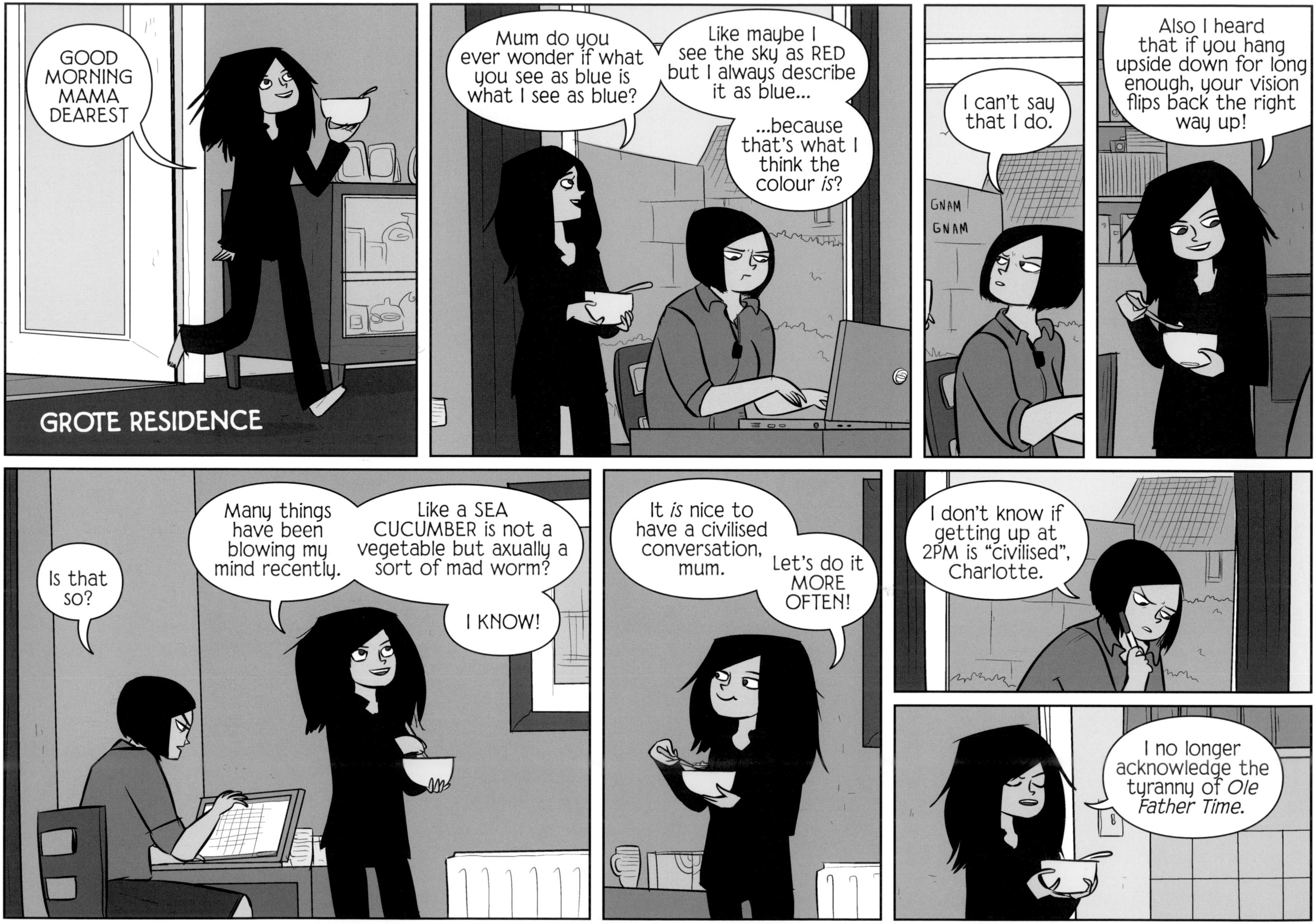
GOOD MORNING MAMA DEAREST
GROTE RESIDENCE
Mum do you ever wonder if what you see as blue is what I see as blue?
Like maybe I see the sky as RED but I always describe it as blue...
...because that's what I think the colour *is*?
GNAM GNAM
I can't say that I do.
Also I heard that if you hang upside down for long enough, your vision flips back the right way up!
Is that so?
Many things have been blowing my mind recently.
Like a SEA CUCUMBER is not a vegetable but axually a sort of mad worm?
I KNOW!
It *is* nice to have a civilised conversation, mum.
Let's do it MORE OFTEN!
I don't know if getting up at 2PM is "civilised", Charlotte.
I no longer acknowledge the tyranny of *Ole Father Time.*

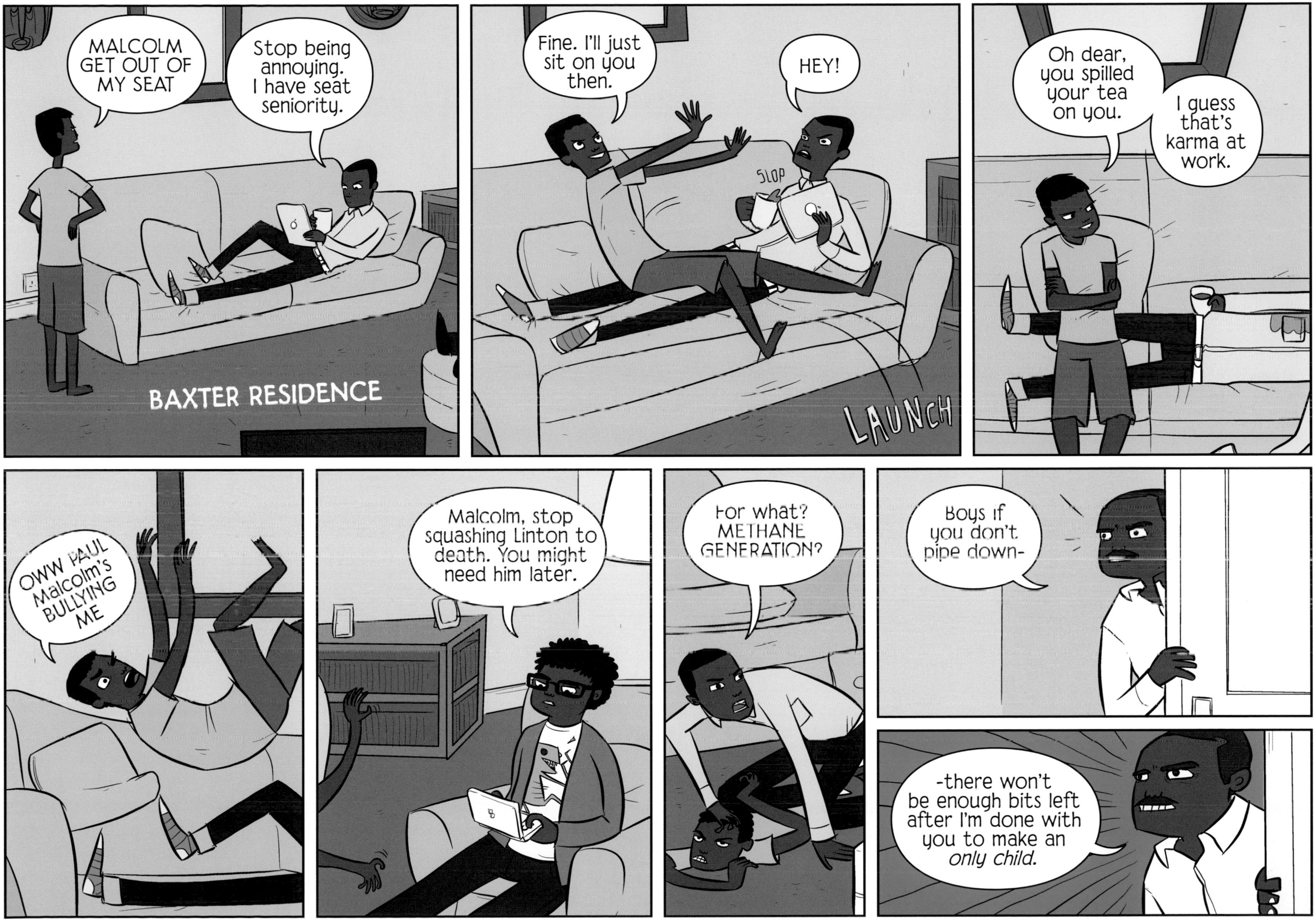
MALCOLM GET OUT OF MY SEAT
Stop being annoying. I have seat seniority.
BAXTER RESIDENCE
Fine. I'll just sit on you then.
HEY!
SLOP
LAUNCH
Oh dear, you spilled your tea on you.
I guess that's karma at work.
OWW PAUL Malcolm's BULLYING ME
Malcolm, stop squashing Linton to death. You might need him later.
For what? METHANE GENERATION?
Boys if you don't pipe down-
-there won't be enough bits left after I'm done with you to make an *only child.*

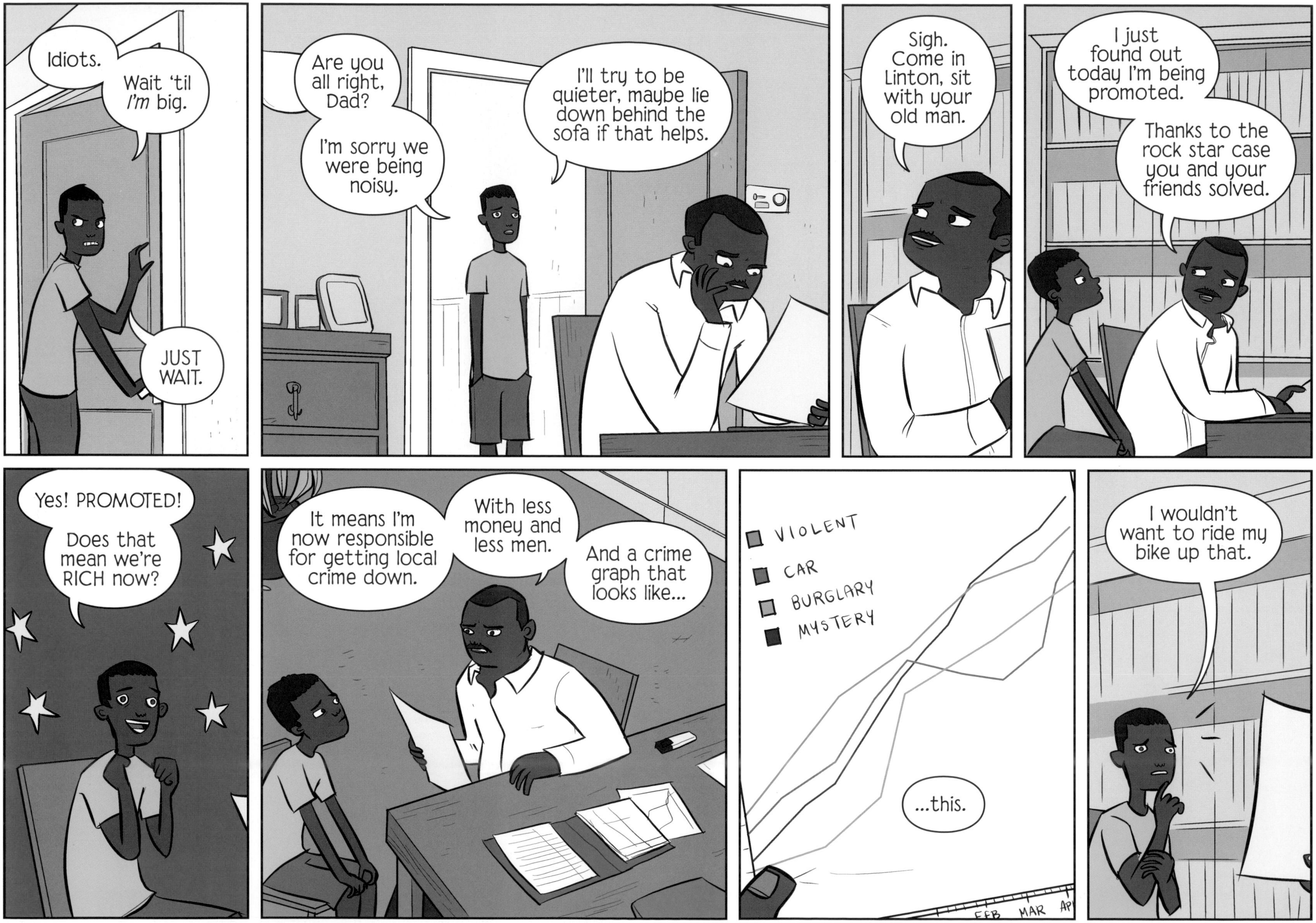

Idiots.
Wait 'til *I'm* big.
JUST WAIT.
Are you all right, Dad?
I'm sorry we were being noisy.
I'll try to be quieter, maybe lie down behind the sofa if that helps.
Sigh. Come in Linton, sit with your old man.
I just found out today I'm being promoted.
Thanks to the rock star case you and your friends solved.
Yes! PROMOTED!
Does that mean we're RICH now?
It means I'm now responsible for getting local crime down.
With less money and less men.
And a crime graph that looks like...
VIOLENT
CAR
BURGLARY
MYSTERY
...this.
FEB MAR
I wouldn't want to ride my bike up that.

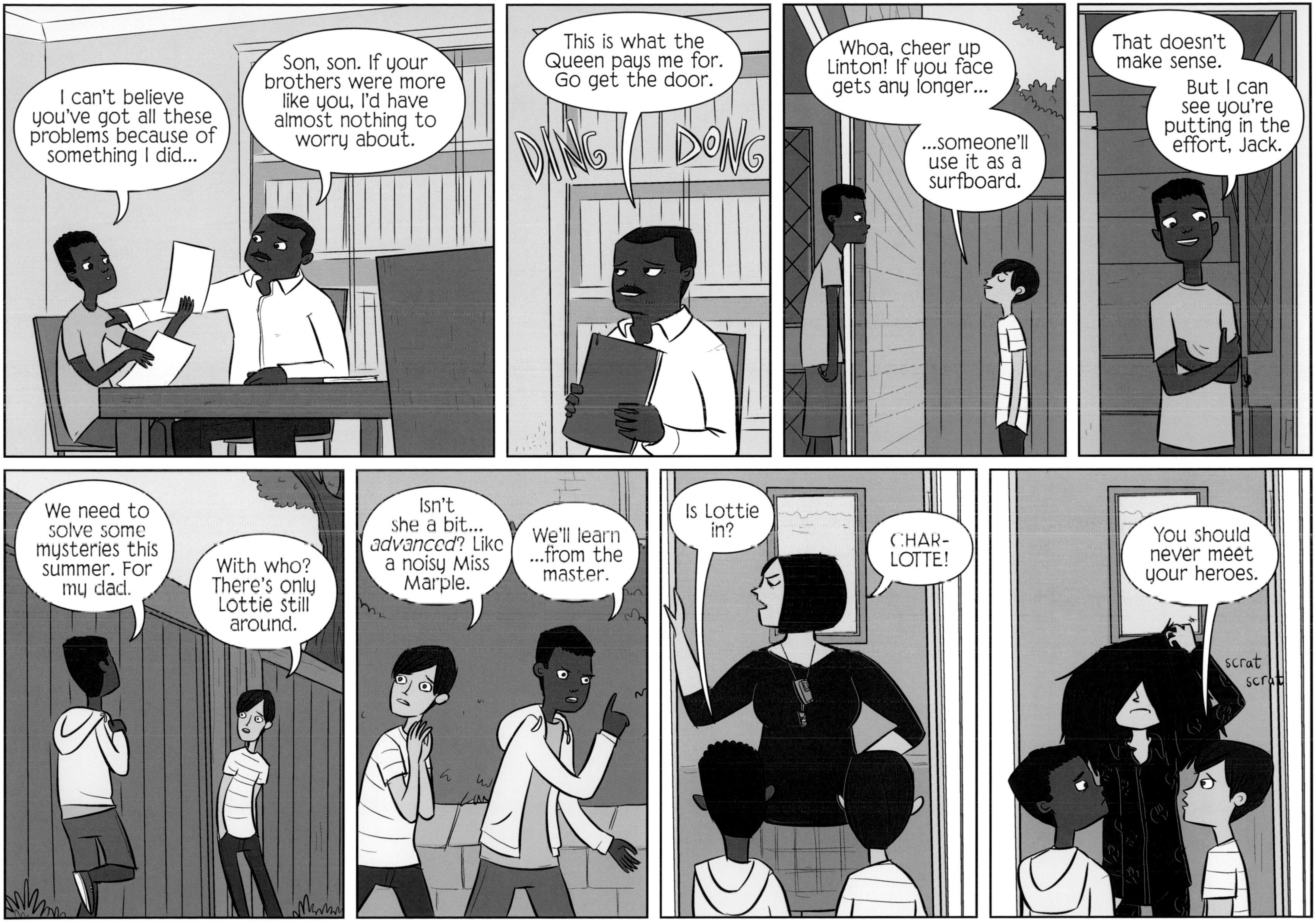
I can't believe you've got all these problems because of something I did...
Son, son. If your brothers were more like you, I'd have almost nothing to worry about.
DING
This is what the Queen pays me for. Go get the door.
DONG
Whoa, cheer up Linton! If you face gets any longer...
...someone'll use it as a surfboard.
That doesn't make sense.
But I can see you're putting in the effort, Jack.
We need to solve some mysteries this summer. For my dad.
With who? There's only Lottie still around.
Isn't she a bit... *advanced*? Like a noisy Miss Marple.
We'll learn ...from the master.
Is Lottie in?
CHAR-LOTTE!
You should never meet your heroes.
scrat
scrat

Bad Machinery, Volume Six

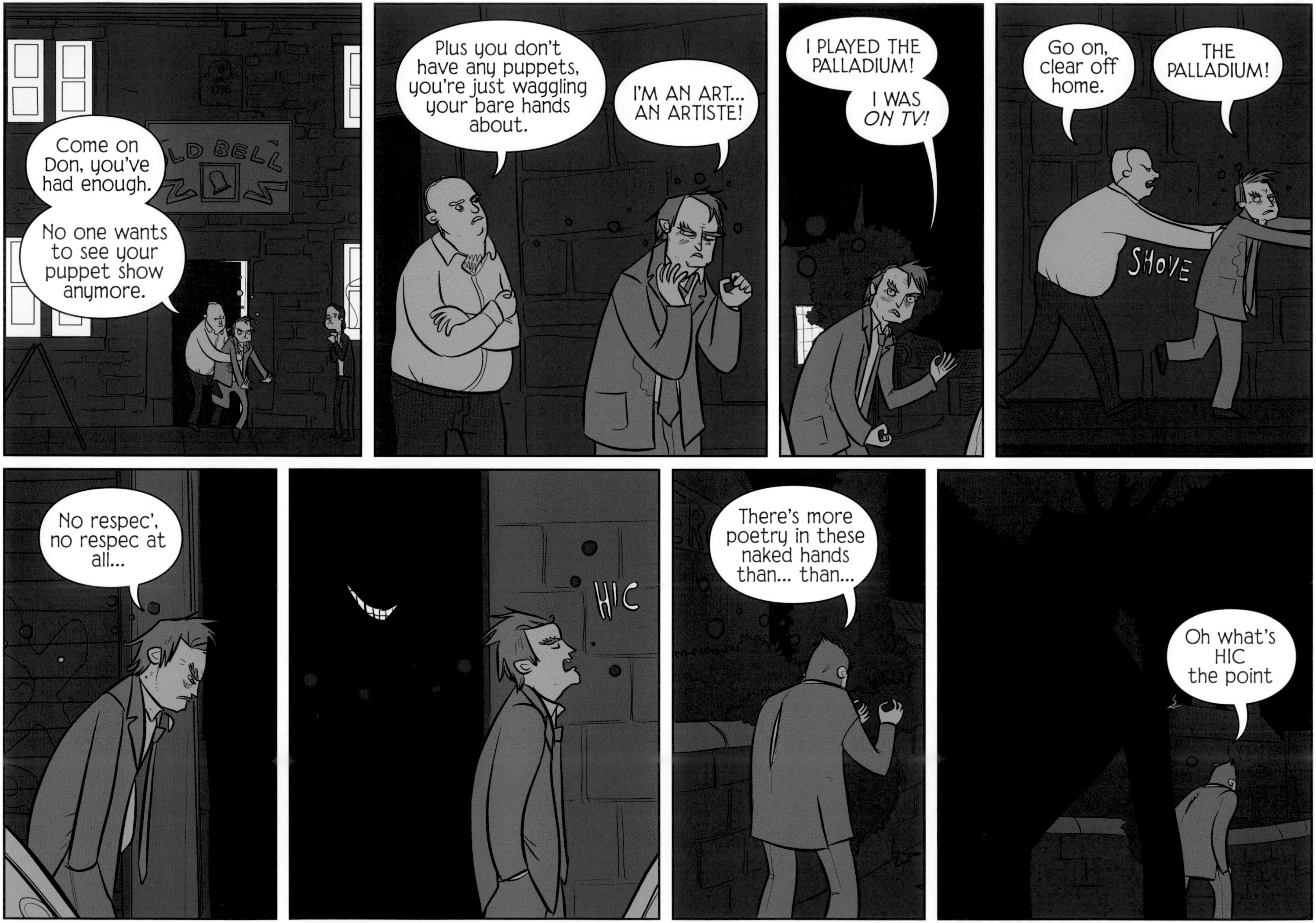
Come on Don, you've had enough.
No one wants to see your puppet show anymore.
Plus you don't have any puppets, you're just waggling your bare hands about.
I'M AN ART... AN ARTISTE!
I PLAYED THE PALLADIUM!
I WAS *ON TV!*
Go on, clear off home.
THE PALLADIUM!
SHOVE
No respec', no respec at all...
HIC
There's more poetry in these naked hands than... than...
Oh what's HIC the point

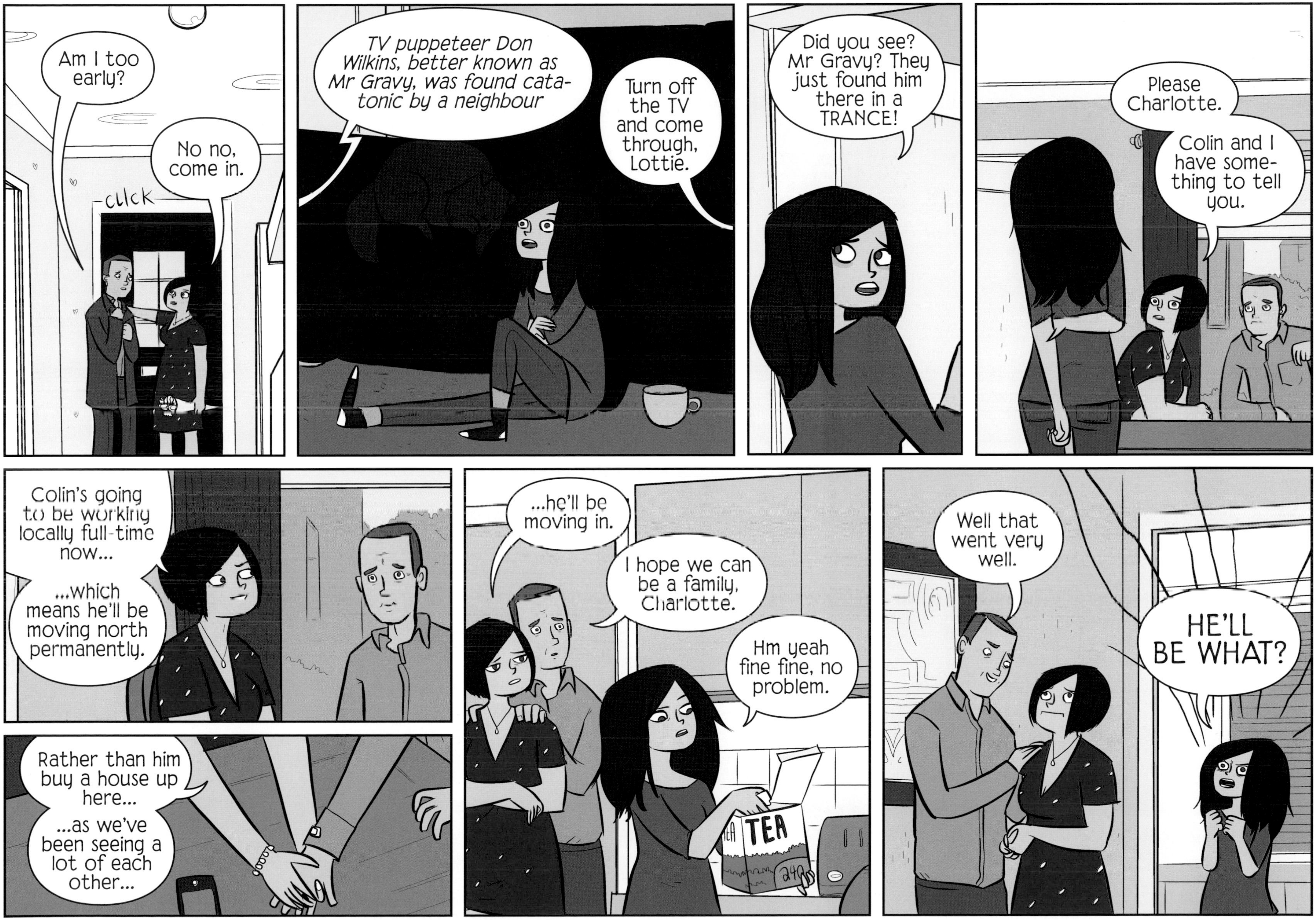
Am I too early?
No no, come in.
CLICK
TV puppeteer Don Wilkins, better known as Mr Gravy, was found catatonic by a neighbour
Turn off the TV and come through, Lottie.
Did you see? Mr Gravy? They just found him there in a TRANCE!
Please Charlotte.
Colin and I have something to tell you.
Colin's going to be working locally full-time now...
...which means he'll be moving north permanently.
Rather than him buy a house up here...
...as we've been seeing a lot of each other...
...he'll be moving in.
I hope we can be a family, Charlotte.
Hm yeah fine fine, no problem.
TEA
Well that went very well.
HE'LL BE WHAT?

Bad Machinery, Volume Six

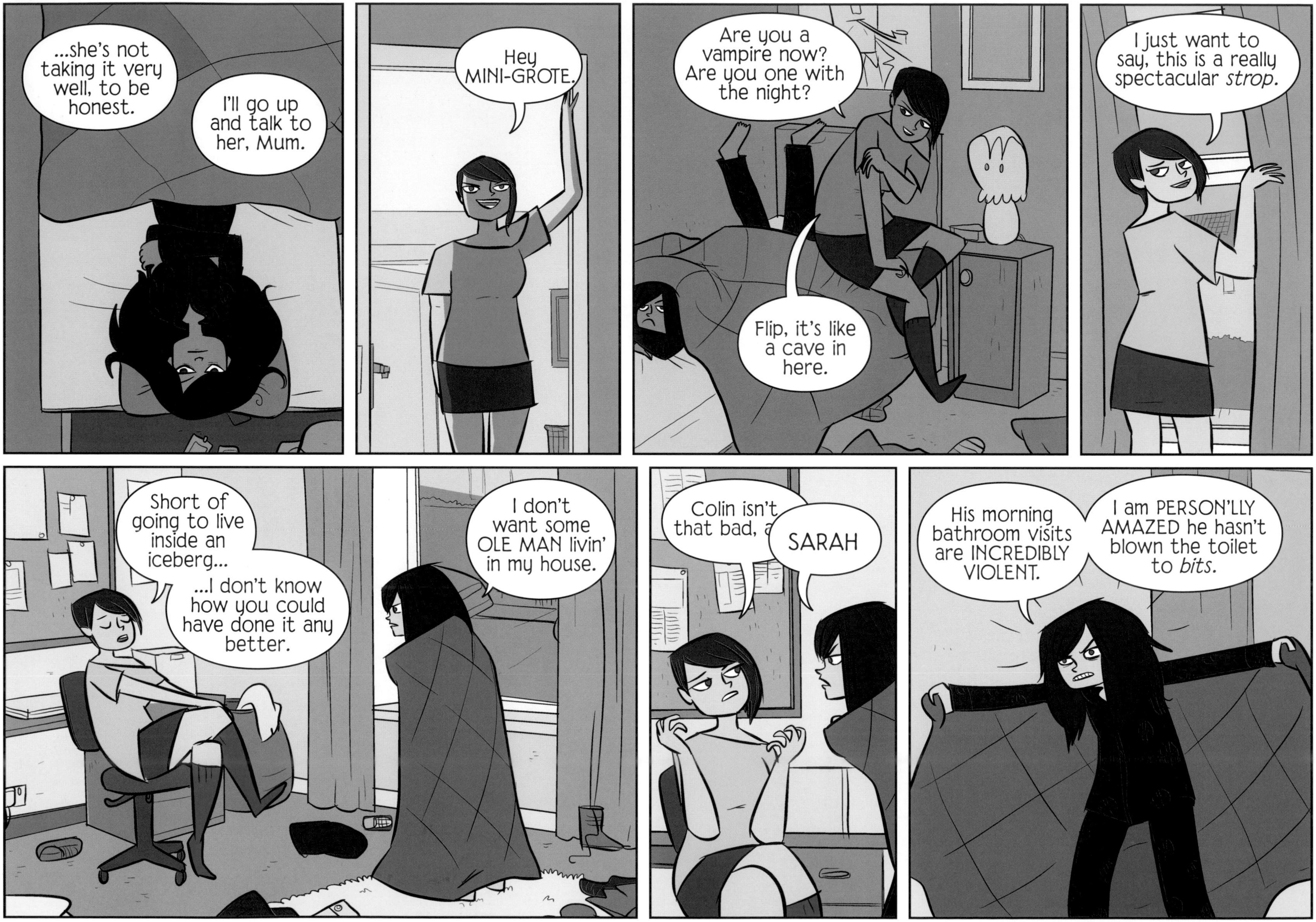

...she's not taking it very well, to be honest.
I'll go up and talk to her, Mum.
Hey MINI-GROTE.
Are you a vampire now? Are you one with the night?
Flip, it's like a cave in here.
I just want to say, this is a really spectacular *strop.*
Short of going to live inside an iceberg...
...I don't know how you could have done it any better.
I don't want some OLE MAN livin' in my house.
Colin isn't that bad, a
SARAH
His morning bathroom visits are INCREDIBLY VIOLENT.
I am PERSON'LLY AMAZED he hasn't blown the toilet to *bits.*

The Case of the Unwelcome Visitor

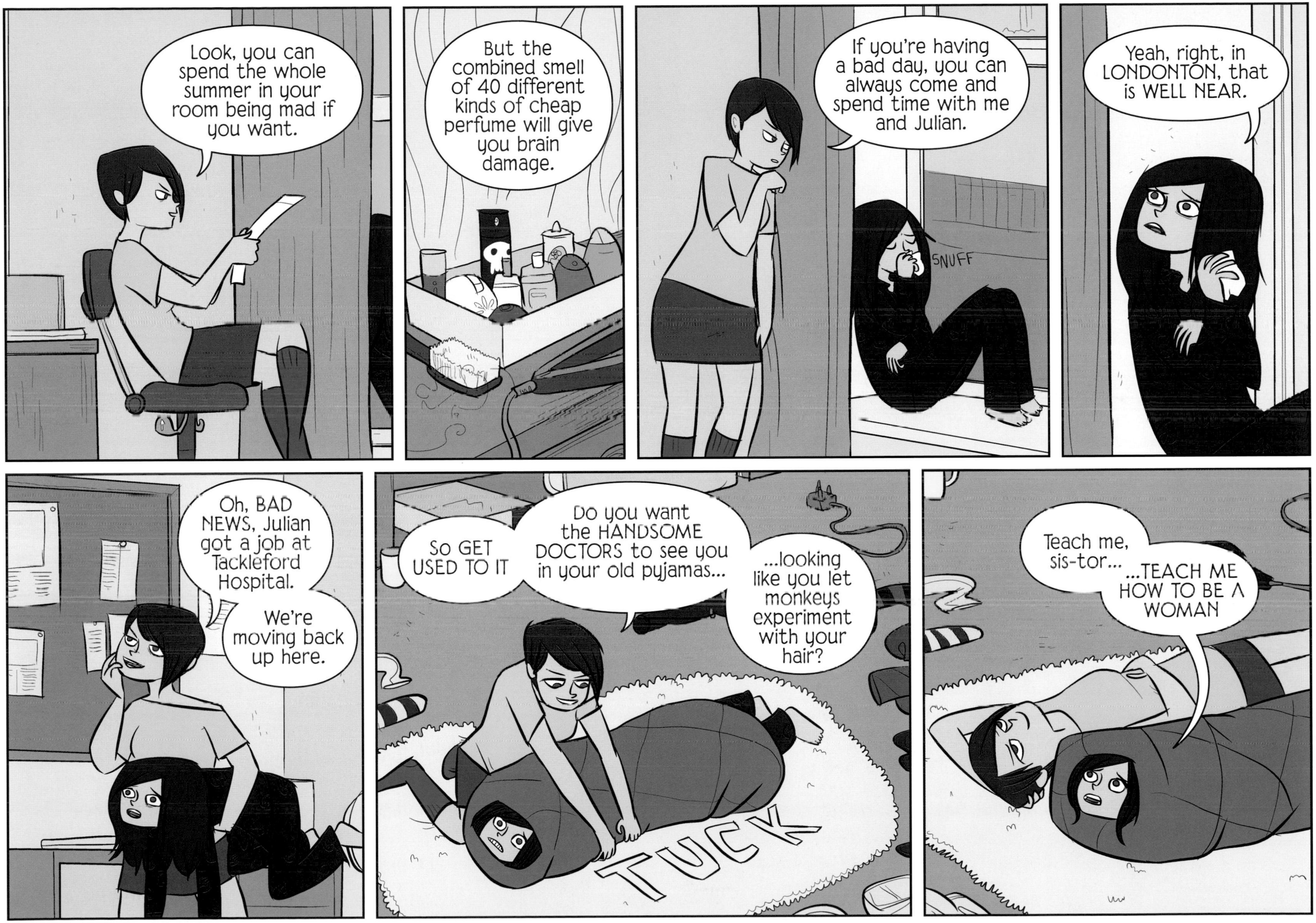

Look, you can spend the whole summer in your room being mad if you want.
But the combined smell of 40 different kinds of cheap perfume will give you brain damage.
If you're having a bad day, you can always come and spend time with me and Julian.
SNUFF
Yeah, right, in LONDONTON, that is WELL NEAR.
Oh, BAD NEWS, Julian got a job at Tackleford Hospital.
We're moving back up here.
So GET USED TO IT
Do you want the HANDSOME DOCTORS to see you in your old pyjamas...
...looking like you let monkeys experiment with your hair?
TUCK
Teach me, sis-tor...
...TEACH ME HOW TO BE A WOMAN

Bad Machinery, Volume Six

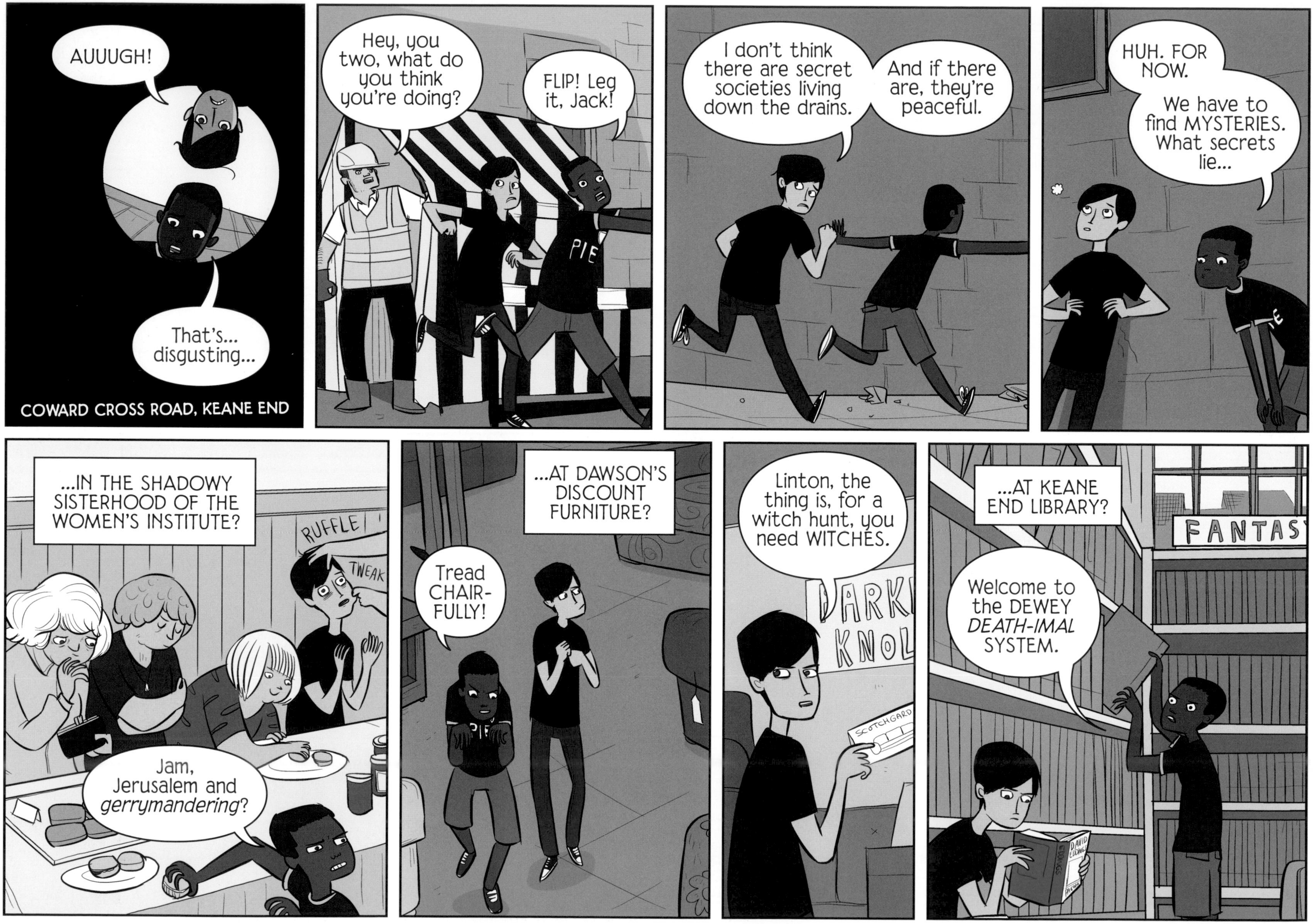

AUUUGH!
That's... disgusting...
COWARD CROSS ROAD, KEANE END
Hey, you two, what do you think you're doing?
FLIP! Leg it, Jack!
PIE
I don't think there are secret societies living down the drains.
And if there are, they're peaceful.
HUH. FOR NOW.
We have to find MYSTERIES. What secrets lie...
...IN THE SHADOWY SISTERHOOD OF THE WOMEN'S INSTITUTE?
RUFFLE
TWEAK
Jam, Jerusalem and *gerrymandering*?
...AT DAWSON'S DISCOUNT FURNITURE?
Tread CHAIR-FULLY!
PIE
Linton, the thing is, for a witch hunt, you need WITCHES.
DARK KNOL
SCOTCHGARD
...AT KEANE END LIBRARY?
FANTAS
Welcome to the DEWEY *DEATH-IMAL* SYSTEM.
DAVID EDDINGS

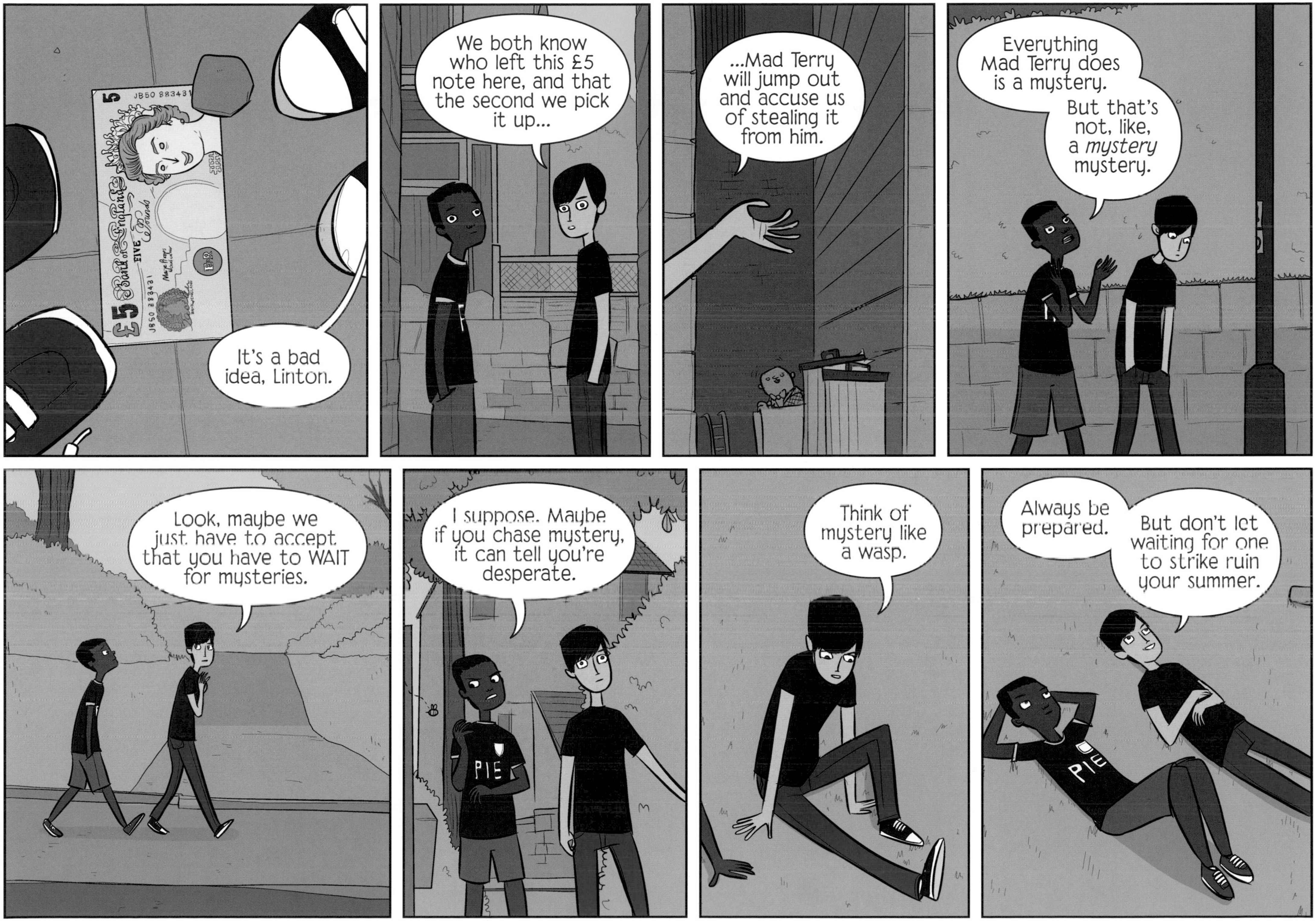
It's a bad idea, Linton.
We both know who left this £5 note here, and that the second we pick it up...
...Mad Terry will jump out and accuse us of stealing it from him.
Everything Mad Terry does is a mystery.
But that's not, like, a *mystery* mystery.
Look, maybe we just have to accept that you have to WAIT for mysteries.
I suppose. Maybe if you chase mystery, it can tell you're desperate.
Think of mystery like a wasp.
Always be prepared.
But don't let waiting for one to strike ruin your summer.

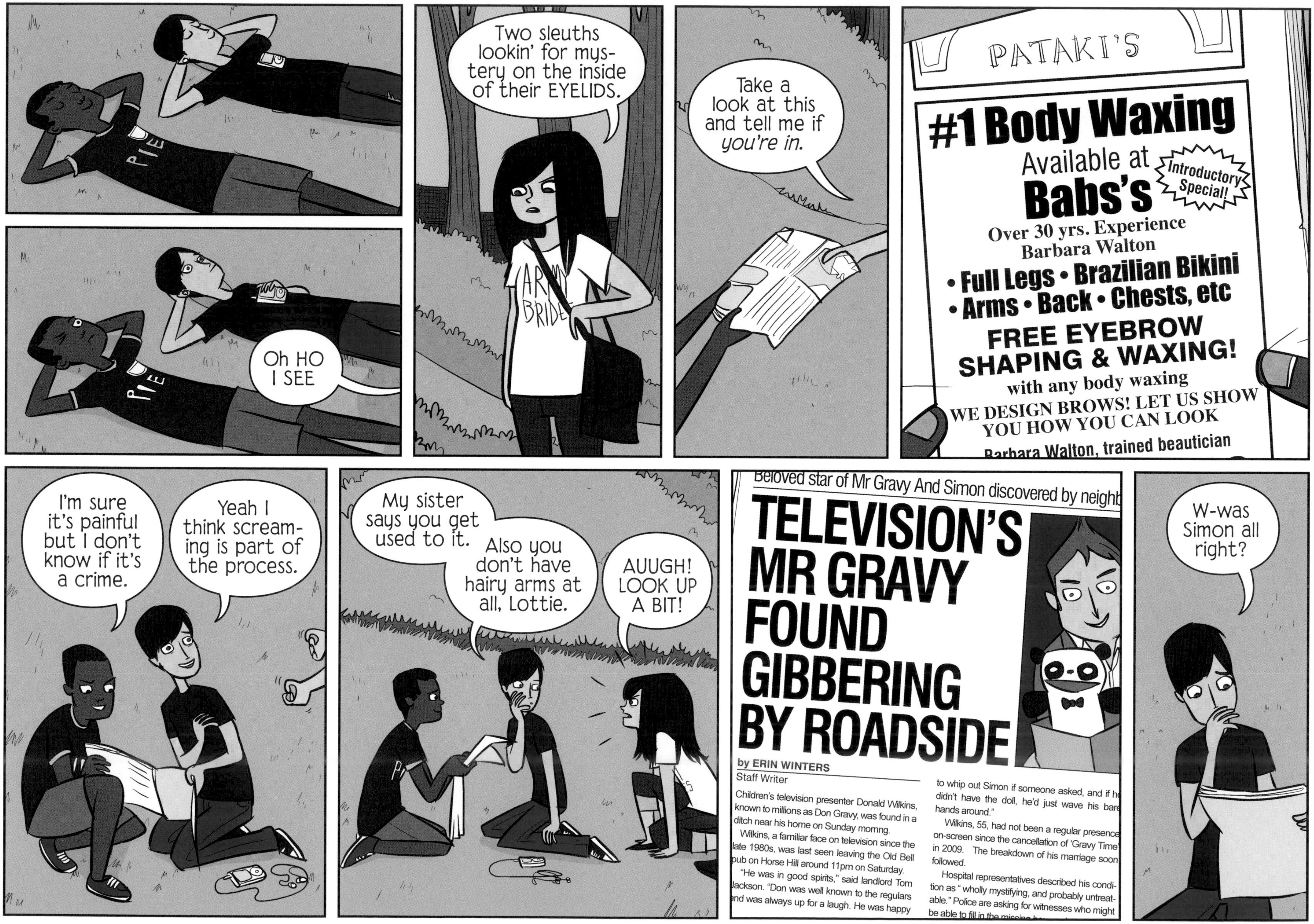
Two sleuths lookin' for mystery on the inside of their EYELIDS.
Oh HO I SEE
Take a look at this and tell me if *you're in*.
PATAKI'S
#1 Body Waxing
Available at
Babs's
Introductory Special!
Over 30 yrs. Experience
Barbara Walton
• Full Legs • Brazilian Bikini
• Arms • Back • Chests, etc
FREE EYEBROW SHAPING & WAXING!
with any body waxing
WE DESIGN BROWS! LET US SHOW YOU HOW YOU CAN LOOK
Barbara Walton, trained beautician
I'm sure it's painful but I don't know if it's a crime.
Yeah I think screaming is part of the process.
My sister says you get used to it.
Also you don't have hairy arms at all, Lottie.
AUUGH! LOOK UP A BIT!
Beloved star of Mr Gravy And Simon discovered by neigh
TELEVISION'S MR GRAVY FOUND GIBBERING BY ROADSIDE
by ERIN WINTERS
Staff Writer
Children's television presenter Donald Wilkins, known to millions as Don Gravy, was found in a ditch near his home on Sunday mornng.
Wilkins, a familiar face on television since the late 1980s, was last seen leaving the Old Bell pub on Horse Hill around 11pm on Saturday.
"He was in good spirits," said landlord Tom Jackson. "Don was well known to the regulars and was always up for a laugh. He was happy to whip out Simon if someone asked, and if h didn't have the doll, he'd just wave his bar hands around."
Wilkins, 55, had not been a regular presence on-screen since the cancellation of 'Gravy Time' in 2009. The breakdown of his marriage soon followed.
Hospital representatives described his condition as " wholly mystifying, and probably untreatable." Police are asking for witnesses who might be able to fill in the
W-was Simon all right?

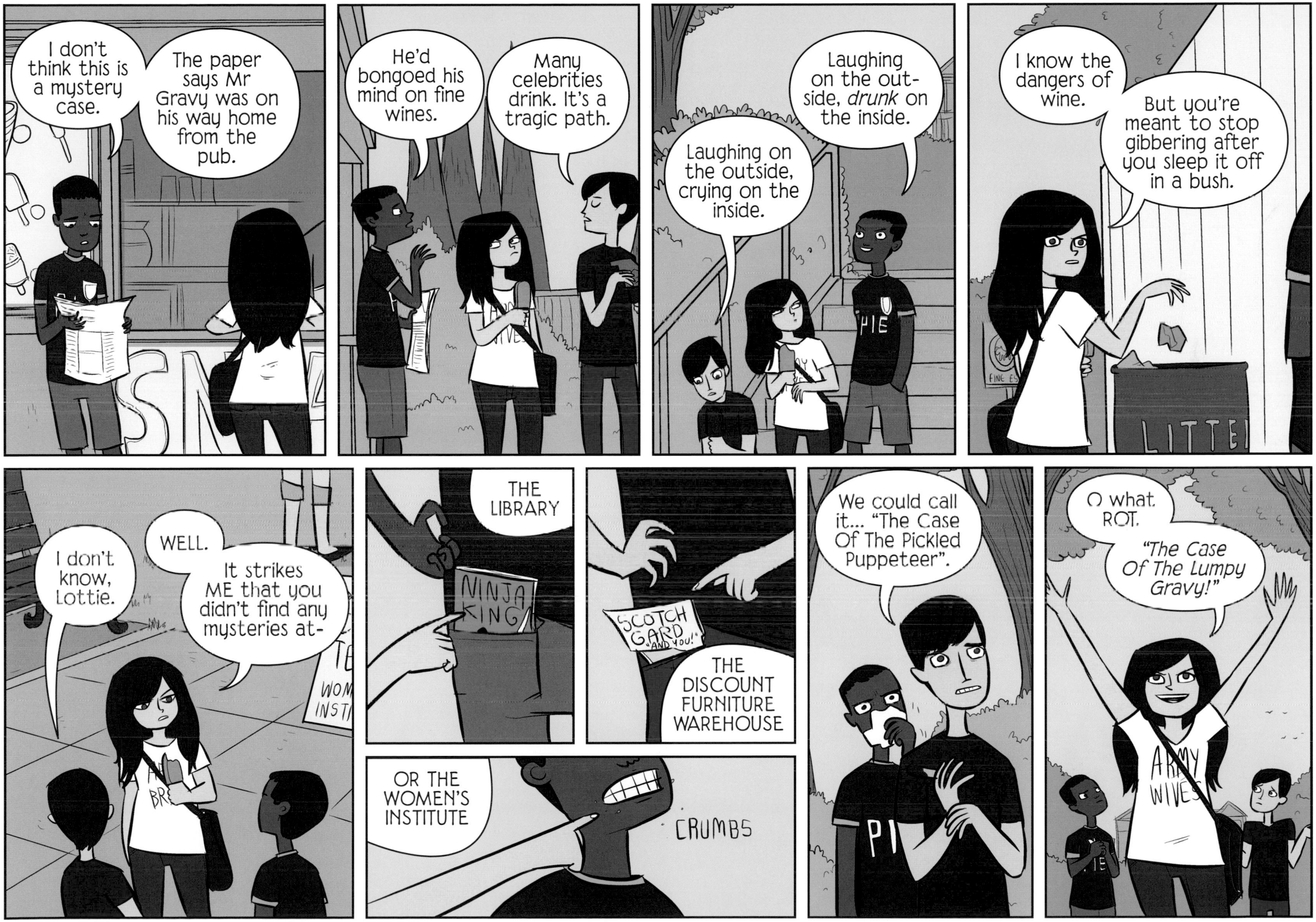
I don't think this is a mystery case.
The paper says Mr Gravy was on his way home from the pub.
He'd bongoed his mind on fine wines.
Many celebrities drink. It's a tragic path.
Laughing on the outside, crying on the inside.
Laughing on the out-side, *drunk* on the inside.
I know the dangers of wine.
But you're meant to stop gibbering after you sleep it off in a bush.
LITTE
I don't know, Lottie.
WELL.
It strikes ME that you didn't find any mysteries at-
THE LIBRARY
NINJA KING
SCOTCH GARD "AND YOU!"
THE DISCOUNT FURNITURE WAREHOUSE
OR THE WOMEN'S INSTITUTE
CRUMBS
We could call it... "The Case Of The Pickled Puppeteer".
O what ROT.
"The Case Of The Lumpy Gravy!"
ARMY WIVES

Bad Machinery, Volume Six

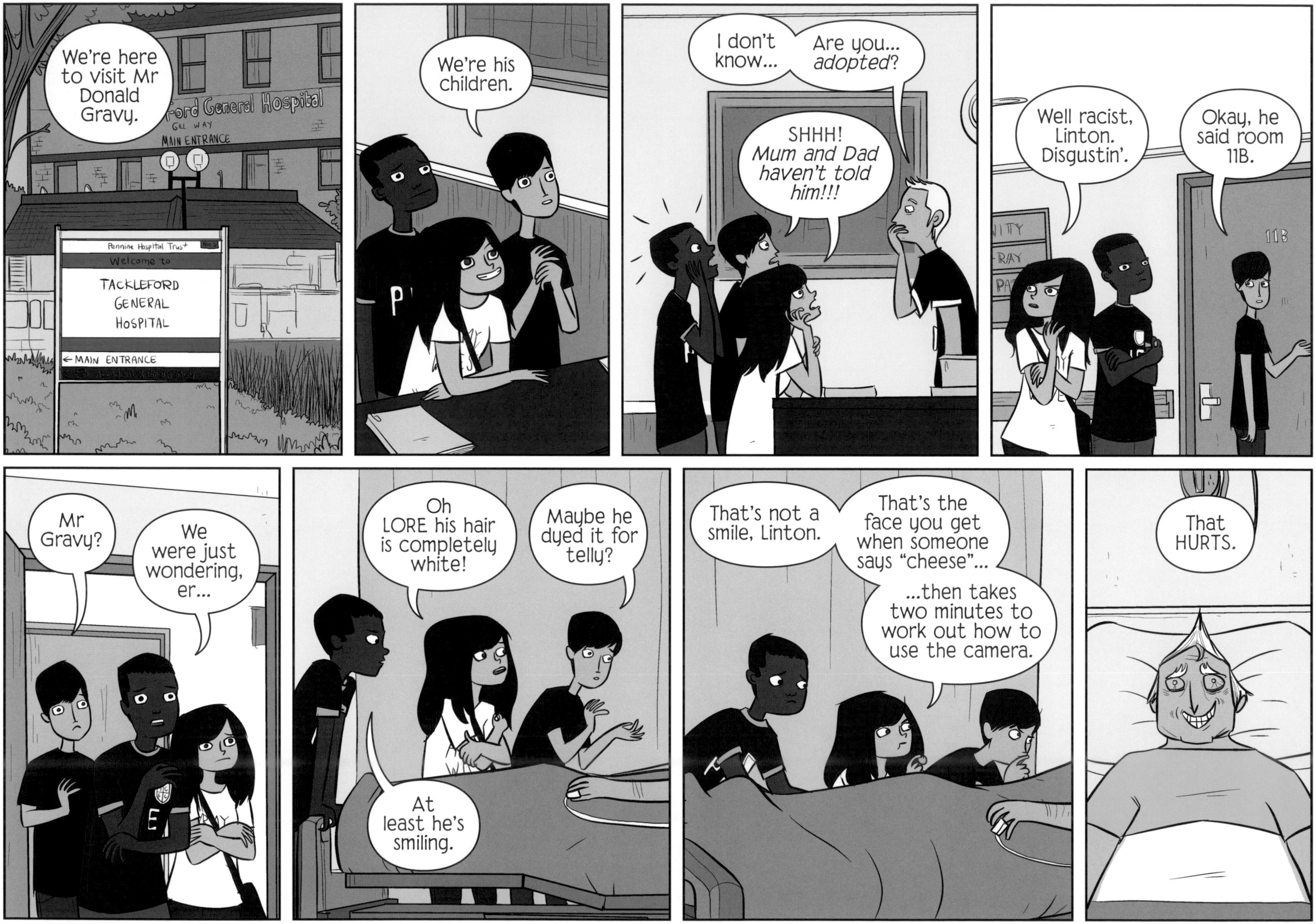
We're here to visit Mr Donald Gravy.
ford General Hospital
GILL WAY
MAIN ENTRANCE
Pennine Hospital Trust
Welcome to
TACKLEFORD GENERAL HOSPITAL
← MAIN ENTRANCE
We're his children.
I don't know...
Are you... *adopted*?
SHHH! *Mum and Dad haven't told him!!!*
Well racist, Linton. Disgustin'.
Okay, he said room 11B.
11B
Mr Gravy?
We were just wondering, er...
Oh LORE his hair is completely white!
Maybe he dyed it for telly?
At least he's smiling.
That's not a smile, Linton.
That's the face you get when someone says "cheese"...
...then takes two minutes to work out how to use the camera.
That HURTS.

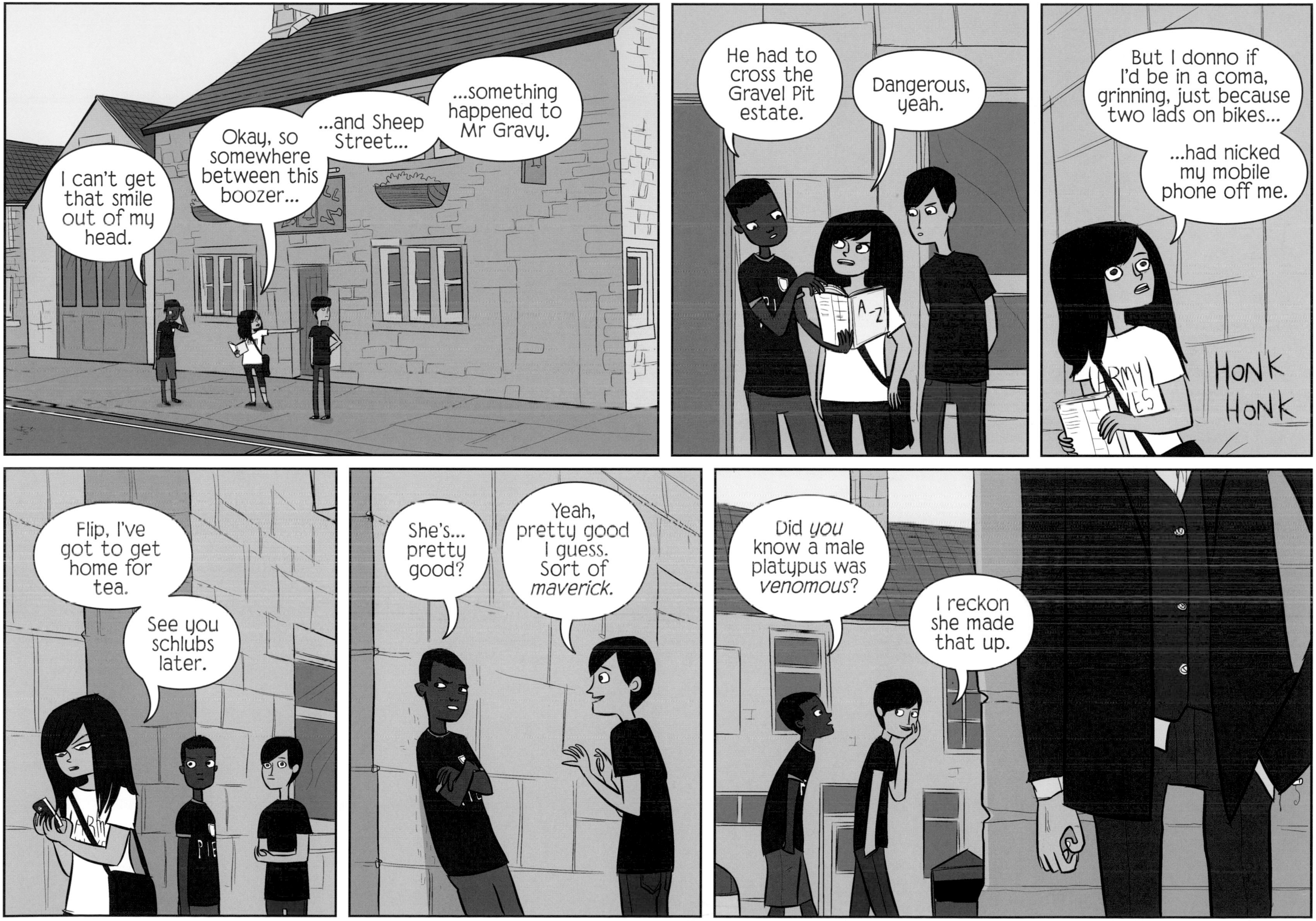
I can't get that smile out of my head.
Okay, so somewhere between this boozer...
...and Sheep Street...
...something happened to Mr Gravy.
He had to cross the Gravel Pit estate.
Dangerous, yeah.
A-Z
But I donno if I'd be in a coma, grinning, just because two lads on bikes...
...had nicked my mobile phone off me.
HONK HONK
Flip, I've got to get home for tea.
See you schlubs later.
She's... pretty good?
Yeah, pretty good I guess. Sort of *maverick.*
Did *you* know a male platypus was *venomous*?
I reckon she made that up.

Bad Machinery, Volume Six

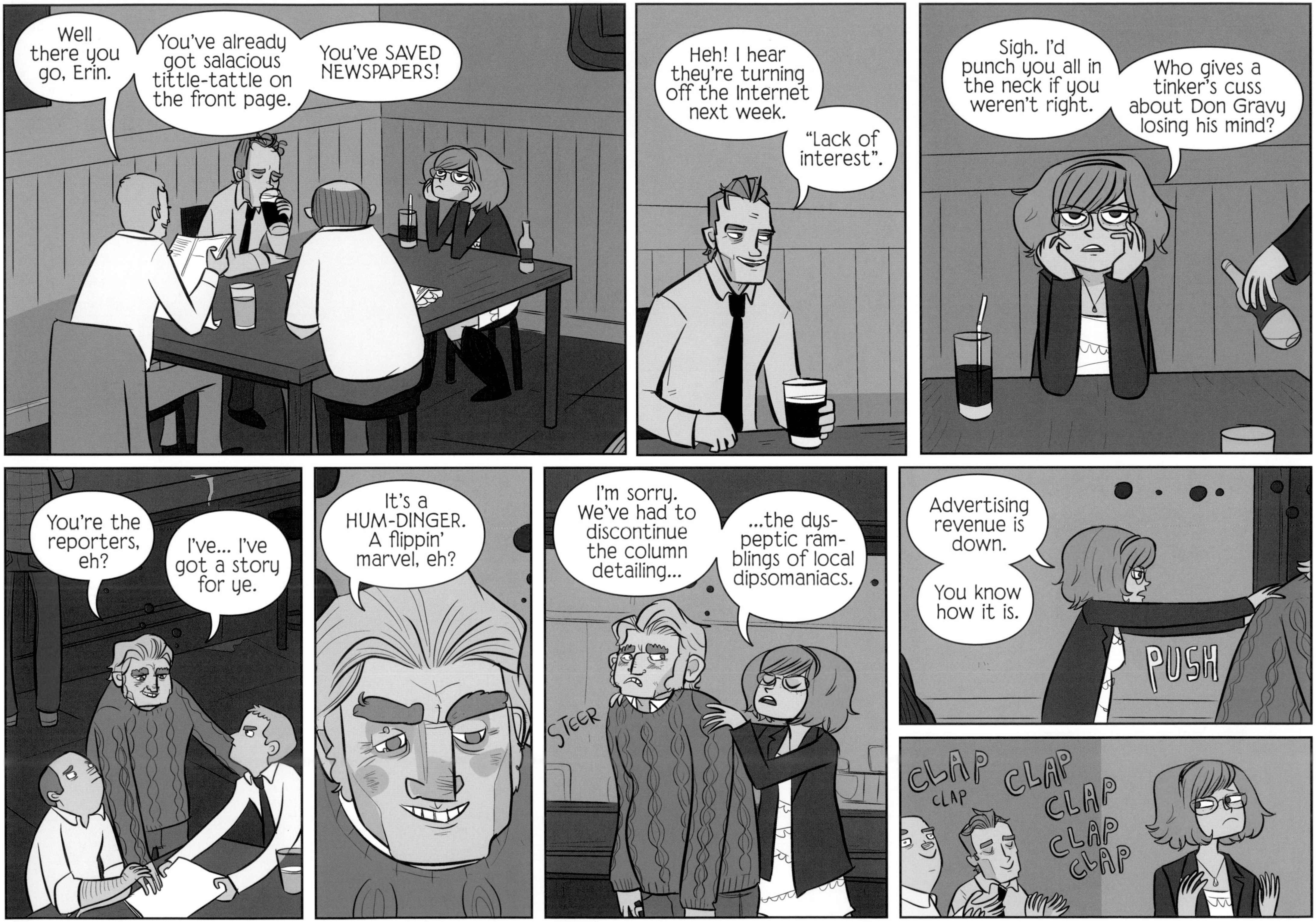
Well there you go, Erin.
You've already got salacious tittle-tattle on the front page.
You've SAVED NEWSPAPERS!
Heh! I hear they're turning off the Internet next week.
"Lack of interest".
Sigh. I'd punch you all in the neck if you weren't right.
Who gives a tinker's cuss about Don Gravy losing his mind?
You're the reporters, eh?
I've... I've got a story for ye.
It's a HUM-DINGER. A flippin' marvel, eh?
I'm sorry. We've had to discontinue the column detailing...
...the dys-peptic ram-blings of local dipsomaniacs.
STEER
Advertising revenue is down.
You know how it is.
PUSH
CLAP
CLAP
CLAP
CLAP
CLAP
CLAP
CLAP

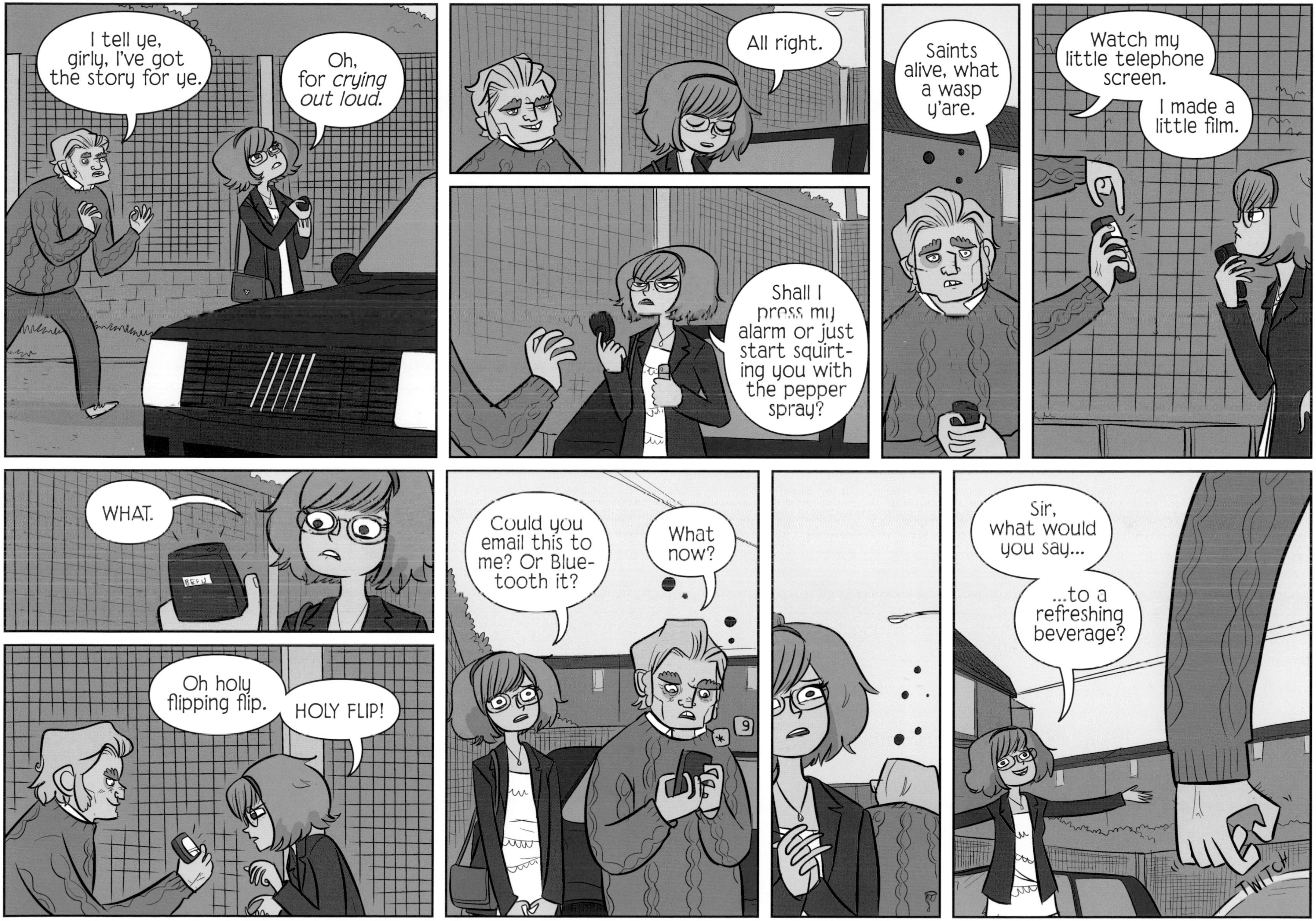
I tell ye, girly, I've got the story for ye.
Oh, for *crying out loud.*
All right.
Shall I press my alarm or just start squirting you with the pepper spray?
Saints alive, what a wasp y'are.
Watch my little telephone screen.
I made a little film.
WHAT.
BEEF
Oh holy flipping flip.
HOLY FLIP!
Could you email this to me? Or Bluetooth it?
What now?
Sir, what would you say...
...to a refreshing beverage?
TWITCH

Bad Machinery, Volume Six

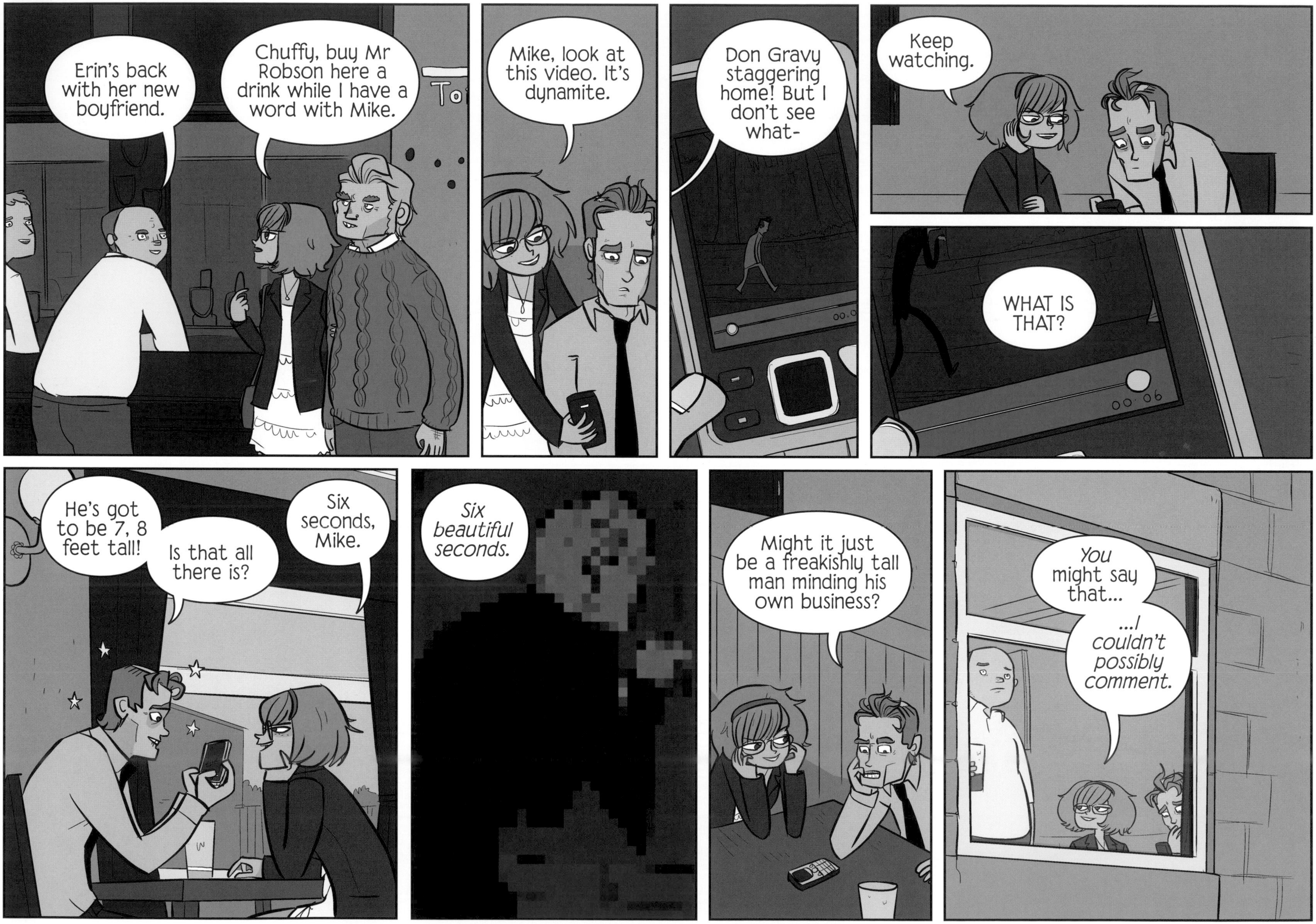
Erin's back with her new boyfriend.
Chuffy, buy Mr Robson here a drink while I have a word with Mike.
Toi
Mike, look at this video. It's dynamite.
Don Gravy staggering home! But I don't see what-
Keep watching.
WHAT IS THAT?
00·06
He's got to be 7, 8 feet tall!
Is that all there is?
Six seconds, Mike.
Six beautiful seconds.
Might it just be a freakishly tall man minding his own business?
You might say that...
...*I couldn't possibly comment.*

The Case of the Unwelcome Visitor

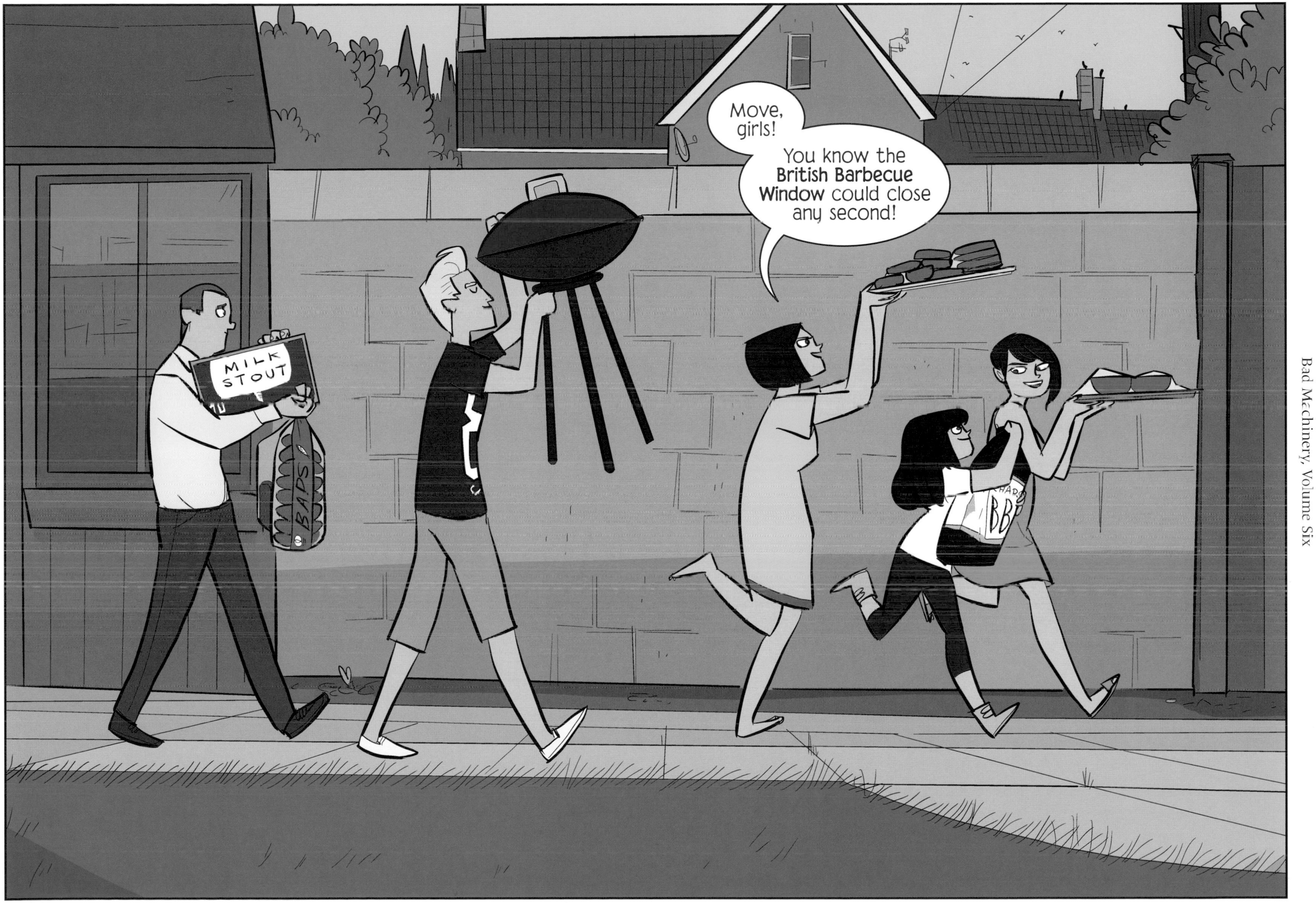
Move, girls!
You know the **British Barbecue Window** could close any second!
MILK STOUT
BAPS

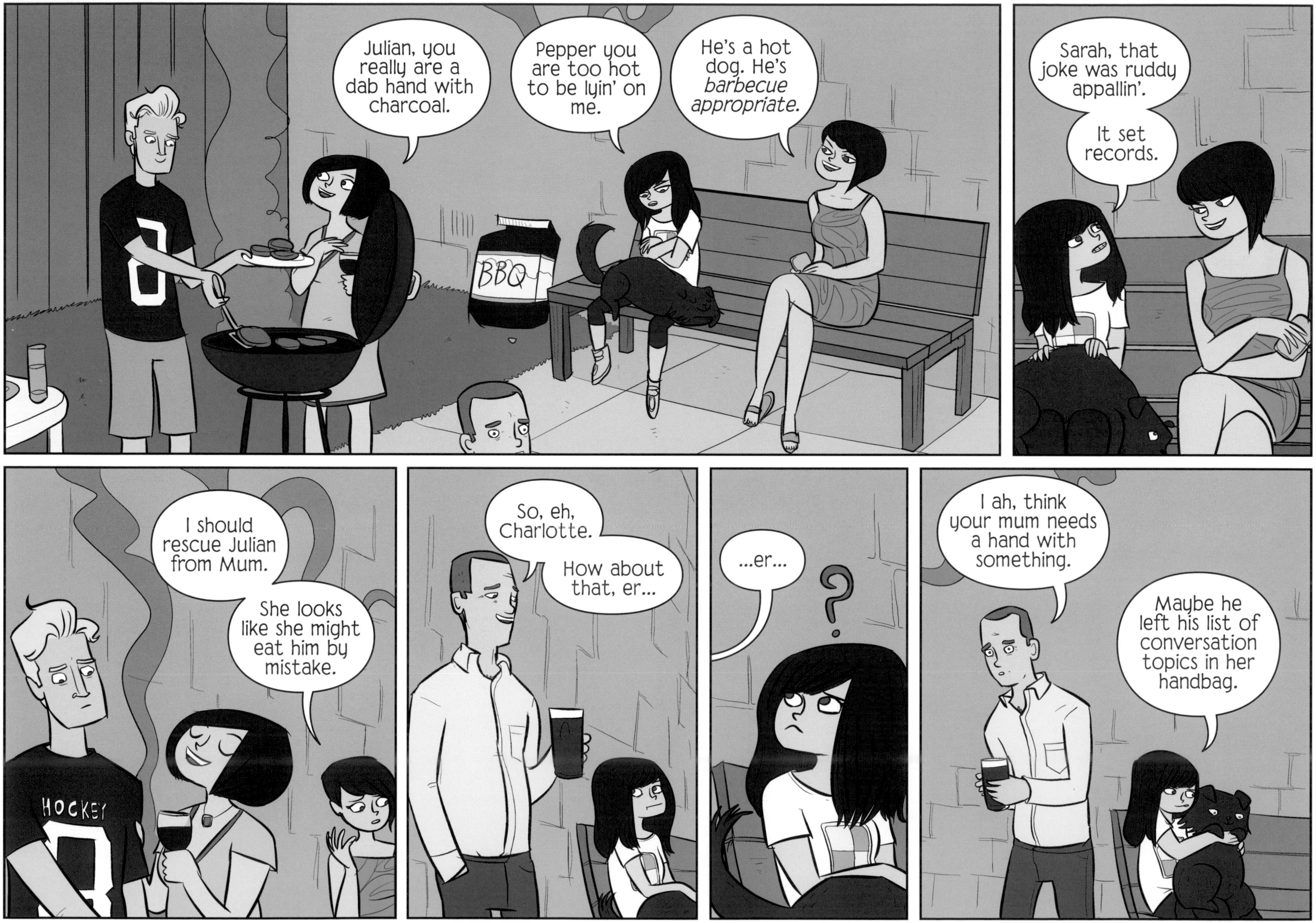
Julian, you really are a dab hand with charcoal.
Pepper you are too hot to be lyin' on me.
He's a hot dog. He's *barbecue appropriate*.
BBQ
Sarah, that joke was ruddy appallin'.
It set records.
I should rescue Julian from Mum.
She looks like she might eat him by mistake.
HOCKEY
So, eh, Charlotte.
How about that, er...
...er...
?
I ah, think your mum needs a hand with something.
Maybe he left his list of conversation topics in her handbag.

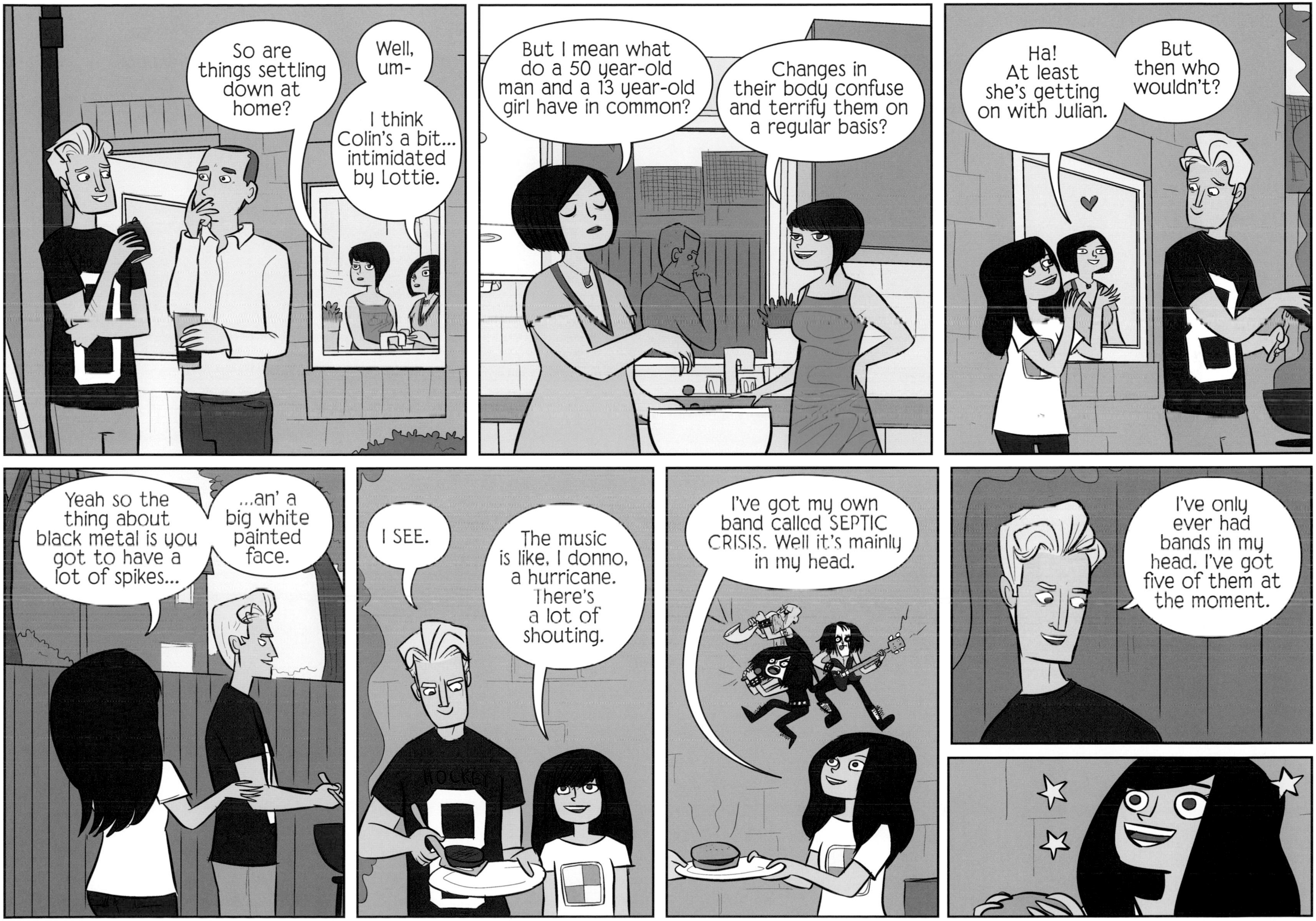

So are things settling down at home?
Well, um-
I think Colin's a bit... intimidated by Lottie.
But I mean what do a 50 year-old man and a 13 year-old girl have in common?
Changes in their body confuse and terrify them on a regular basis?
Ha! At least she's getting on with Julian.
But then who wouldn't?
Yeah so the thing about black metal is you got to have a lot of spikes...
...an' a big white painted face.
I SEE.
The music is like, I donno, a hurricane. There's a lot of shouting.
I've got my own band called SEPTIC CRISIS. Well it's mainly in my head.
I've only ever had bands in my head. I've got five of them at the moment.

Bad Machinery, Volume Six

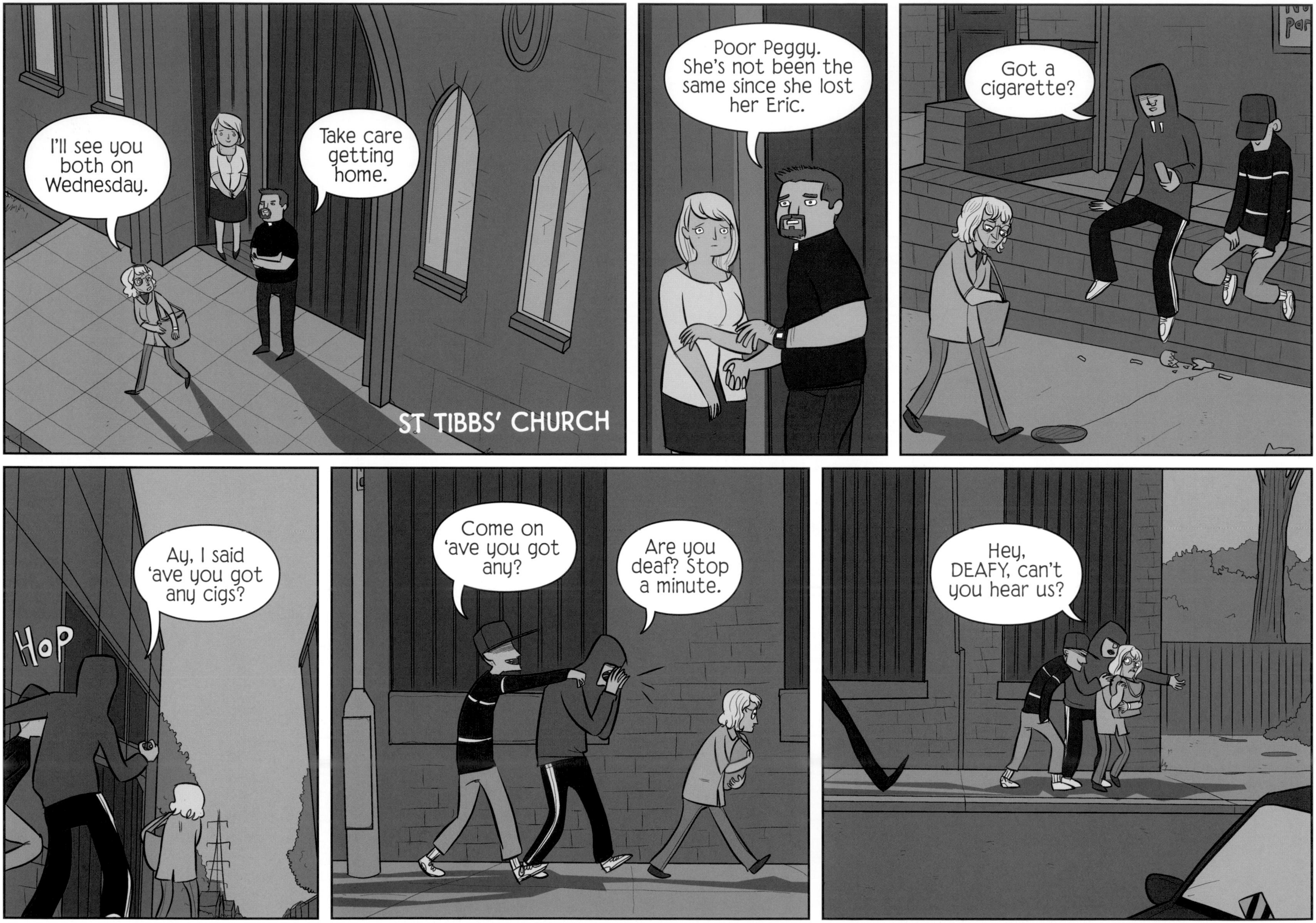
I'll see you both on Wednesday.
Take care getting home.
ST TIBBS' CHURCH
Poor Peggy. She's not been the same since she lost her Eric.
Got a cigarette?
Ay, I said 'ave you got any cigs?
HOP
Come on 'ave you got any?
Are you deaf? Stop a minute.
Hey, DEAFY, can't you hear us?

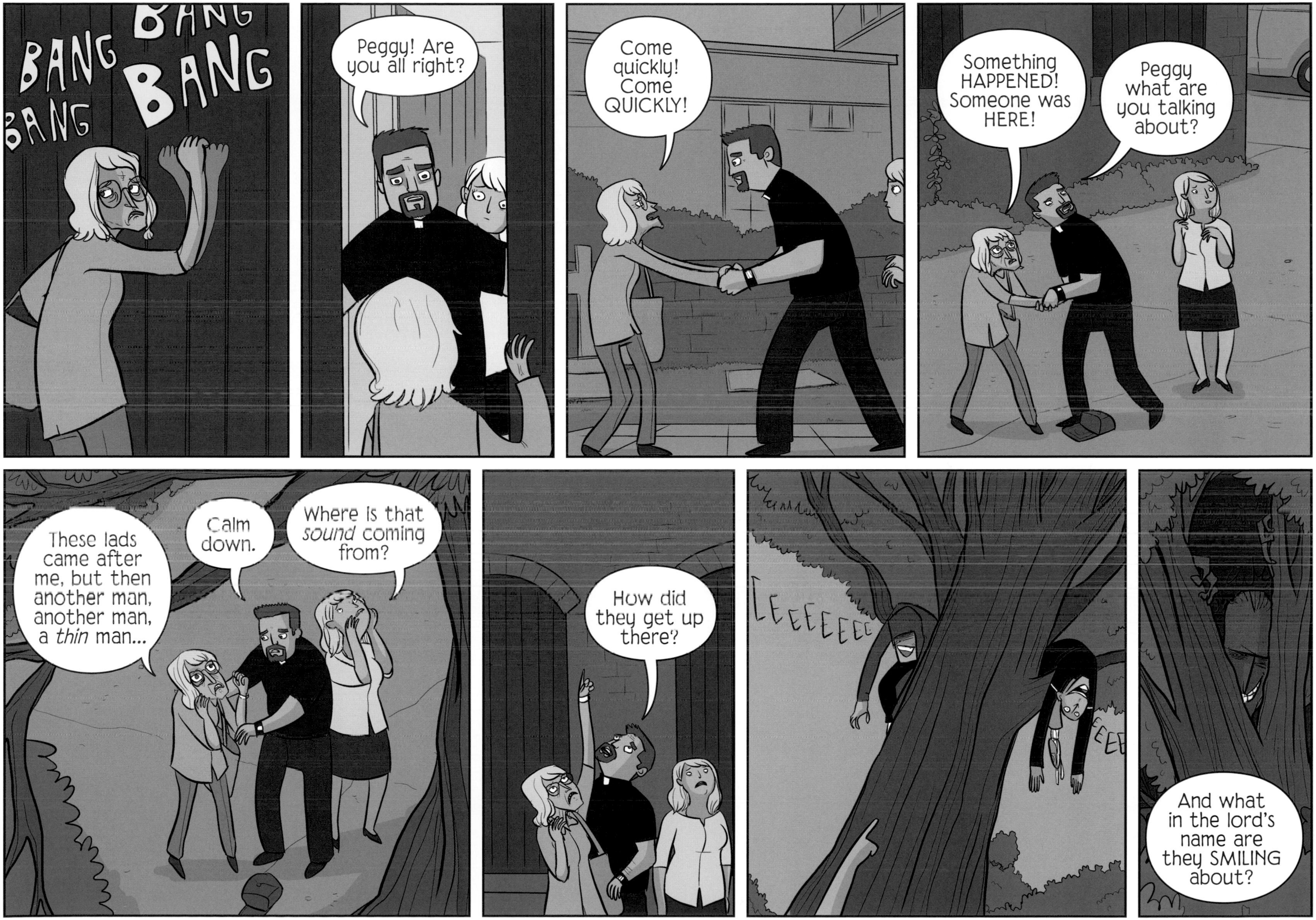
BANG BANG BANG BANG
Peggy! Are you all right?
Come quickly! Come QUICKLY!
Something HAPPENED! Someone was HERE!
Peggy what are you talking about?
These lads came after me, but then another man, another man, a *thin* man...
Calm down.
Where is that *sound* coming from?
How did they get up there?
EEEEEEEE
EEEE
And what in the lord's name are they SMILING about?

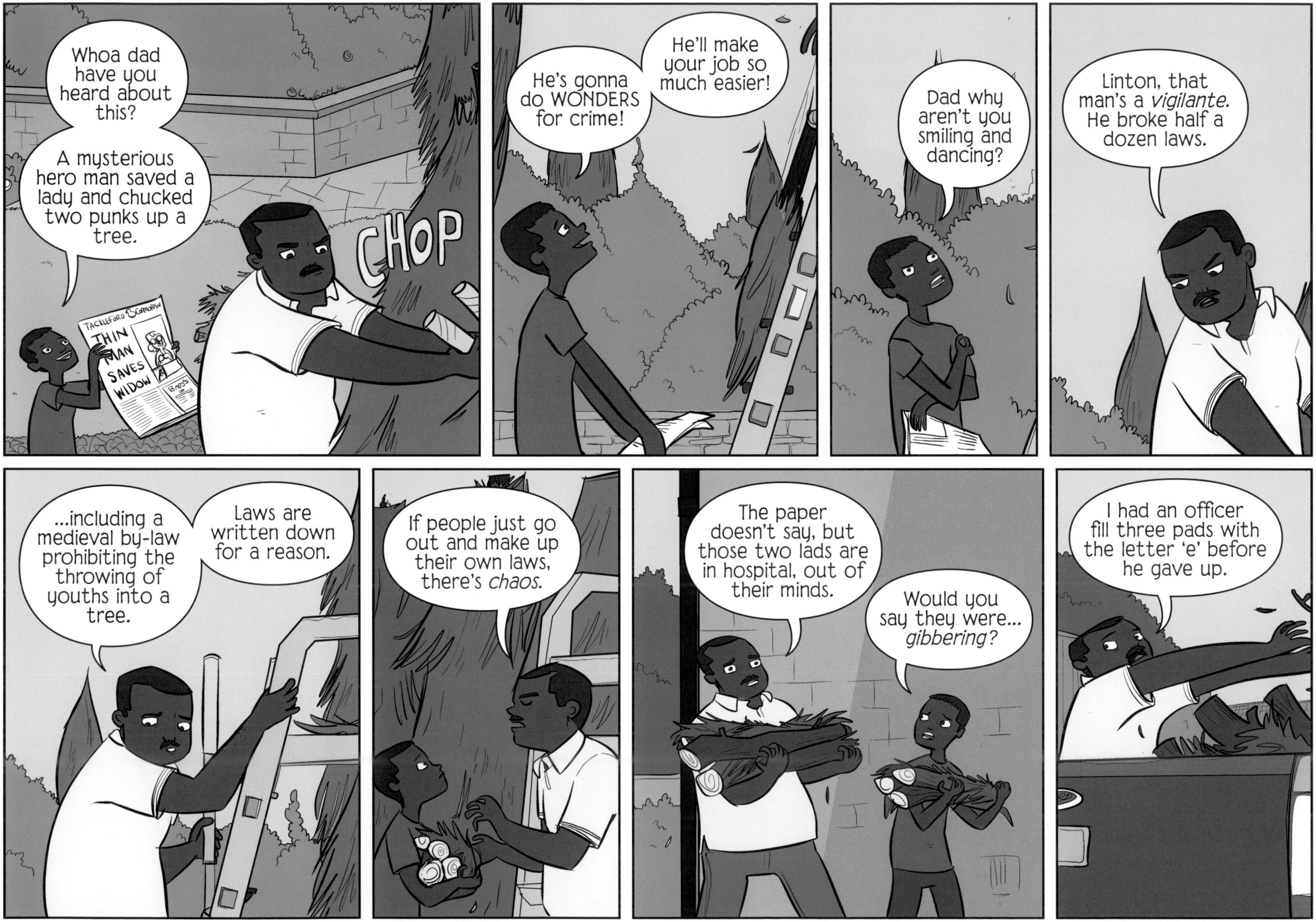
Whoa dad have you heard about this?
A mysterious hero man saved a lady and chucked two punks up a tree.
CHOP
THIN MAN SAVES WIDOW
He's gonna do WONDERS for crime!
He'll make your job so much easier!
Dad why aren't you smiling and dancing?
Linton, that man's a *vigilante.* He broke half a dozen laws.
...including a medieval by-law prohibiting the throwing of youths into a tree.
Laws are written down for a reason.
If people just go out and make up their own laws, there's *chaos.*
The paper doesn't say, but those two lads are in hospital, out of their minds.
Would you say they were... *gibbering?*
I had an officer fill three pads with the letter 'e' before he gave up.

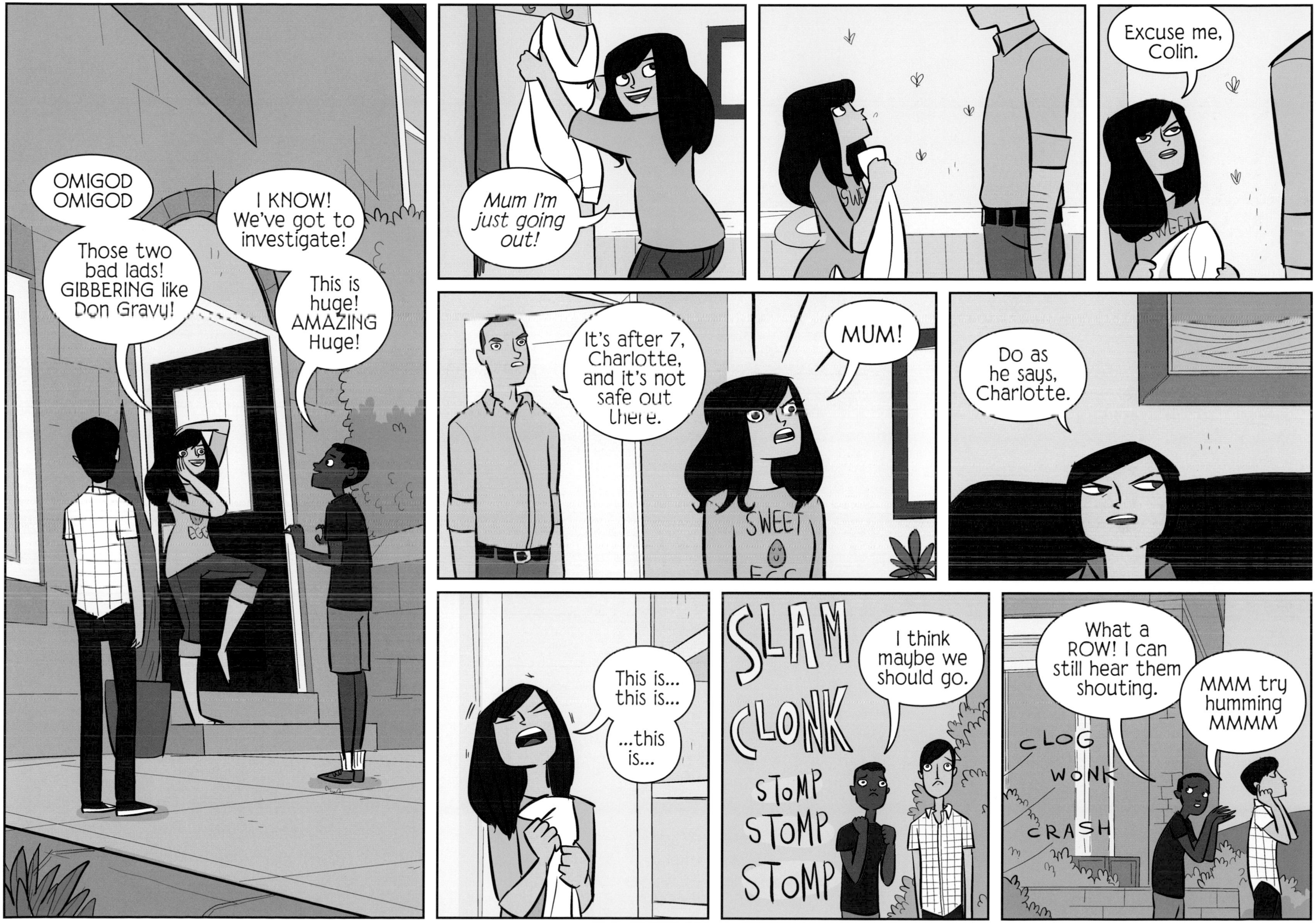
OMIGOD OMIGOD
Those two bad lads! GIBBERING like Don Gravy!
I KNOW! We've got to investigate!
This is huge! AMAZING Huge!
Mum I'm just going out!
Excuse me, Colin.
It's after 7, Charlotte, and it's not safe out there.
MUM!
Do as he says, Charlotte.
This is... this is...
...this is...
SLAM
CLONK
STOMP
STOMP
STOMP
I think maybe we should go.
What a ROW! I can still hear them shouting.
MMM try humming MMMM
CLOG
WONK
CRASH

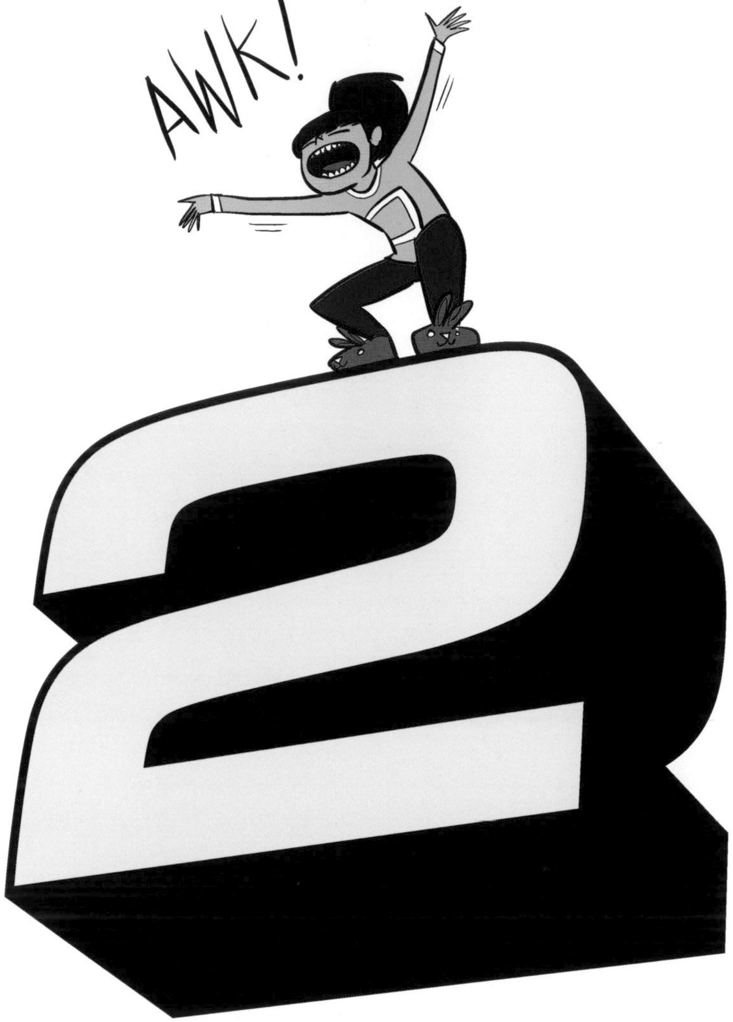
AWK!

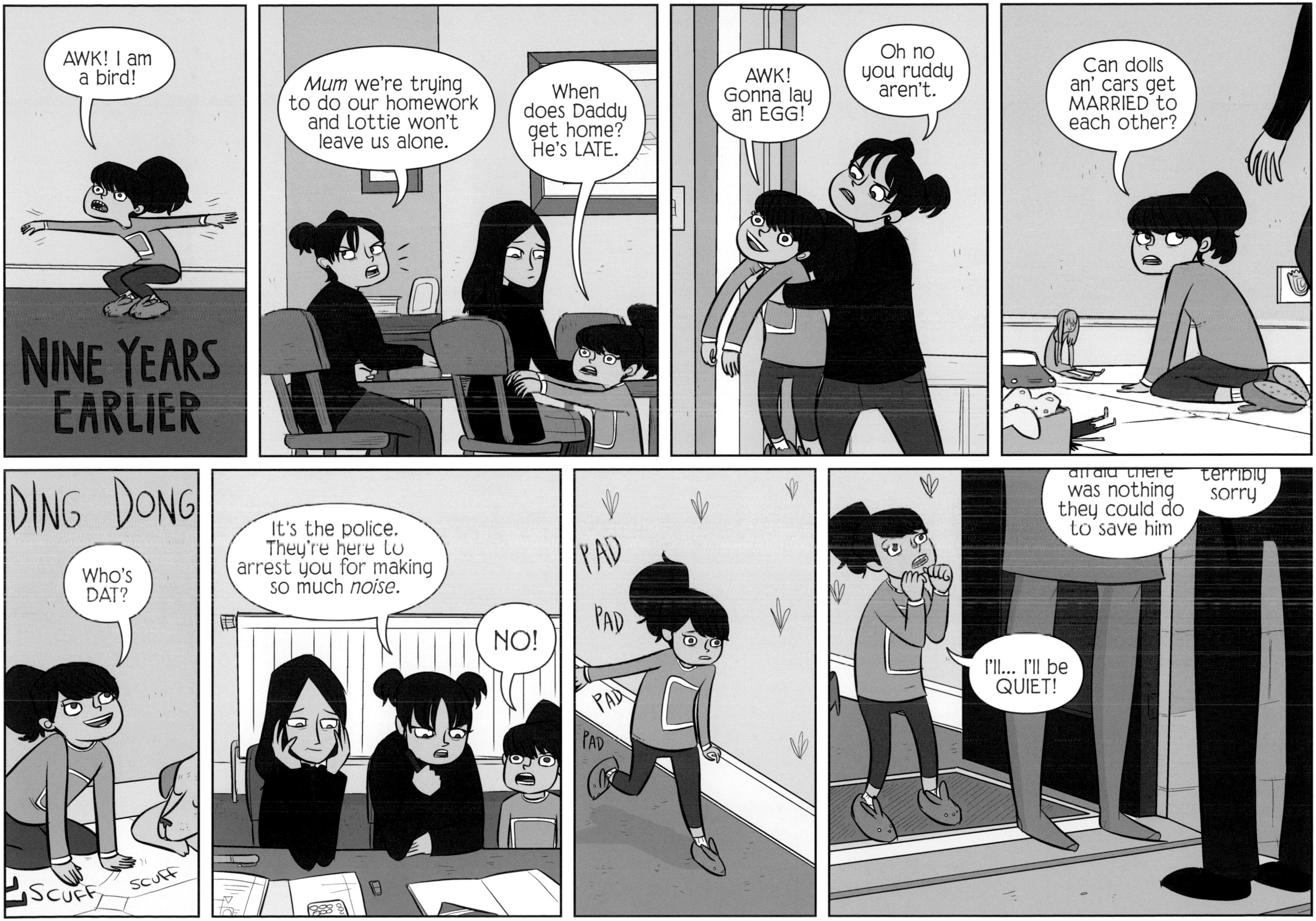
AWK! I am a bird!
NINE YEARS EARLIER
Mum we're trying to do our homework and Lottie won't leave us alone.
When does Daddy get home? He's LATE.
AWK! Gonna lay an EGG!
Oh no you ruddy aren't.
Can dolls an' cars get MARRIED to each other?
DING DONG
Who's DAT?
SCUFF
SCUFF
It's the police. They're here to arrest you for making so much *noise*.
NO!
PAD
PAD
PAD
PAD
was nothing they could do to save him
terribly sorry
I'll... I'll be QUIET!

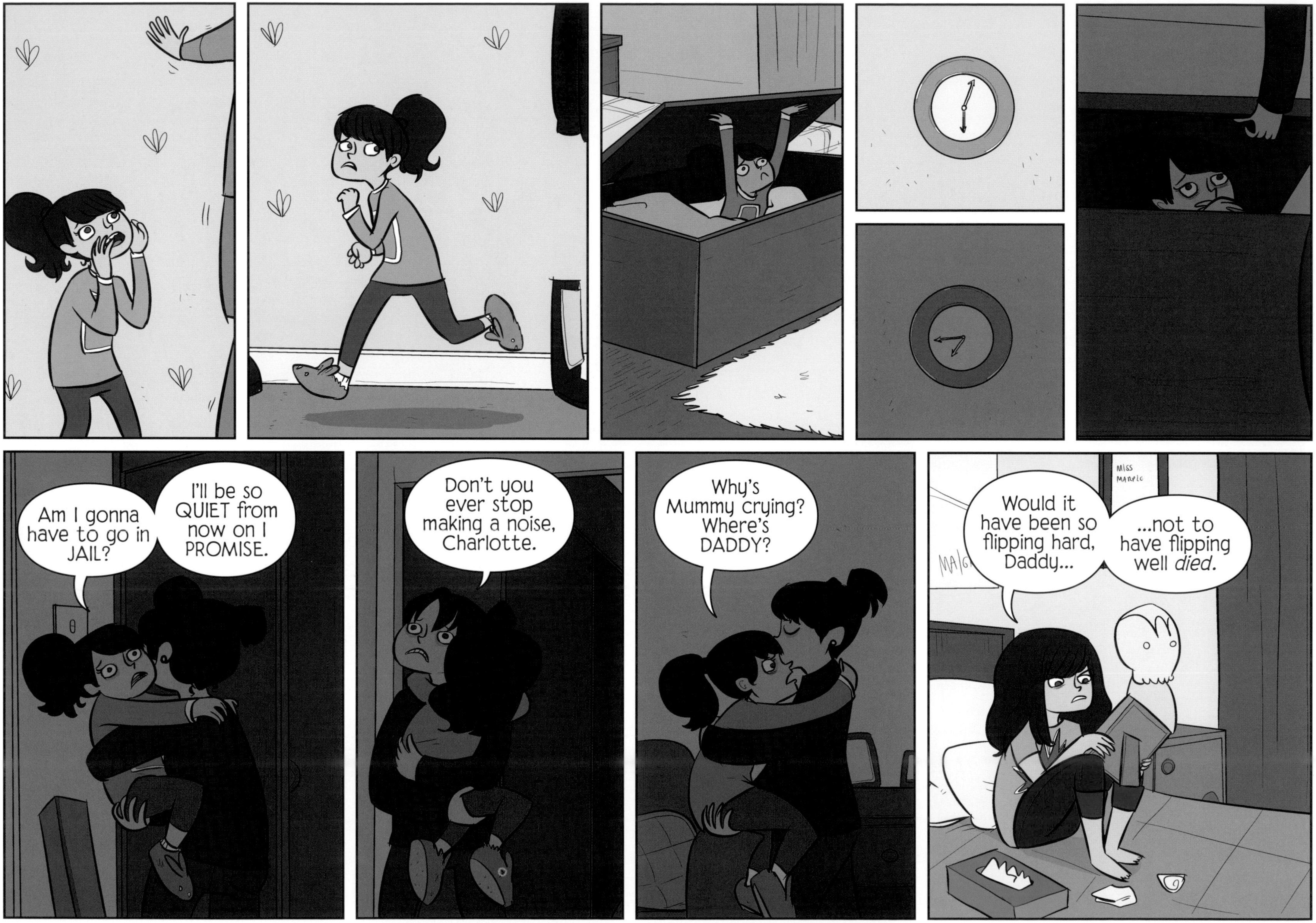
Am I gonna have to go in JAIL?
I'll be so QUIET from now on I PROMISE.
Don't you ever stop making a noise, Charlotte.
Why's Mummy crying? Where's DADDY?
MISS MARPLE
Would it have been so flipping hard, Daddy...
...not to have flipping well *died*.

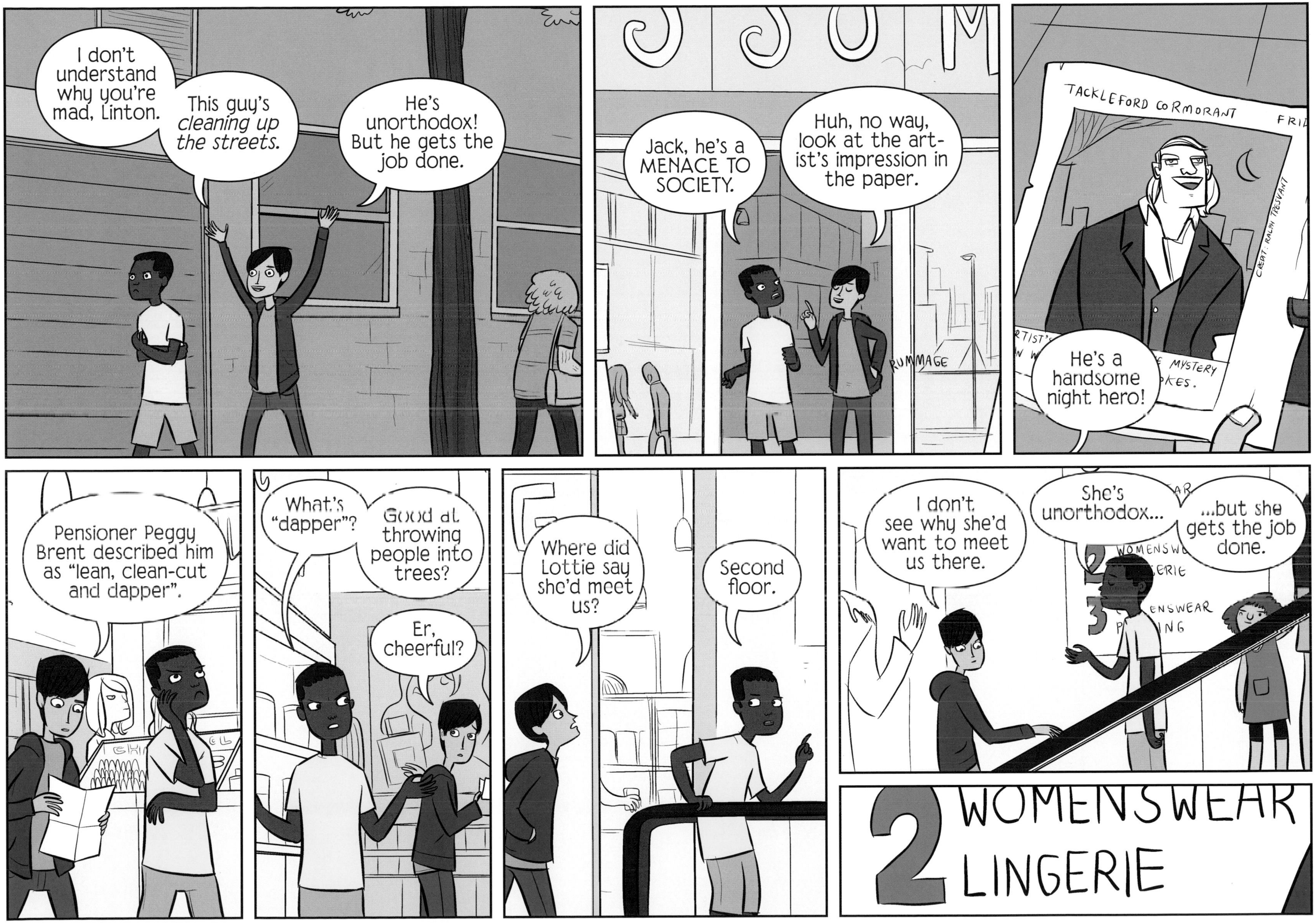
I don't understand why you're mad, Linton.
This guy's *cleaning up the streets.*
He's unorthodox! But he gets the job done.
Jack, he's a MENACE TO SOCIETY.
Huh, no way, look at the artist's impression in the paper.
RUMMAGE
TACKLEFORD CORMORANT
CREDIT: RALPH TRESVANT
He's a handsome night hero!
Pensioner Peggy Brent described him as "lean, clean-cut and dapper".
What's "dapper"?
Good at throwing people into trees?
Er, cheerful?
Where did Lottie say she'd meet us?
Second floor.
I don't see why she'd want to meet us there.
She's unorthodox...
...but she gets the job done.
2 WOMENSWEAR
LINGERIE

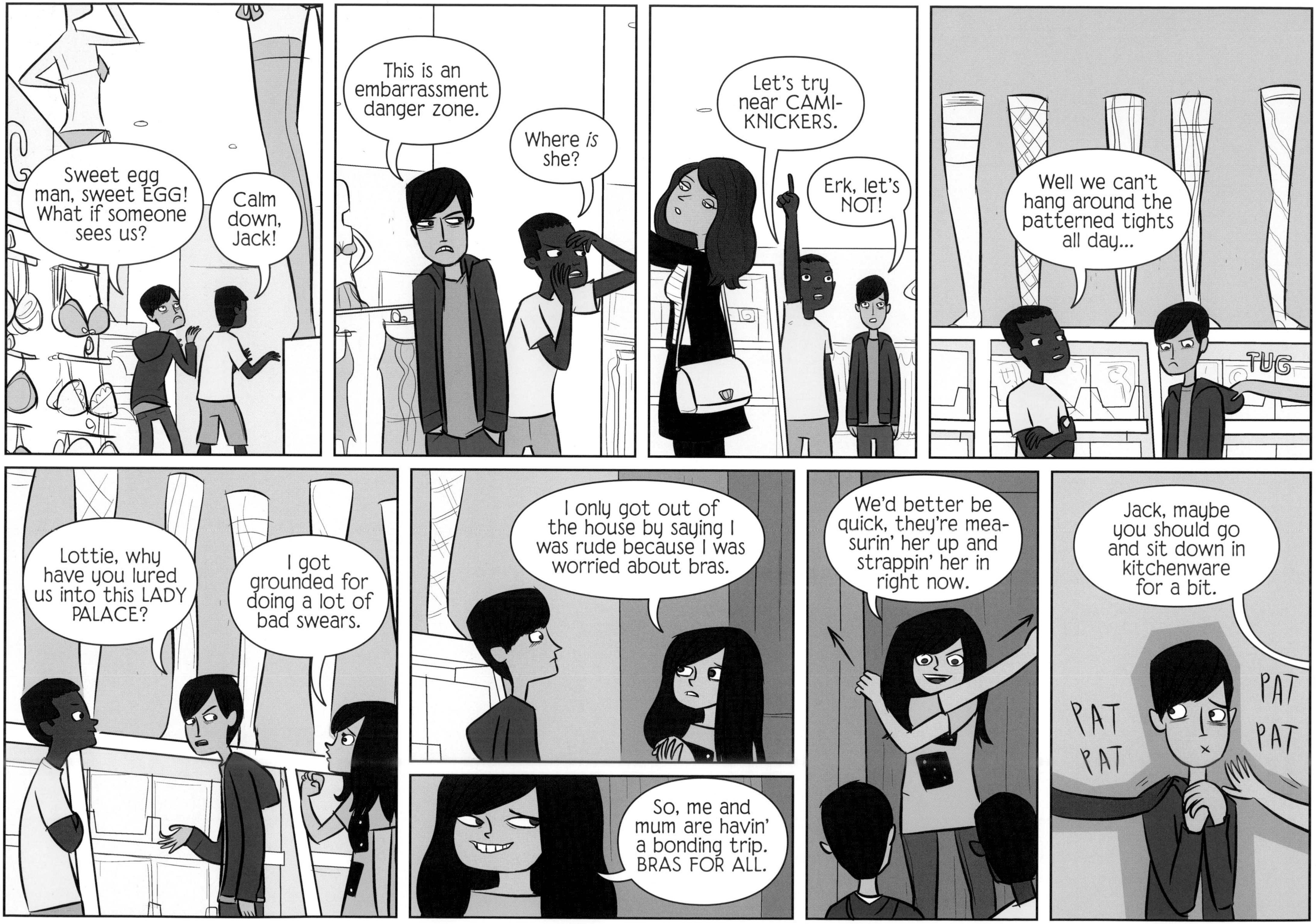
Sweet egg man, sweet EGG! What if someone sees us?
Calm down, Jack!
This is an embarrassment danger zone.
Where *is* she?
Let's try near CAMI-KNICKERS.
Erk, let's NOT!
Well we can't hang around the patterned tights all day...
TUG
Lottie, why have you lured us into this LADY PALACE?
I got grounded for doing a lot of bad swears.
I only got out of the house by saying I was rude because I was worried about bras.
So, me and mum are havin' a bonding trip. BRAS FOR ALL.
We'd better be quick, they're mea-surin' her up and strappin' her in right now.
Jack, maybe you should go and sit down in kitchenware for a bit.
PAT PAT
PAT PAT

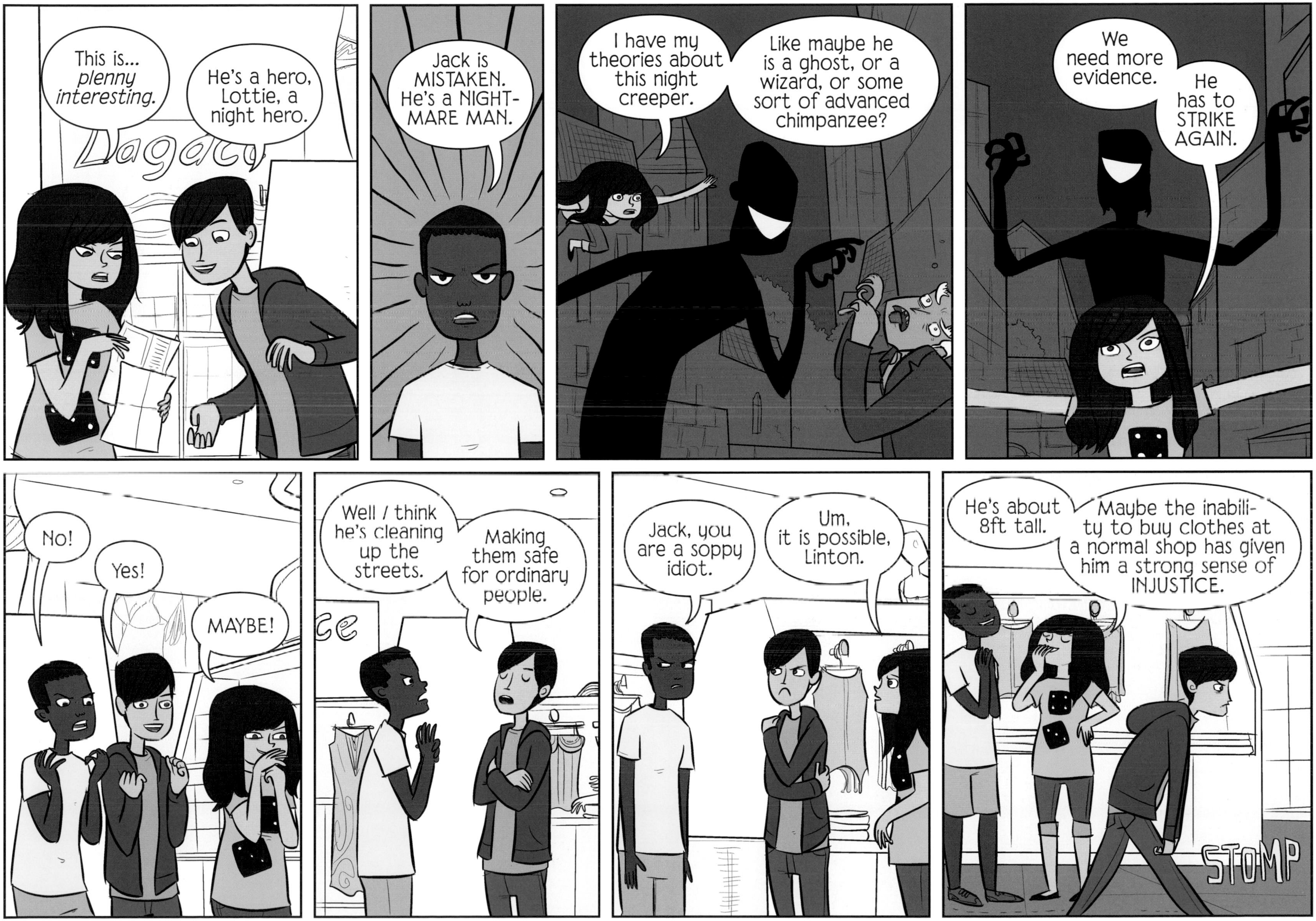
This is... *plenny interesting.*
He's a hero, Lottie, a night hero.
Jack is MISTAKEN. He's a NIGHT-MARE MAN.
I have my theories about this night creeper.
Like maybe he is a ghost, or a wizard, or some sort of advanced chimpanzee?
We need more evidence.
He has to STRIKE AGAIN.
No!
Yes!
MAYBE!
Well *I* think he's cleaning up the streets.
Making them safe for ordinary people.
Jack, you are a soppy idiot.
Um, it is possible, Linton.
He's about 8ft tall.
Maybe the inability to buy clothes at a normal shop has given him a strong sense of INJUSTICE.
STOMP

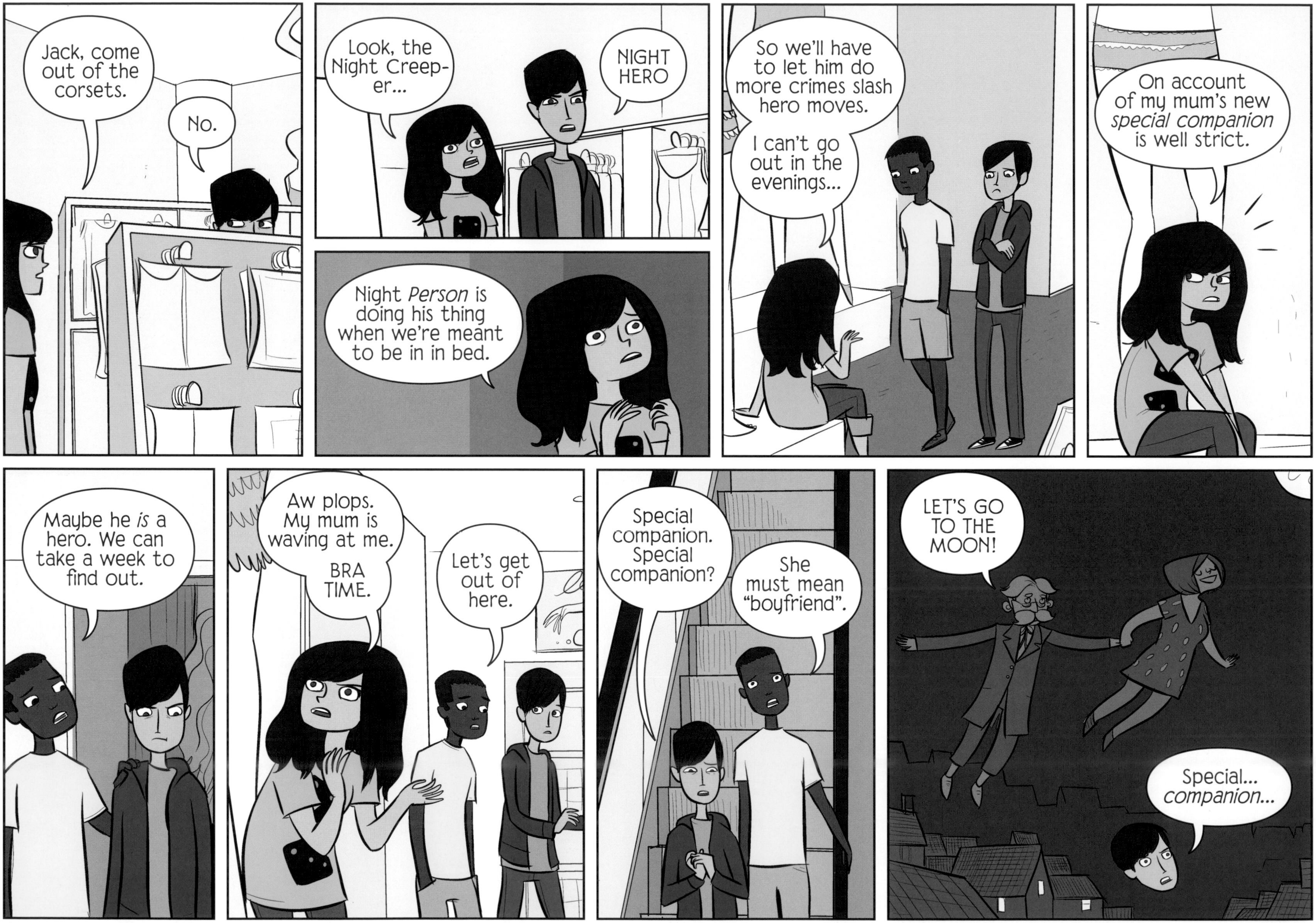
Jack, come out of the corsets.
No.
Look, the Night Creep- er...
NIGHT HERO
Night *Person* is doing his thing when we're meant to be in in bed.
So we'll have to let him do more crimes slash hero moves.
I can't go out in the evenings...
On account of my mum's new *special companion* is well strict.
Maybe he *is* a hero. We can take a week to find out.
Aw plops. My mum is waving at me.
BRA TIME.
Let's get out of here.
Special companion. Special companion?
She must mean "boyfriend".
LET'S GO TO THE MOON!
Special... *companion*...

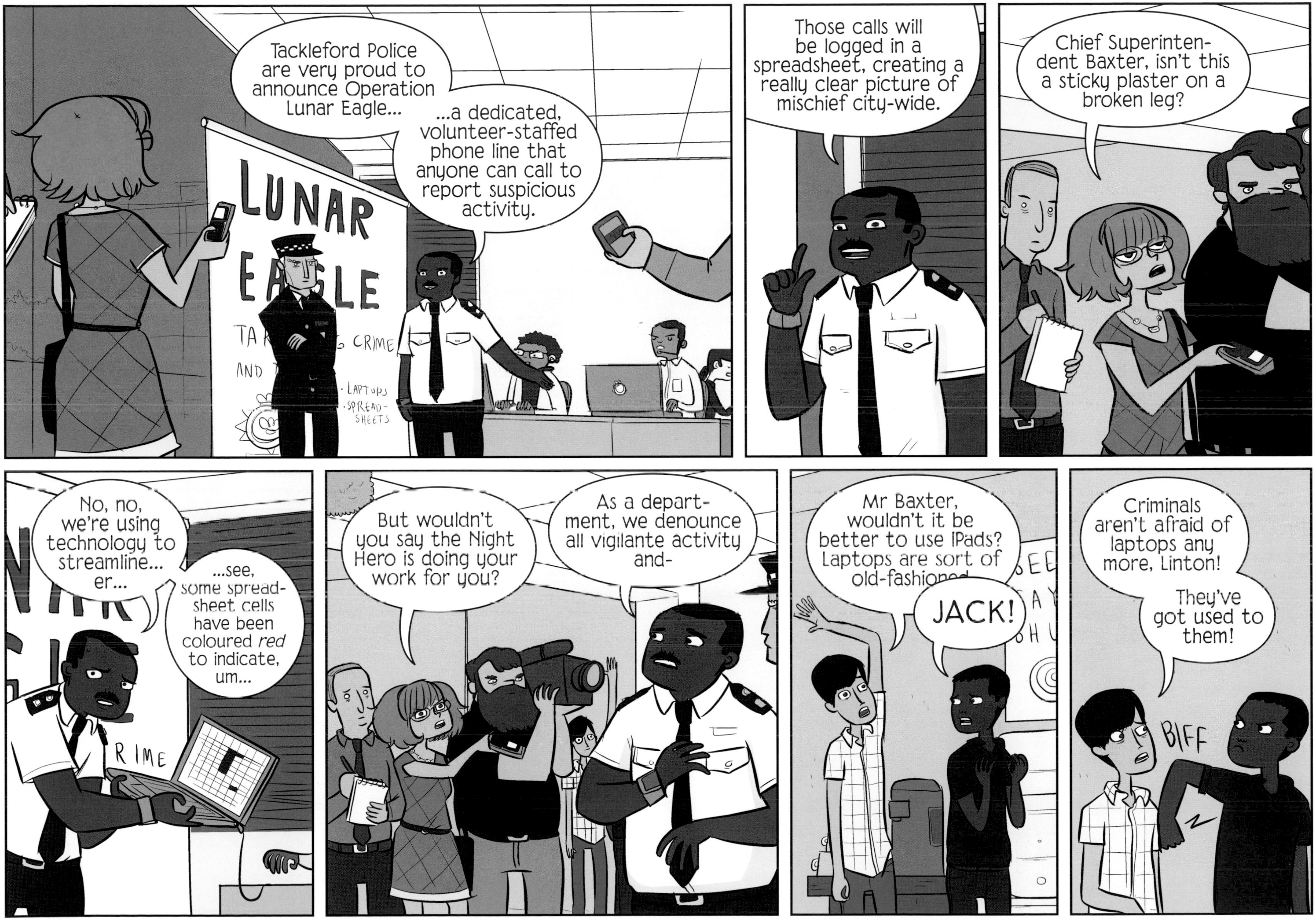
Tackleford Police are very proud to announce Operation Lunar Eagle...
...a dedicated, volunteer-staffed phone line that anyone can call to report suspicious activity.
LUNAR EAGLE
CRIME
AND
· LAPTOPS
· SPREAD-SHEETS
Those calls will be logged in a spreadsheet, creating a really clear picture of mischief city-wide.
Chief Superintendent Baxter, isn't this a sticky plaster on a broken leg?
No, no, we're using technology to streamline... er...
...see, some spreadsheet cells have been coloured *red* to indicate, um...
RIME
But wouldn't you say the Night Hero is doing your work for you?
As a department, we denounce all vigilante activity and-
Mr Baxter, wouldn't it be better to use IPads? Laptops are sort of old-fashioned
JACK!
Criminals aren't afraid of laptops any more, Linton!
They've got used to them!
BIFF

Bad Machinery, Volume Six

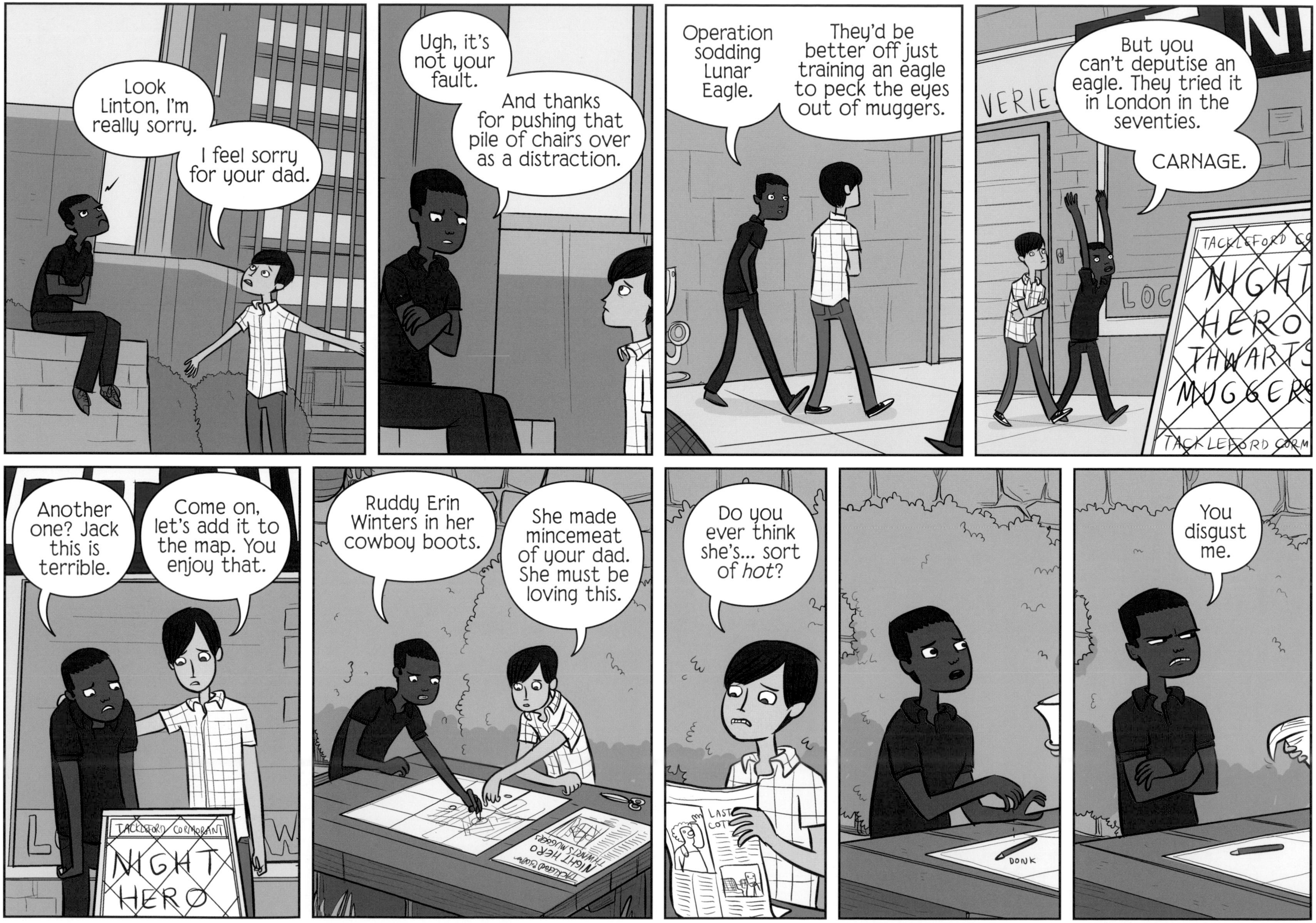
Look Linton, I'm really sorry.
I feel sorry for your dad.
Ugh, it's not your fault.
And thanks for pushing that pile of chairs over as a distraction.
Operation sodding Lunar Eagle.
They'd be better off just training an eagle to peck the eyes out of muggers.
But you can't deputise an eagle. They tried it in London in the seventies.
CARNAGE.
Another one? Jack this is terrible.
Come on, let's add it to the map. You enjoy that.
NIGHT HERO
Ruddy Erin Winters in her cowboy boots.
She made mincemeat of your dad. She must be loving this.
Do you ever think she's... sort of *hot*?
DONK
You disgust me.

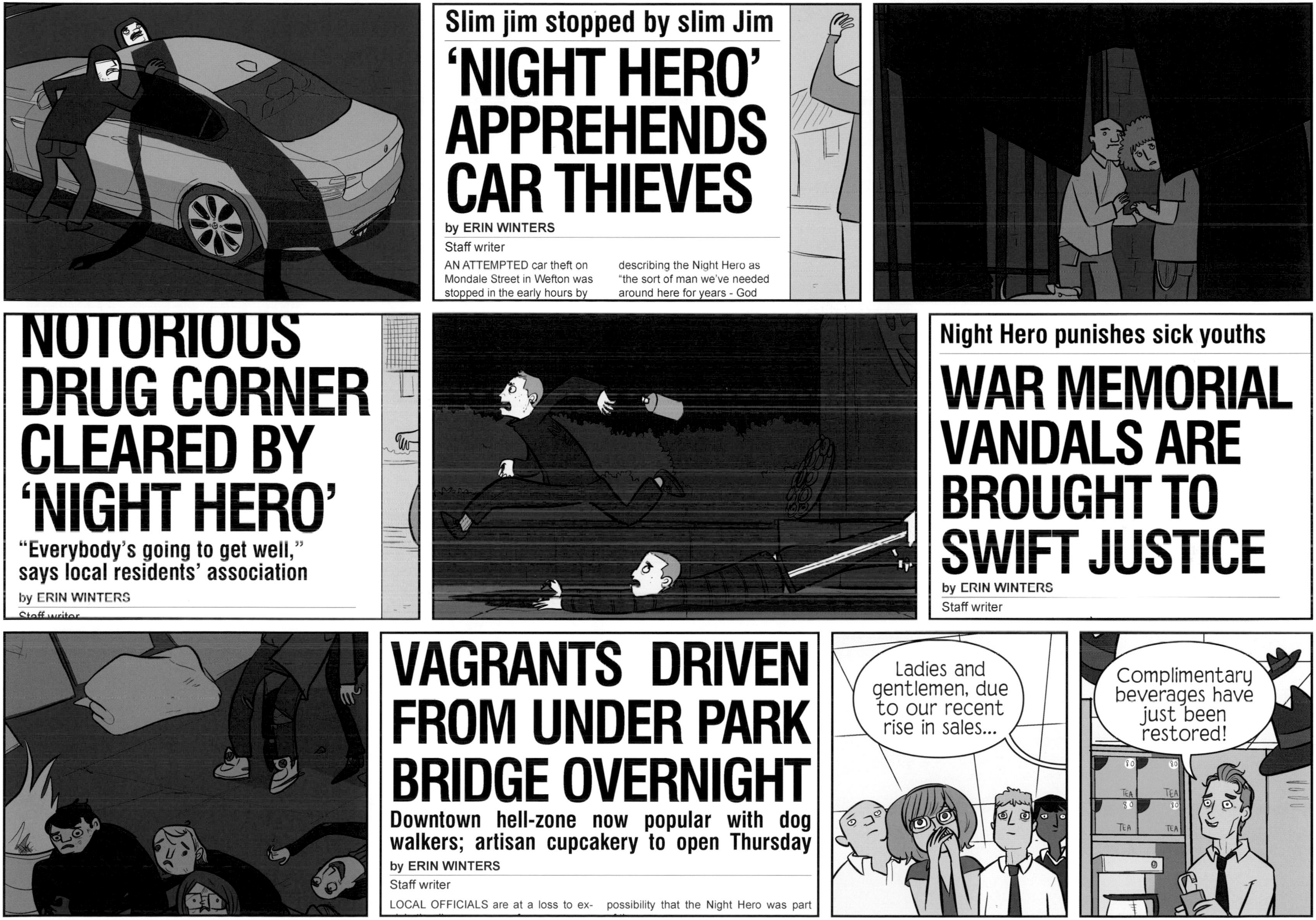

Slim jim stopped by slim Jim
'NIGHT HERO' APPREHENDS CAR THIEVES
by ERIN WINTERS
Staff writer
AN ATTEMPTED car theft on Mondale Street in Wefton was stopped in the early hours by
describing the Night Hero as "the sort of man we've needed around here for years - God
NOTORIOUS DRUG CORNER CLEARED BY 'NIGHT HERO'
"Everybody's going to get well," says local residents' association
by ERIN WINTERS
Night Hero punishes sick youths
WAR MEMORIAL VANDALS ARE BROUGHT TO SWIFT JUSTICE
by ERIN WINTERS
Staff writer
VAGRANTS DRIVEN FROM UNDER PARK BRIDGE OVERNIGHT
Downtown hell-zone now popular with dog walkers; artisan cupcakery to open Thursday
by ERIN WINTERS
Staff writer
LOCAL OFFICIALS are at a loss to ex-
possibility that the Night Hero was part
Ladies and gentlemen, due to our recent rise in sales...
Complimentary beverages have just been restored!

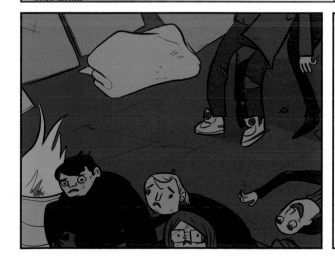

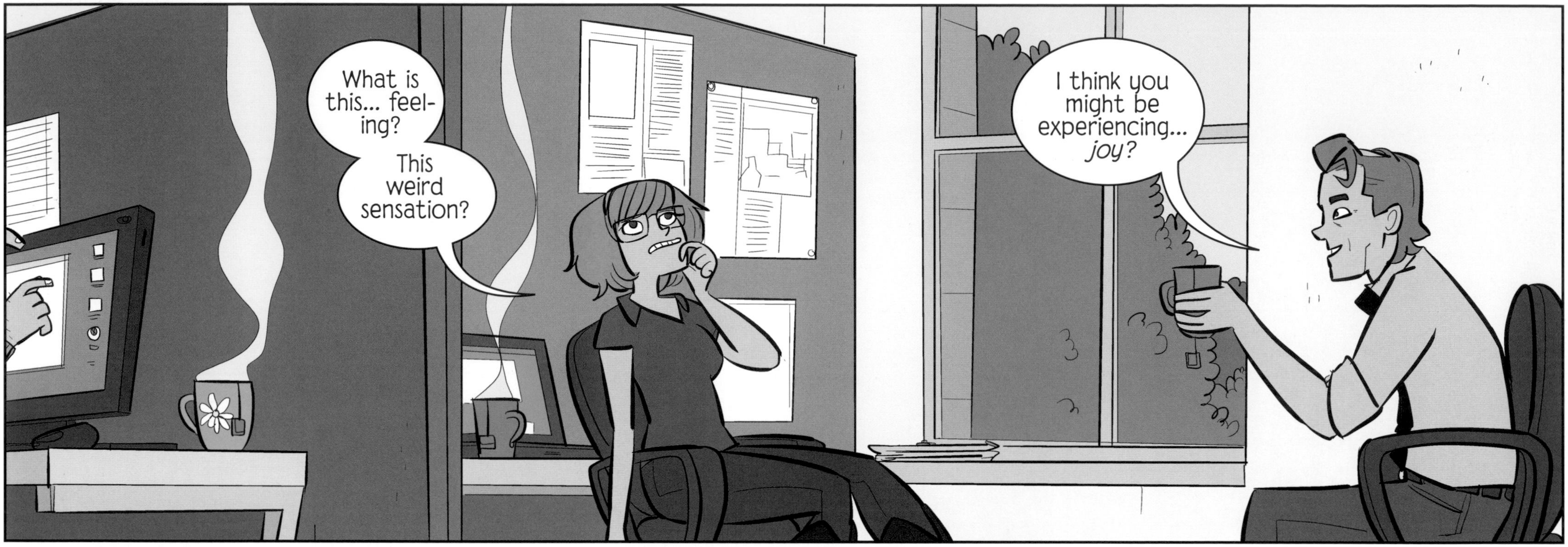
What is this... feel-ing?
This weird sensation?
I think you might be experiencing... *joy*?

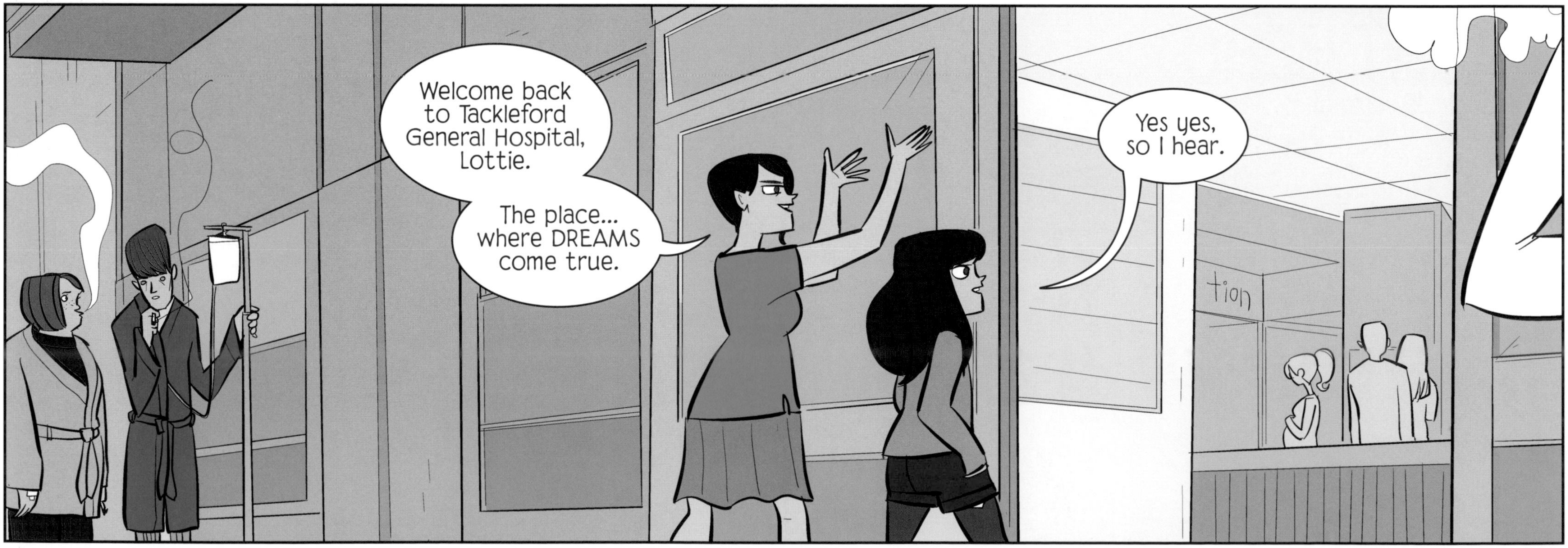
Welcome back to Tackleford General Hospital, Lottie.
The place... where DREAMS come true.
Yes yes, so I hear.

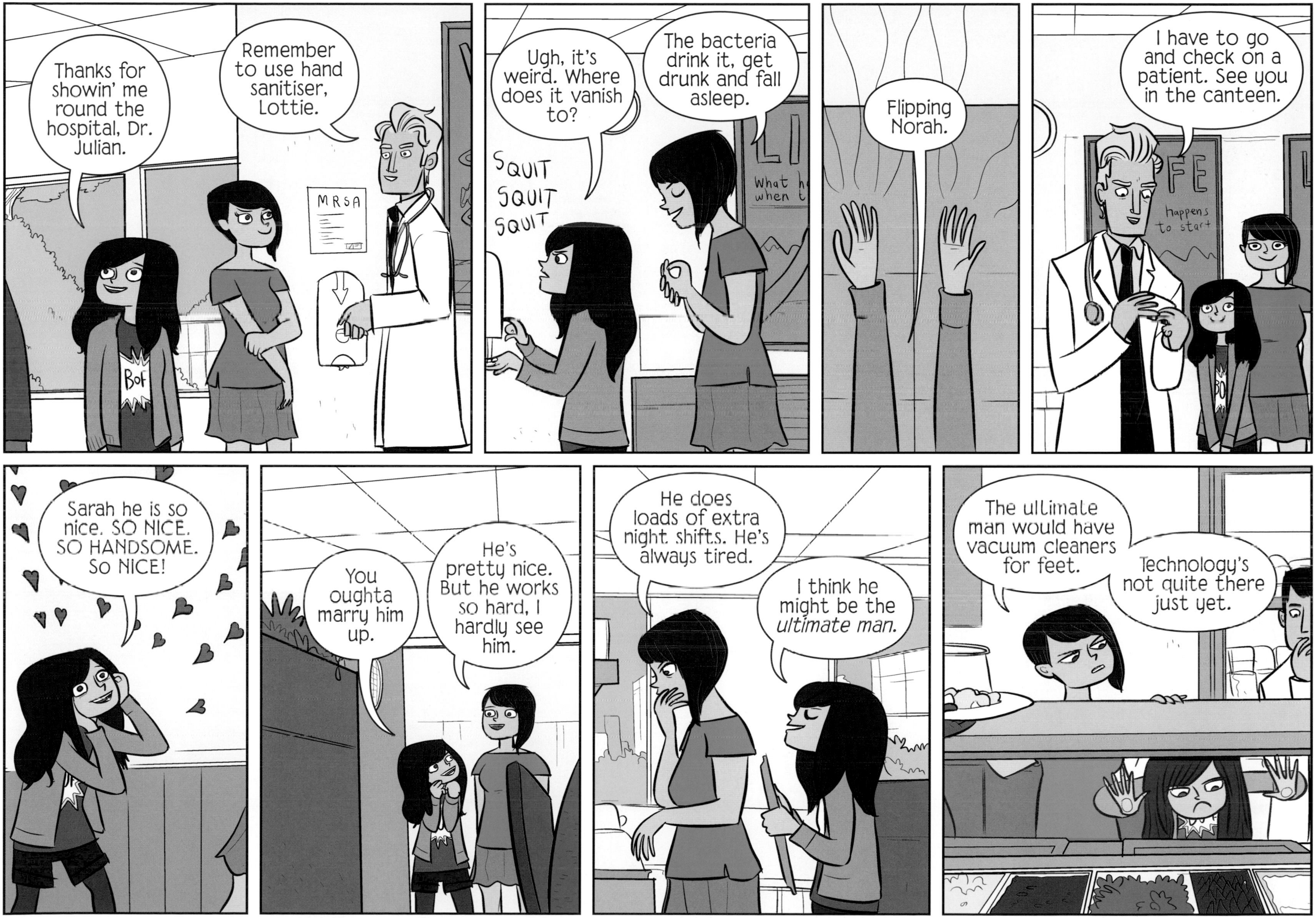

Thanks for showin' me round the hospital, Dr. Julian.
Remember to use hand sanitiser, Lottie.
MRSA
Ugh, it's weird. Where does it vanish to?
SQUIT SQUIT SQUIT
The bacteria drink it, get drunk and fall asleep.
Flipping Norah.
I have to go and check on a patient. See you in the canteen.
happens to start
Sarah he is so nice. SO NICE. SO HANDSOME. So NICE!
You oughta marry him up.
He's pretty nice. But he works so hard, I hardly see him.
He does loads of extra night shifts. He's always tired.
I think he might be the *ultimate man.*
The ultimate man would have vacuum cleaners for feet.
Technology's not quite there just yet.

Bad Machinery, Volume Six

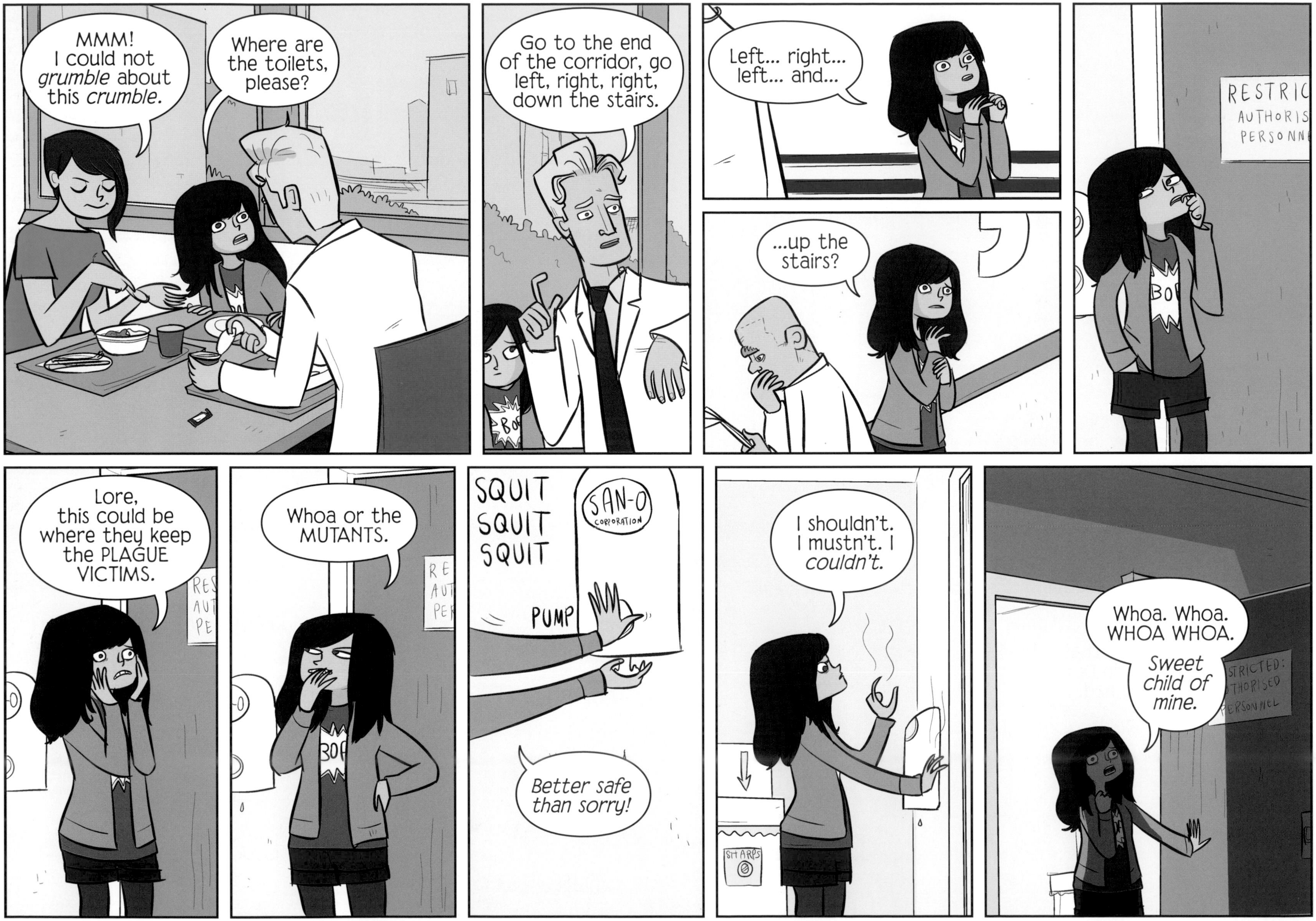
MMM! I could not *grumble* about this *crumble*.
Where are the toilets, please?
Go to the end of the corridor, go left, right, right, down the stairs.
Left... right... left... and...
...up the stairs?
RESTRIC AUTHORIS PERSONNE
Lore, this could be where they keep the PLAGUE VICTIMS.
Whoa or the MUTANTS.
SQUIT SQUIT SQUIT
SAN-O CORPORATION
PUMP
Better safe than sorry!
I shouldn't. I mustn't. I *couldn't.*
SHARPS
Whoa. Whoa. WHOA WHOA.
Sweet child of mine.
STRICTED: THORISED PERSONNEL

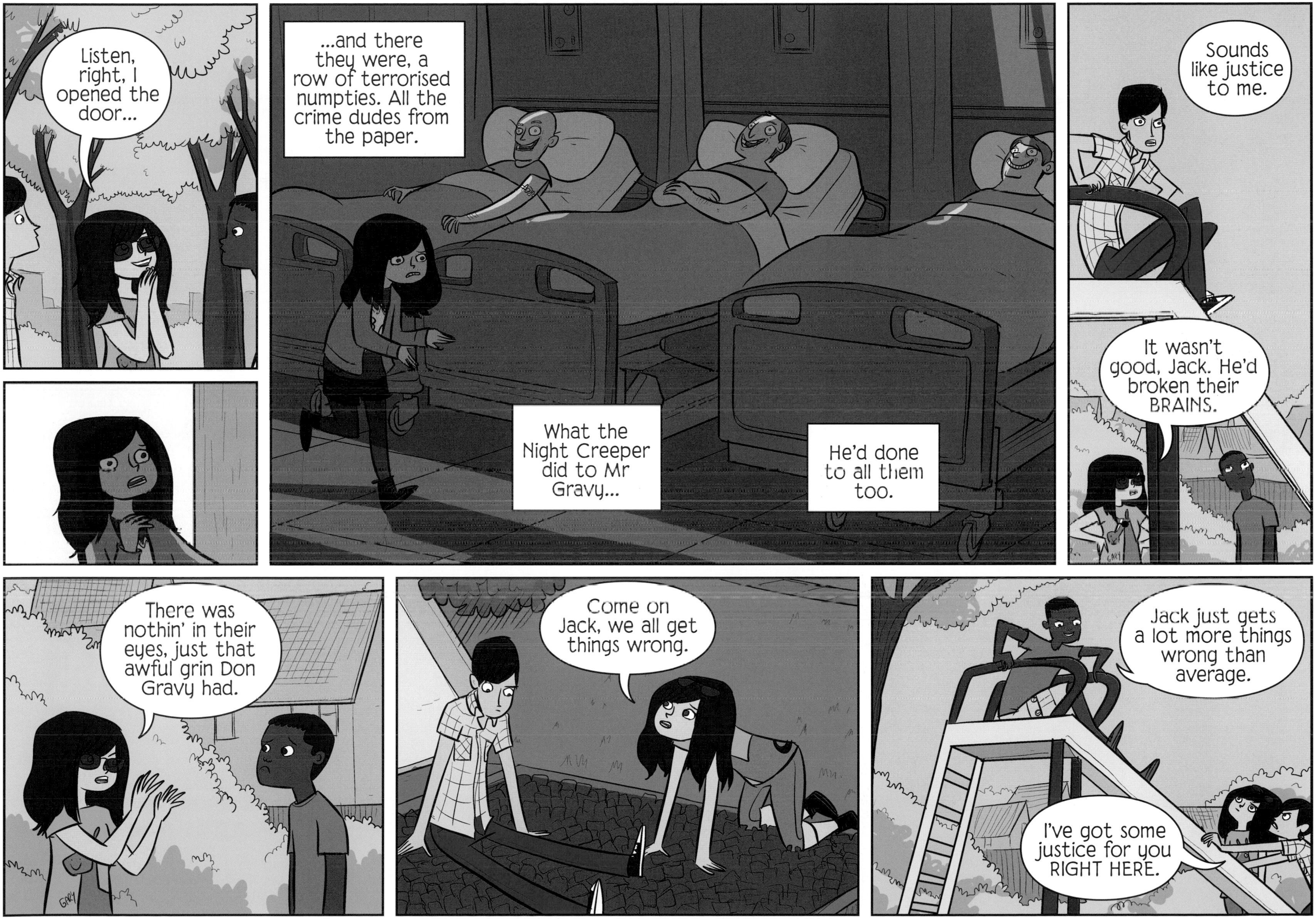
Listen, right, I opened the door...
...and there they were, a row of terrorised numpties. All the crime dudes from the paper.
What the Night Creeper did to Mr Gravy...
He'd done to all them too.
Sounds like justice to me.
It wasn't good, Jack. He'd broken their BRAINS.
There was nothin' in their eyes, just that awful grin Don Gravy had.
Come on Jack, we all get things wrong.
Jack just gets a lot more things wrong than average.
I've got some justice for you RIGHT HERE.

Bad Machinery, Volume Six

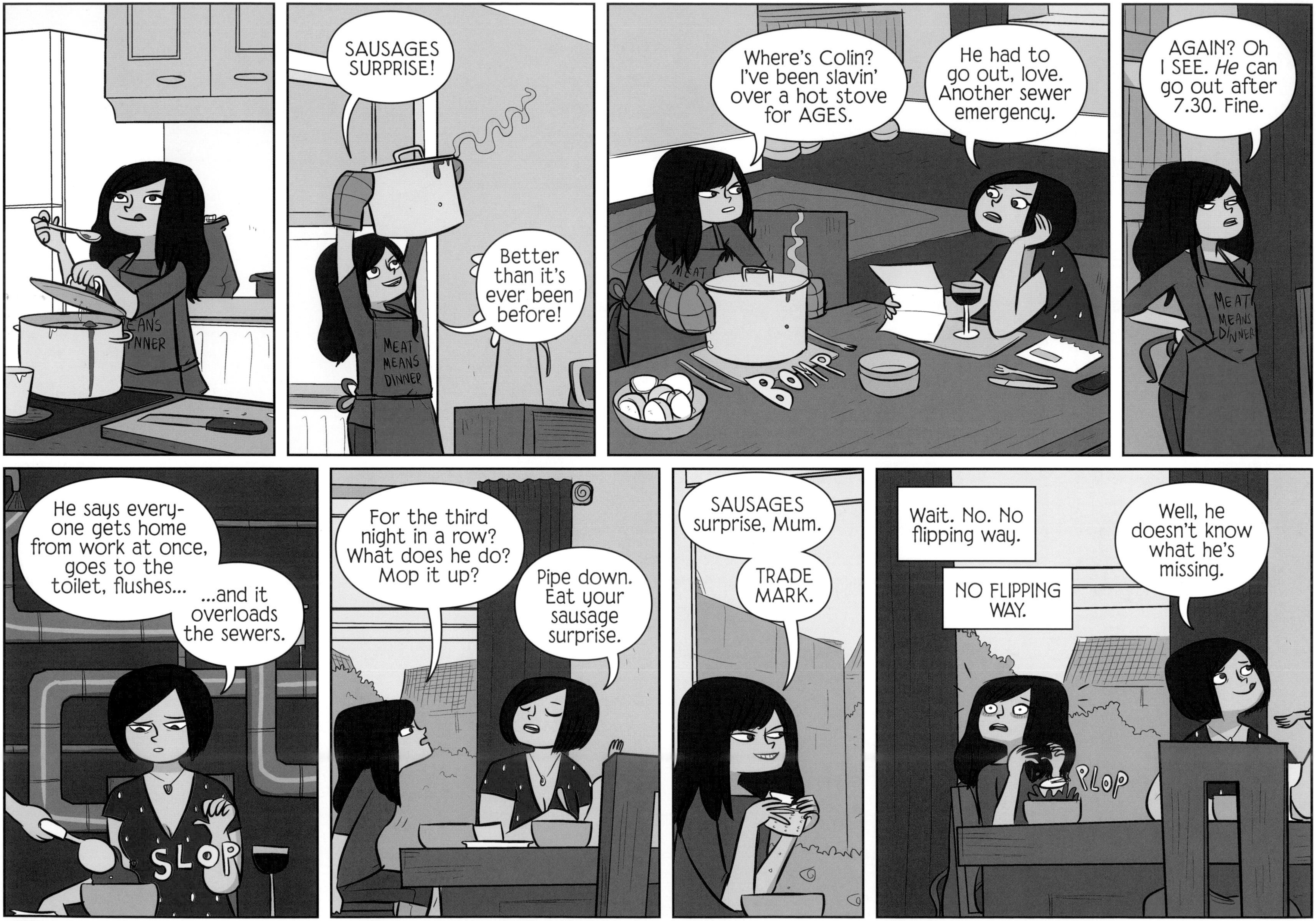
MEANS DINNER
SAUSAGES SURPRISE!
MEAT MEANS DINNER
Better than it's ever been before!
Where's Colin? I've been slavin' over a hot stove for AGES.
He had to go out, love. Another sewer emergency.
BOMP
AGAIN? Oh I SEE. *He* can go out after 7.30. Fine.
MEAT MEANS DINNER
He says every-one gets home from work at once, goes to the toilet, flushes...
...and it overloads the sewers.
SLOP
For the third night in a row? What does he do? Mop it up?
Pipe down. Eat your sausage surprise.
SAUSAGES surprise, Mum.
TRADE MARK.
Wait. No. No flipping way.
NO FLIPPING WAY.
Well, he doesn't know what he's missing.
PLOP

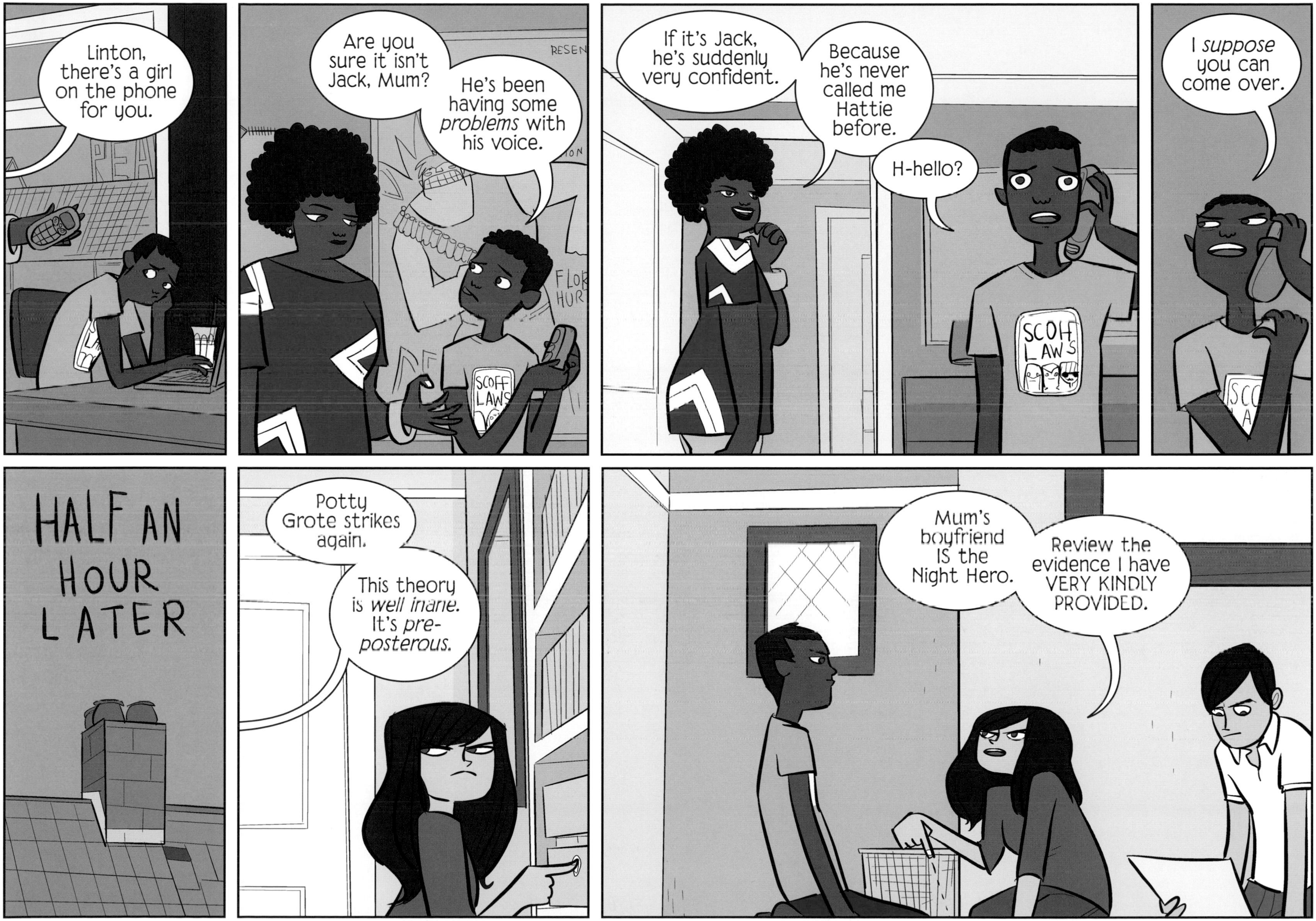
Linton, there's a girl on the phone for you.
Are you sure it isn't Jack, Mum?
He's been having some *problems* with his voice.
If it's Jack, he's suddenly very confident.
Because he's never called me Hattie before.
H-hello?
I *suppose* you can come over.
HALF AN HOUR LATER
Potty Grote strikes again.
This theory is *well inane*. It's *pre-posterous*.
Mum's boyfriend IS the Night Hero.
Review the evidence I have VERY KINDLY PROVIDED.

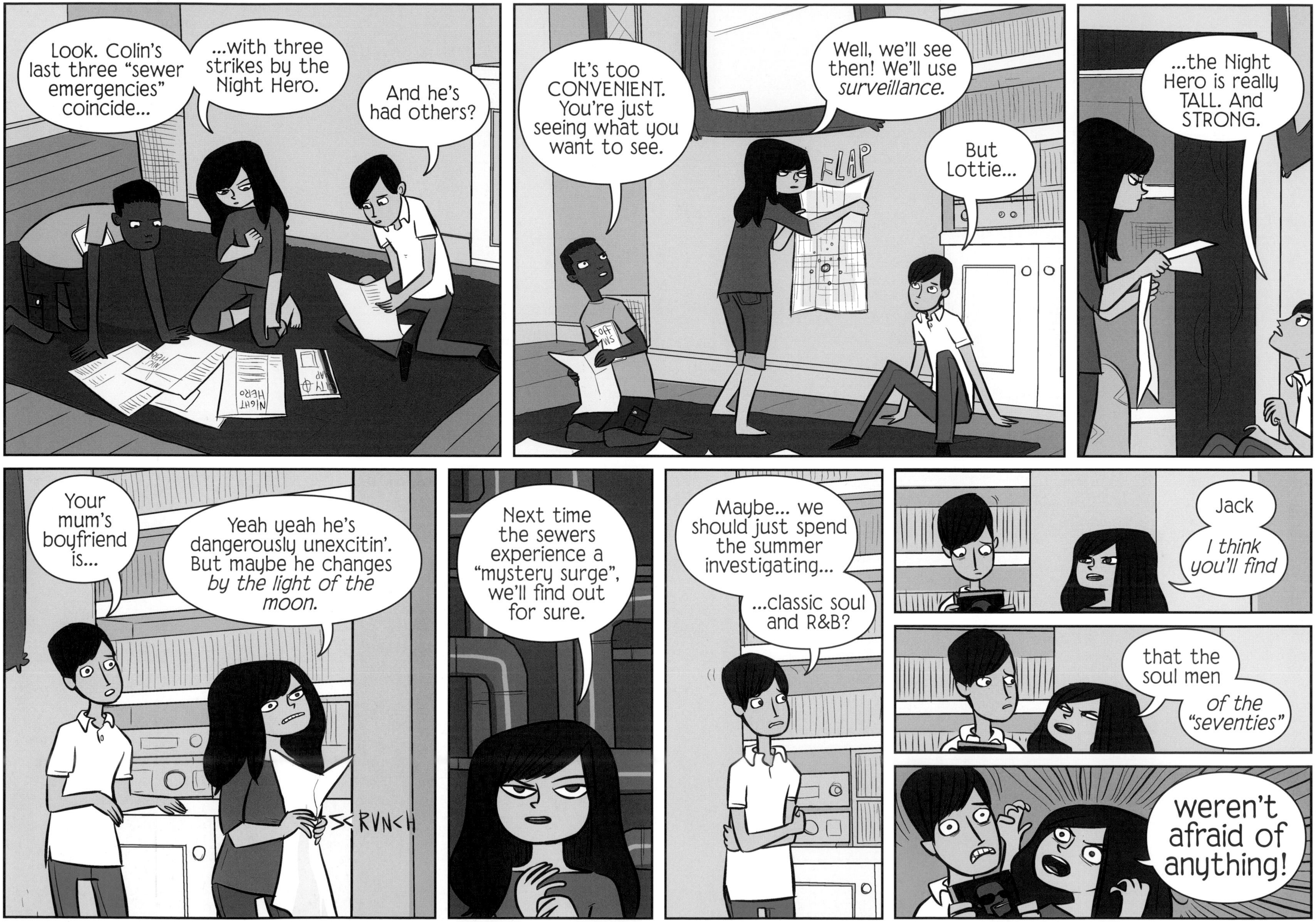
Look. Colin's last three "sewer emergencies" coincide...
...with three strikes by the Night Hero.
And he's had others?
NIGHT HERO
It's too CONVENIENT. You're just seeing what you want to see.
Well, we'll see then! We'll use *surveillance.*
FLAP
But Lottie...
...the Night Hero is really TALL. And STRONG.
Your mum's boyfriend is...
Yeah yeah he's dangerously unexcitin'. But maybe he changes *by the light of the moon.*
SCRUNCH
Next time the sewers experience a "mystery surge", we'll find out for sure.
Maybe... we should just spend the summer investigating...
...classic soul and R&B?
Jack
I think you'll find
that the soul men
of the "seventies"
weren't afraid of anything!

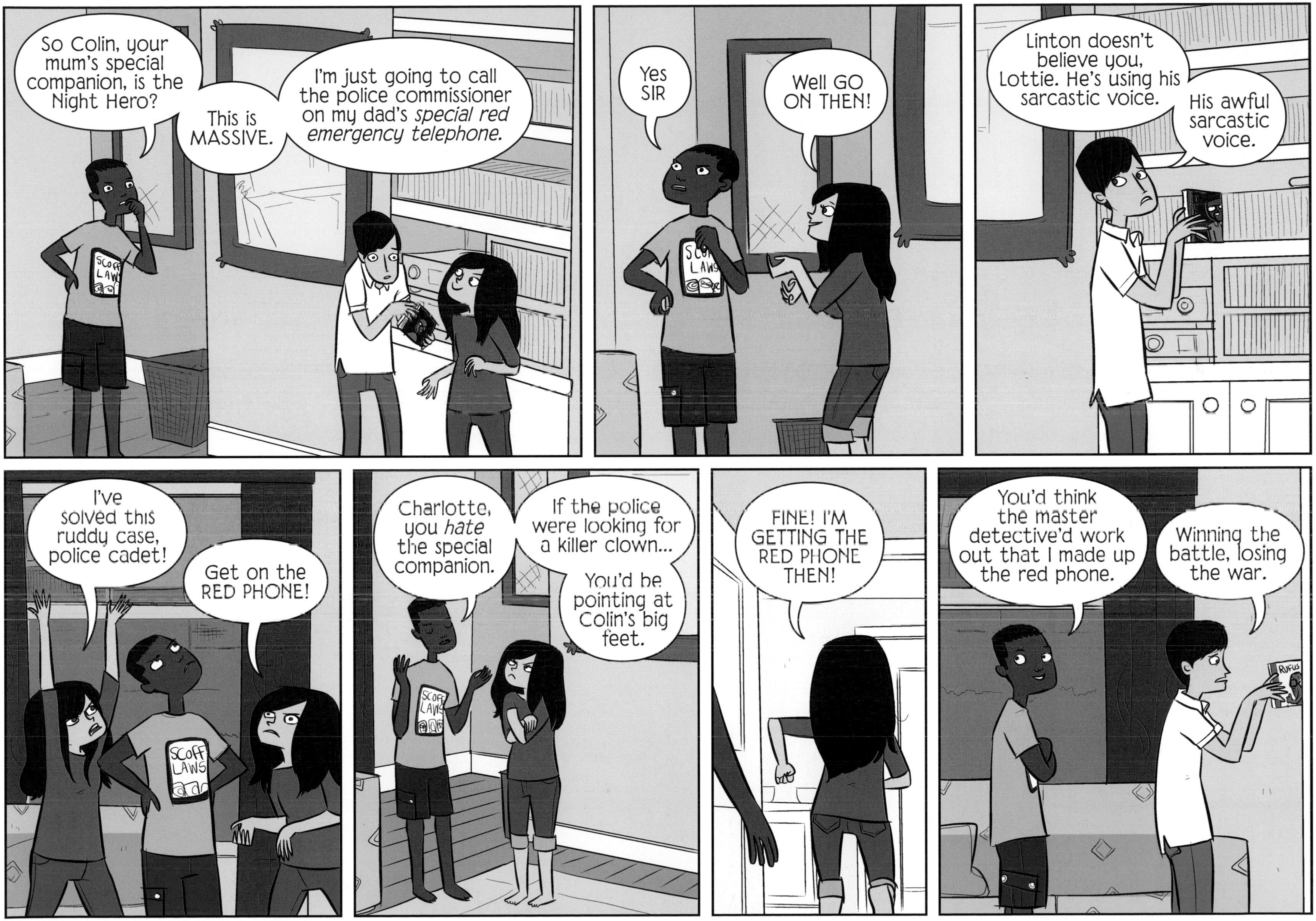
So Colin, your mum's special companion, is the Night Hero?
This is MASSIVE.
I'm just going to call the police commissioner on my dad's *special red emergency telephone.*
Yes SIR
Well GO ON THEN!
Linton doesn't believe you, Lottie. He's using his sarcastic voice.
His awful sarcastic voice.
I've solved this ruddy case, police cadet!
Get on the RED PHONE!
Charlotte, you *hate* the special companion.
If the police were looking for a killer clown...
You'd be pointing at Colin's big feet.
FINE! I'M GETTING THE RED PHONE THEN!
You'd think the master detective'd work out that I made up the red phone.
Winning the battle, losing the war.
SCOFF LAWS
RUFUS

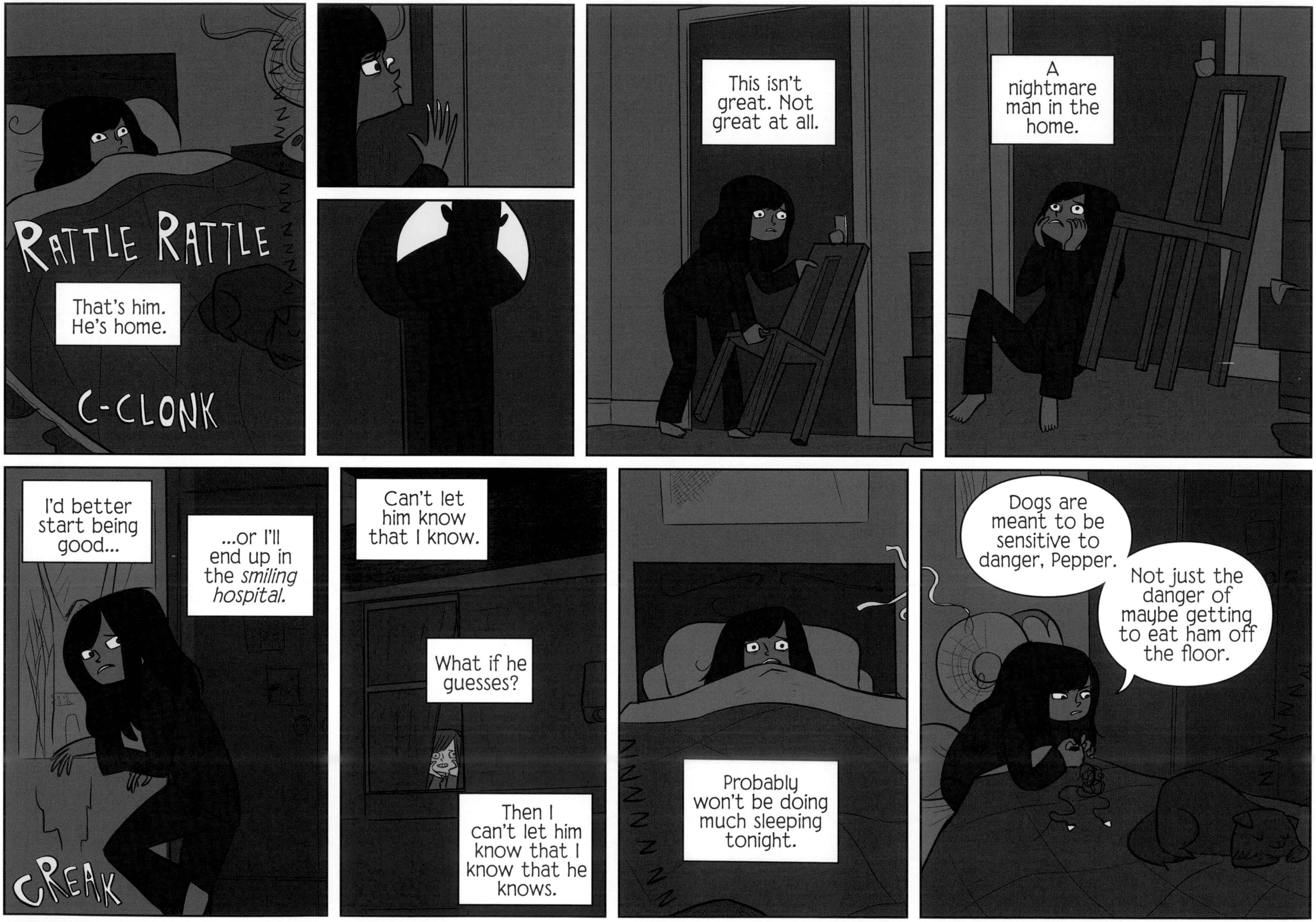
RATTLE RATTLE
That's him. He's home.
C-CLONK
This isn't great. Not great at all.
A nightmare man in the home.
I'd better start being good...
...or I'll end up in the *smiling hospital.*
CREAK
Can't let him know that I know.
What if he guesses?
Then I can't let him know that I know that he knows.
Probably won't be doing much sleeping tonight.
Dogs are meant to be sensitive to danger, Pepper.
Not just the danger of maybe getting to eat ham off the floor.

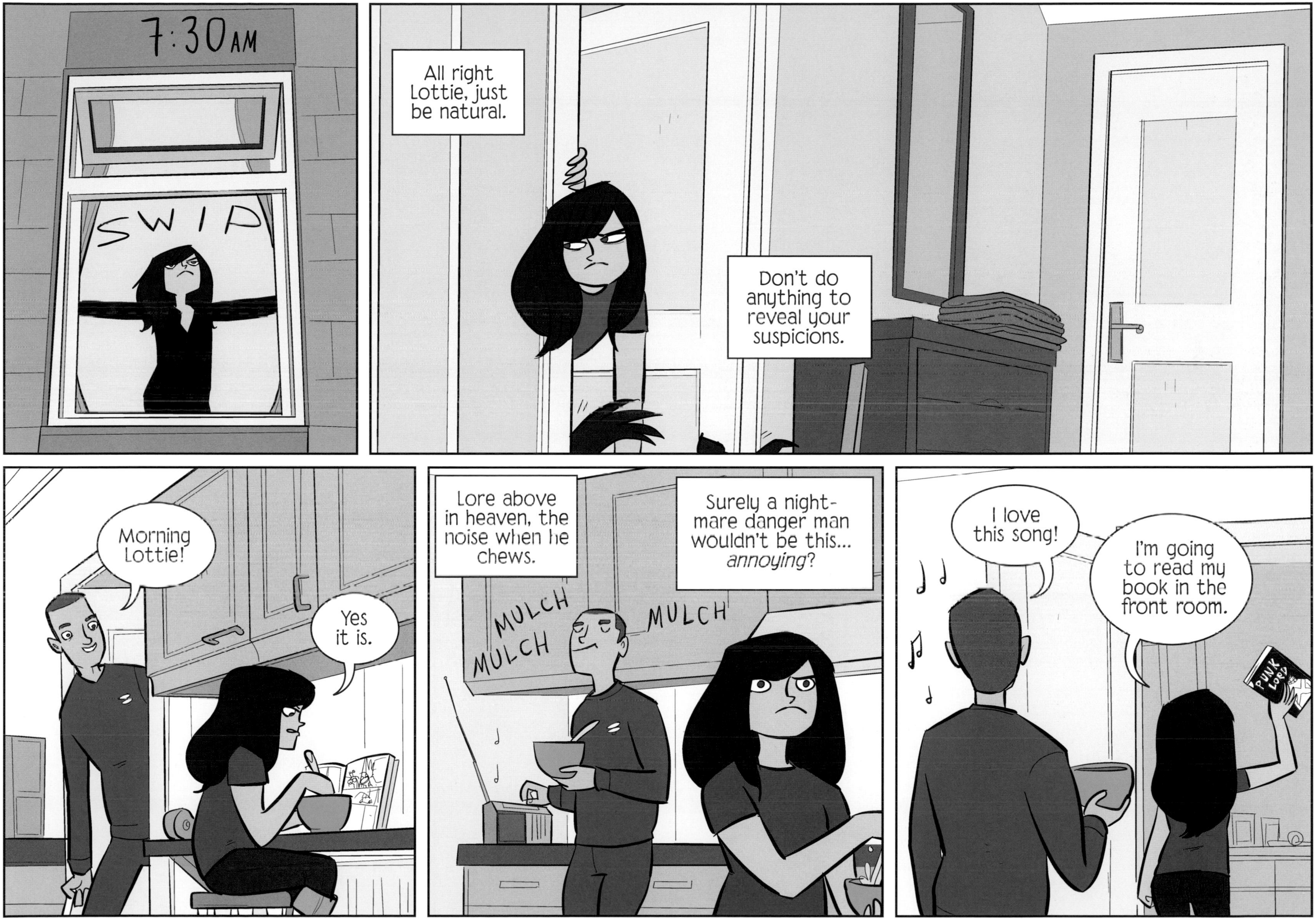

7:30AM
SWIP
All right Lottie, just be natural.
Don't do anything to reveal your suspicions.
Morning Lottie!
Yes it is.
Lore above in heaven, the noise when he chews.
Surely a night-mare danger man wouldn't be this... *annoying*?
MULCH
MULCH
MULCH
I love this song!
I'm going to read my book in the front room.
PUNK LORD

Bad Machinery, Volume Six

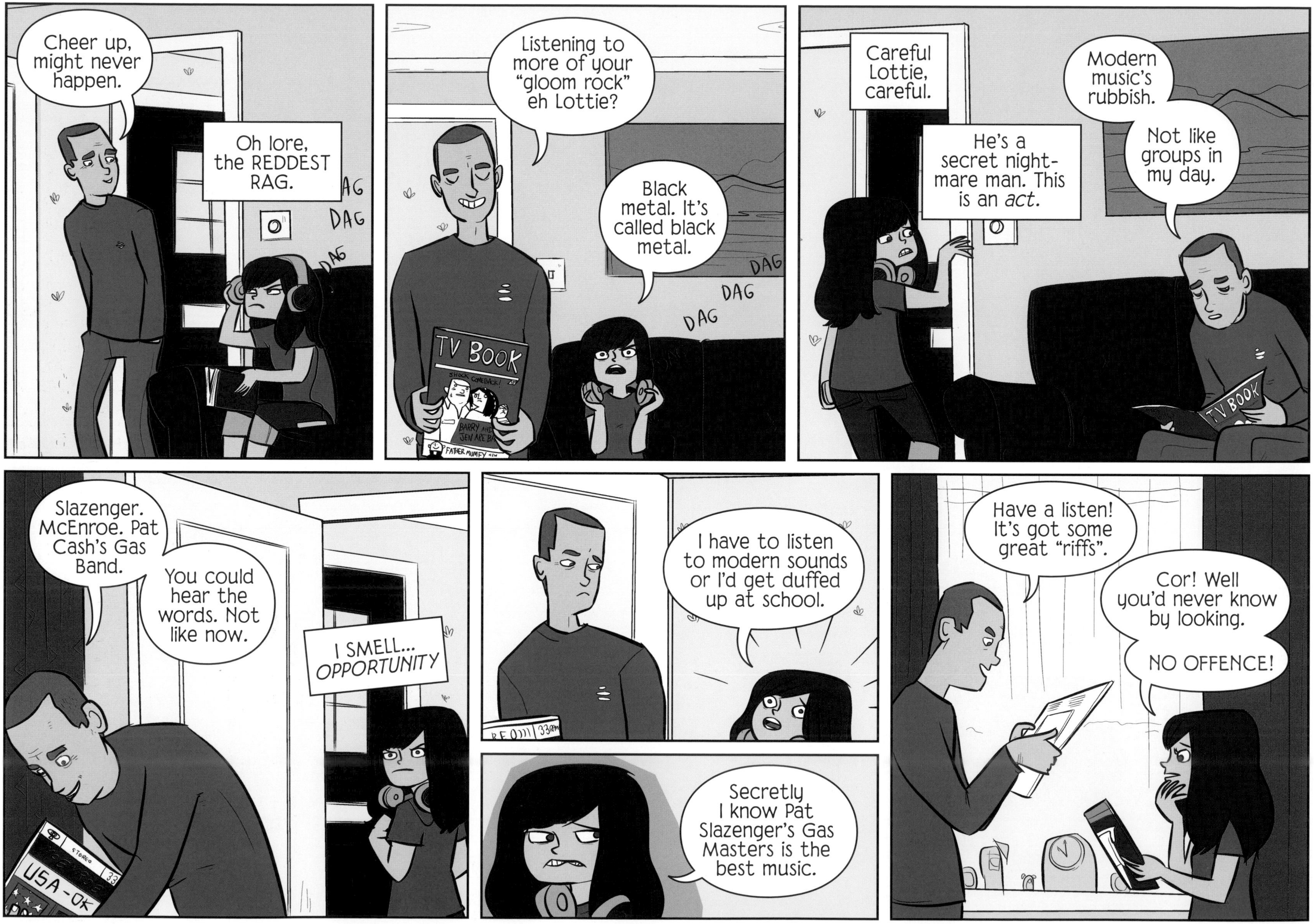
Cheer up, might never happen.
Oh lore, the REDDEST RAG.
DAG DAG DAG
Listening to more of your "gloom rock" eh Lottie?
Black metal. It's called black metal.
DAG DAG DAG
TV BOOK
Careful Lottie, careful.
Modern music's rubbish.
He's a secret night-mare man. This is an *act*.
Not like groups in my day.
TV BOOK
Slazenger. McEnroe. Pat Cash's Gas Band.
You could hear the words. Not like now.
I SMELL... *OPPORTUNITY*
USA-OK
I have to listen to modern sounds or I'd get duffed up at school.
Secretly I know Pat Slazenger's Gas Masters is the best music.
Have a listen! It's got some great "riffs".
Cor! Well you'd never know by looking.
NO OFFENCE!

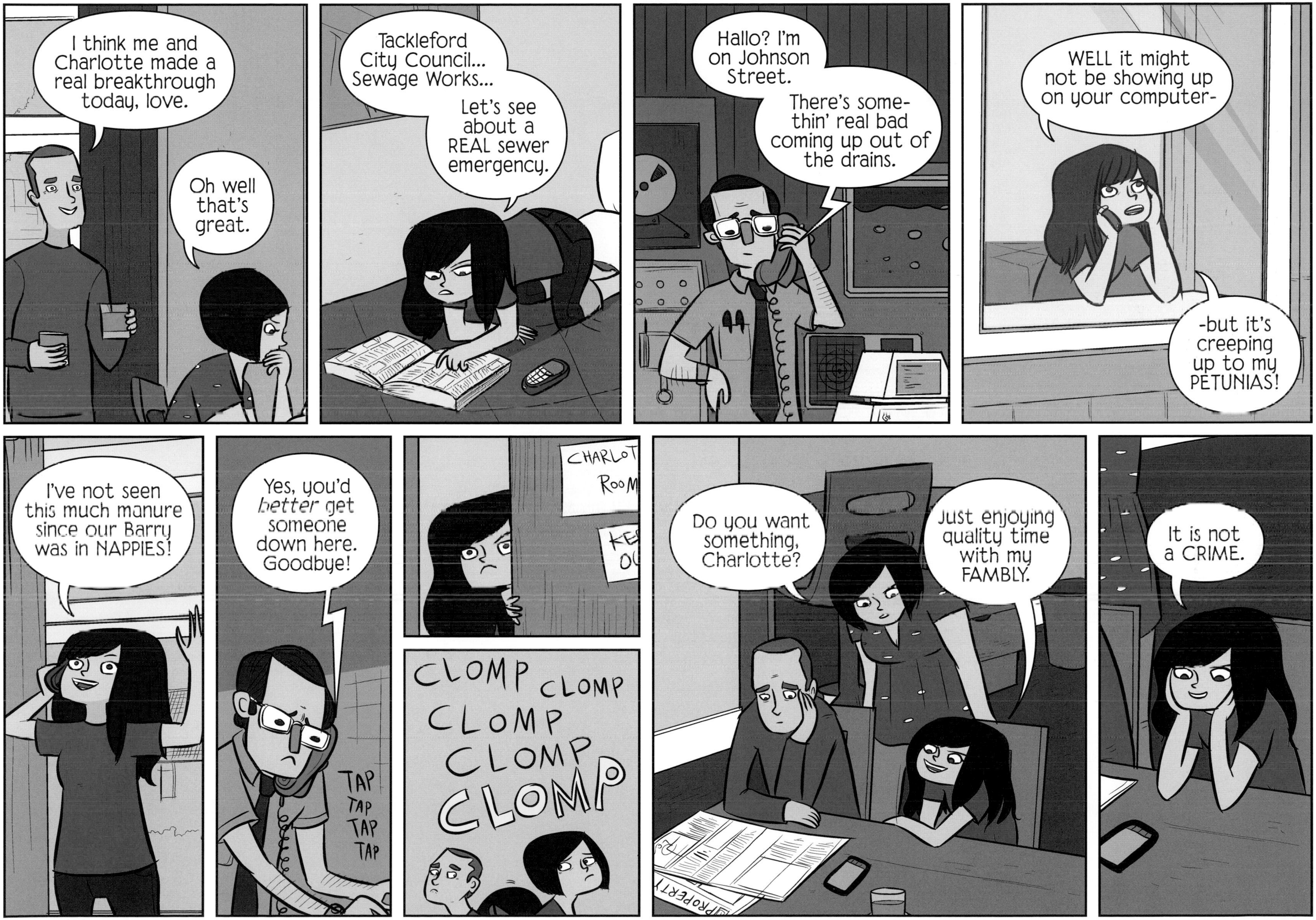
I think me and Charlotte made a real breakthrough today, love.
Oh well that's great.
Tackleford City Council... Sewage Works...
Let's see about a REAL sewer emergency.
Hallo? I'm on Johnson Street.
There's somethin' real bad coming up out of the drains.
WELL it might not be showing up on your computer-
-but it's creeping up to my PETUNIAS!
I've not seen this much manure since our Barry was in NAPPIES!
Yes, you'd *better* get someone down here. Goodbye!
TAP TAP TAP TAP
CHARLOT ROOM
CLOMP CLOMP CLOMP CLOMP CLOMP
Do you want something, Charlotte?
Just enjoying quality time with my FAMBLY.
It is not a CRIME.

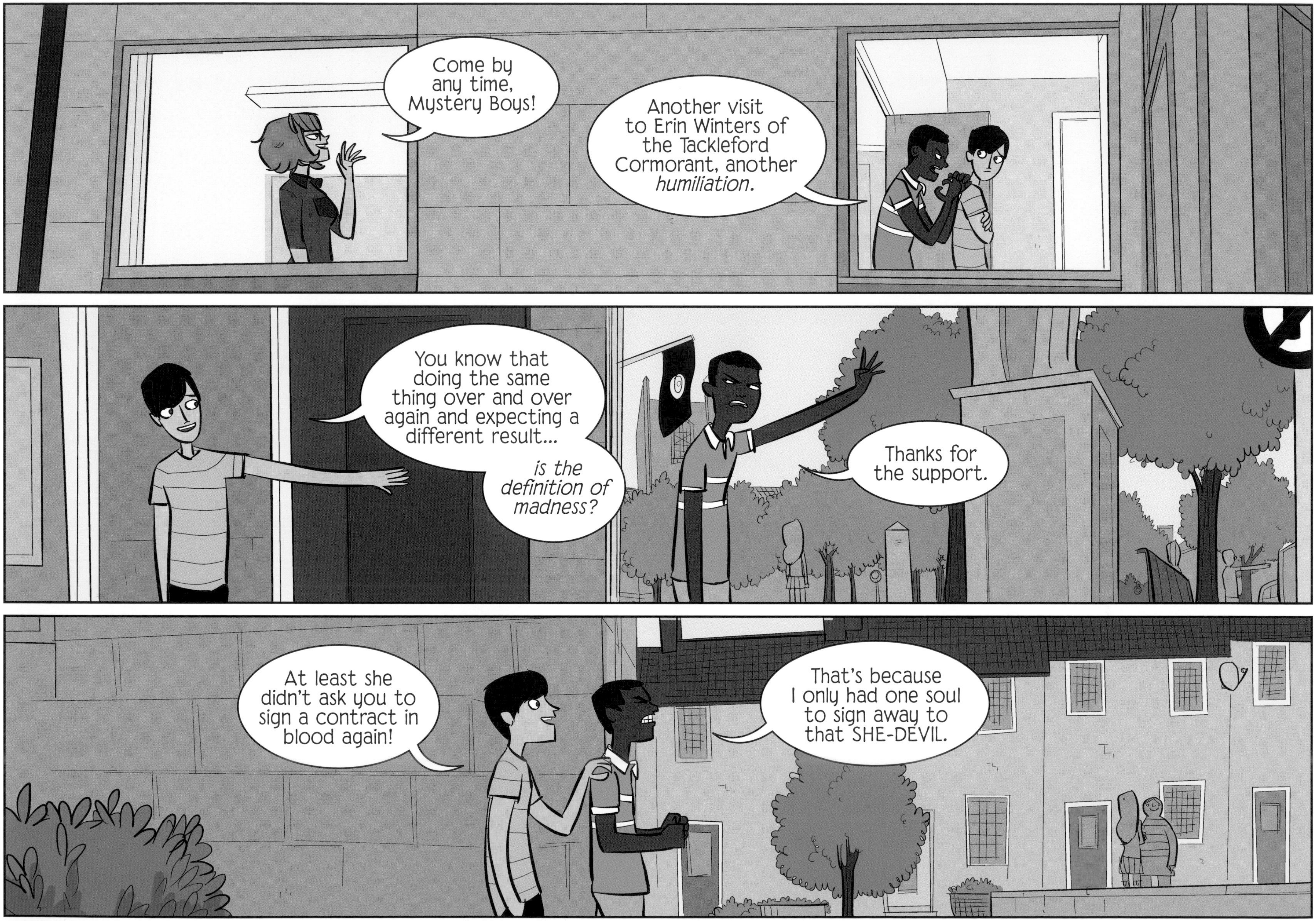
Come by any time, Mystery Boys!
Another visit to Erin Winters of the Tackleford Cormorant, another *humiliation.*
You know that doing the same thing over and over again and expecting a different result...
is the definition of madness?
Thanks for the support.
At least she didn't ask you to sign a contract in blood again!
That's because I only had one soul to sign away to that SHE-DEVIL.

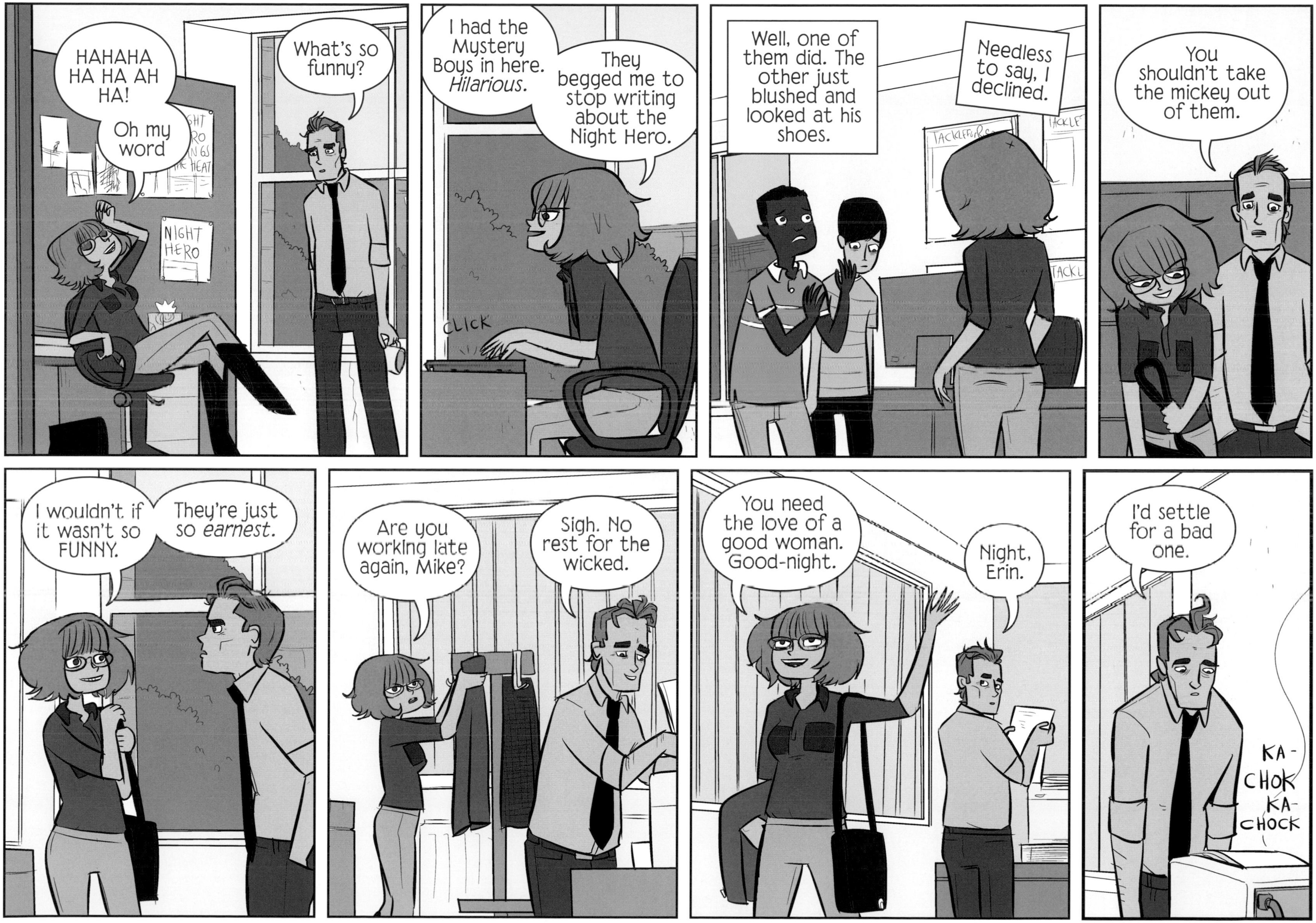
HAHAHA HA HA AH HA!
Oh my word
What's so funny?
NIGHT HERO
I had the Mystery Boys in here. *Hilarious.*
They begged me to stop writing about the Night Hero.
CLICK
Well, one of them did. The other just blushed and looked at his shoes.
Needless to say, I declined.
You shouldn't take the mickey out of them.
I wouldn't if it wasn't so FUNNY.
They're just so *earnest*.
Are you working late again, Mike?
Sigh. No rest for the wicked.
You need the love of a good woman. Good-night.
Night, Erin.
I'd settle for a bad one.
KA-CHOK KA-CHOCK

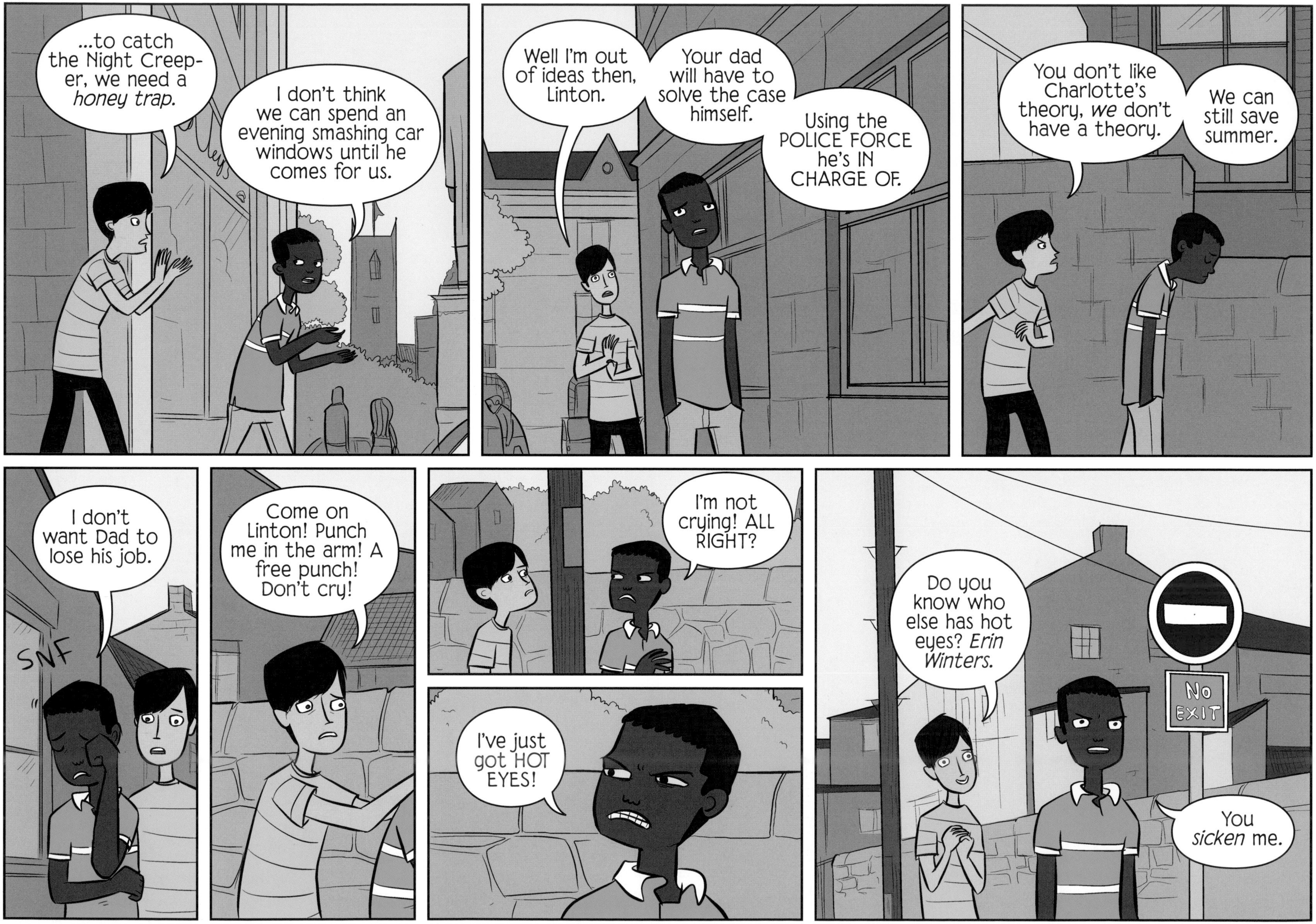
...to catch the Night Creeper, we need a *honey trap.*
I don't think we can spend an evening smashing car windows until he comes for us.
Well I'm out of ideas then, Linton.
Your dad will have to solve the case himself.
Using the POLICE FORCE he's IN CHARGE OF.
You don't like Charlotte's theory, *we* don't have a theory.
We can still save summer.
I don't want Dad to lose his job.
SNF
Come on Linton! Punch me in the arm! A free punch! Don't cry!
I'm not crying! ALL RIGHT?
I've just got HOT EYES!
Do you know who else has hot eyes? *Erin Winters.*
NO EXIT
You *sicken* me.

The Case of the Unwelcome Visitor

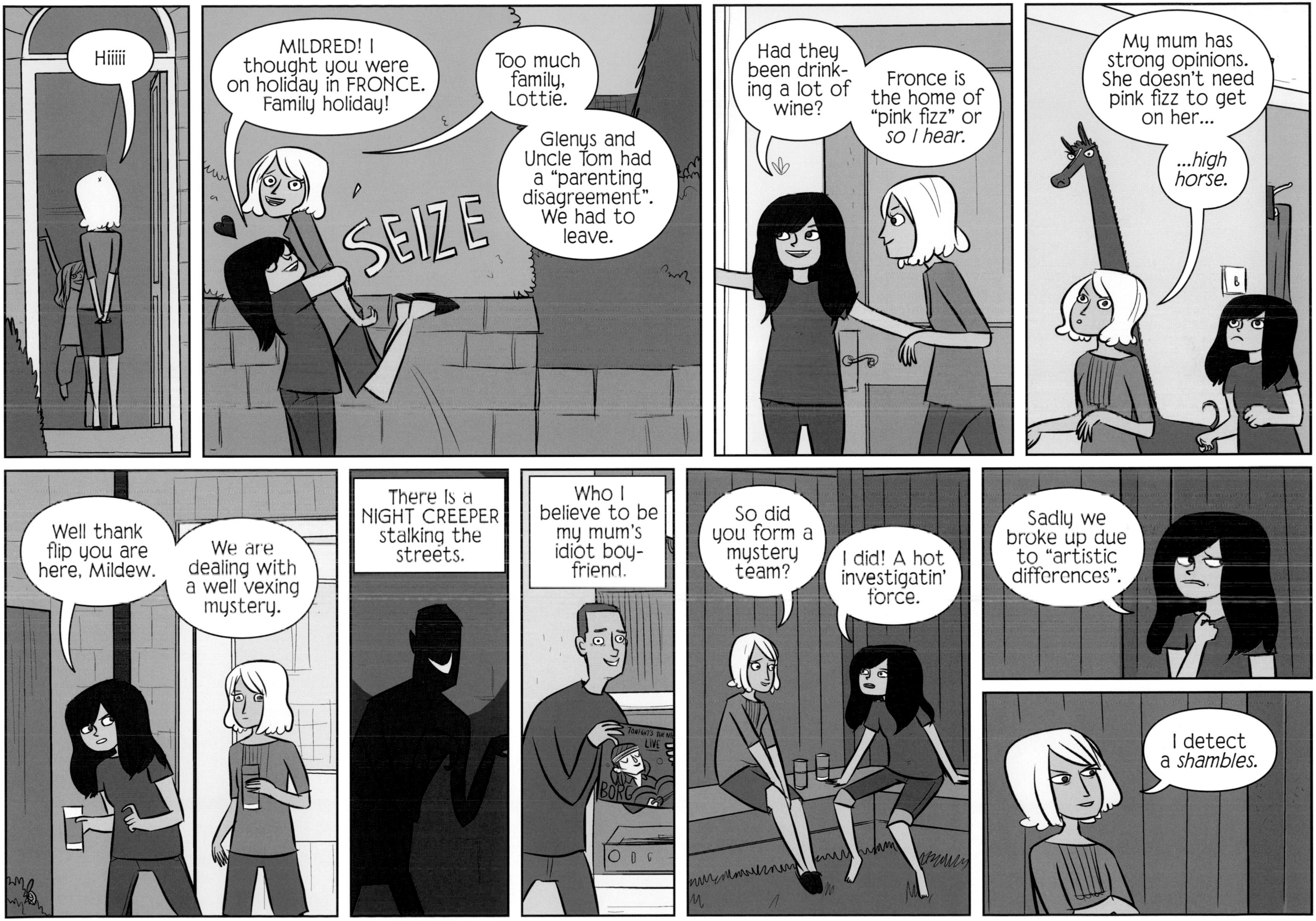
Hiiiii
MILDRED! I thought you were on holiday in FRONCE. Family holiday!
SEIZE
Too much family, Lottie.
Glenys and Uncle Tom had a "parenting disagreement". We had to leave.
Had they been drink-ing a lot of wine?
Fronce is the home of "pink fizz" or *so I hear.*
My mum has strong opinions. She doesn't need pink fizz to get on her...
...high horse.
Well thank flip you are here, Mildew.
We are dealing with a well vexing mystery.
There is a NIGHT CREEPER stalking the streets.
Who I believe to be my mum's idiot boy-friend.
So did you form a mystery team?
I did! A hot investigatin' force.
Sadly we broke up due to "artistic differences".
I detect a *shambles.*

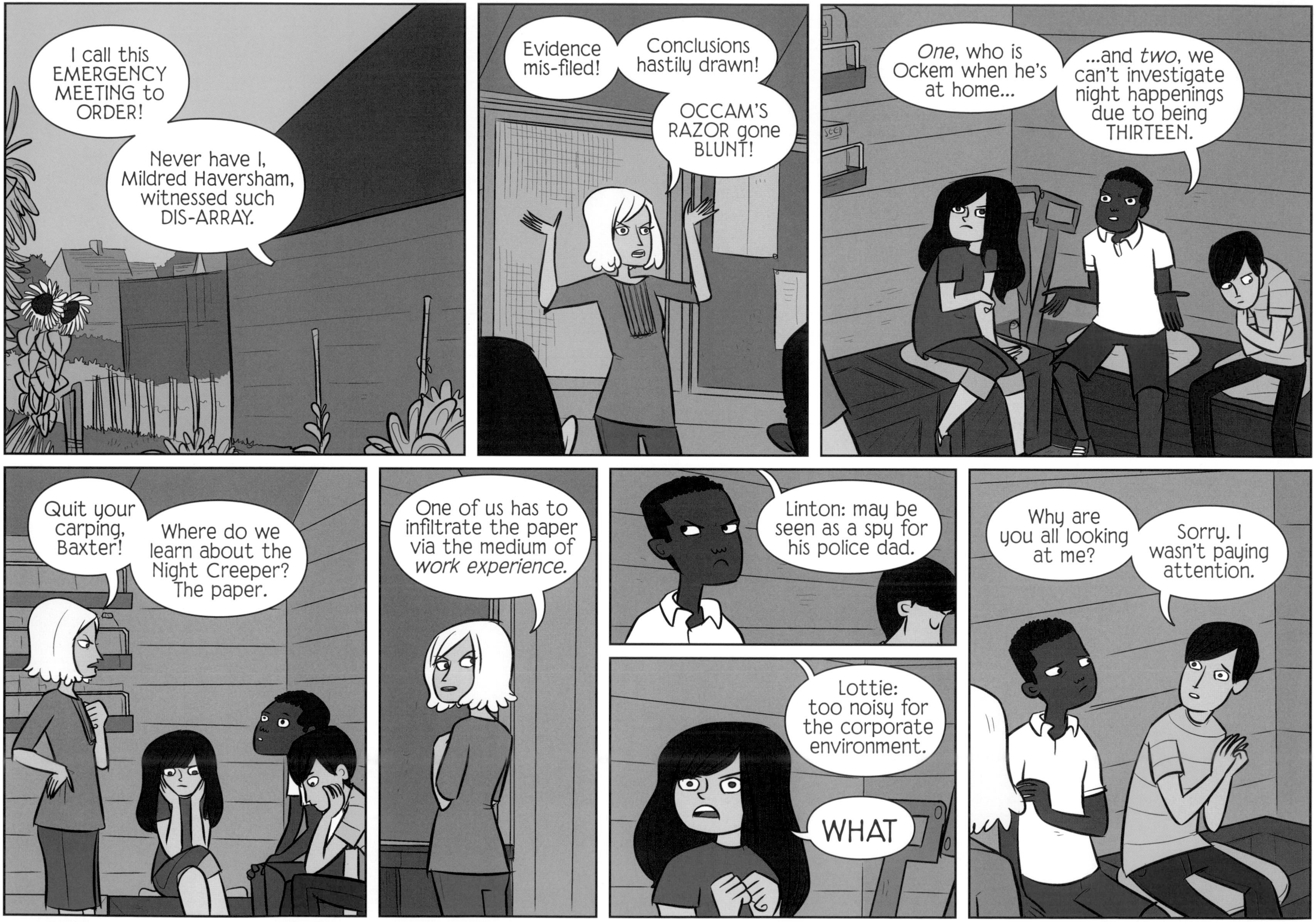
I call this EMERGENCY MEETING to ORDER!
Never have I, Mildred Haversham, witnessed such DIS-ARRAY.
Evidence mis-filed!
Conclusions hastily drawn!
OCCAM'S RAZOR gone BLUNT!
One, who is Ockem when he's at home...
...and *two*, we can't investigate night happenings due to being THIRTEEN.
Quit your carping, Baxter!
Where do we learn about the Night Creeper? The paper.
One of us has to infiltrate the paper via the medium of *work experience*.
Linton: may be seen as a spy for his police dad.
Lottie: too noisy for the corporate environment.
WHAT
Why are you all looking at me?
Sorry. I wasn't paying attention.

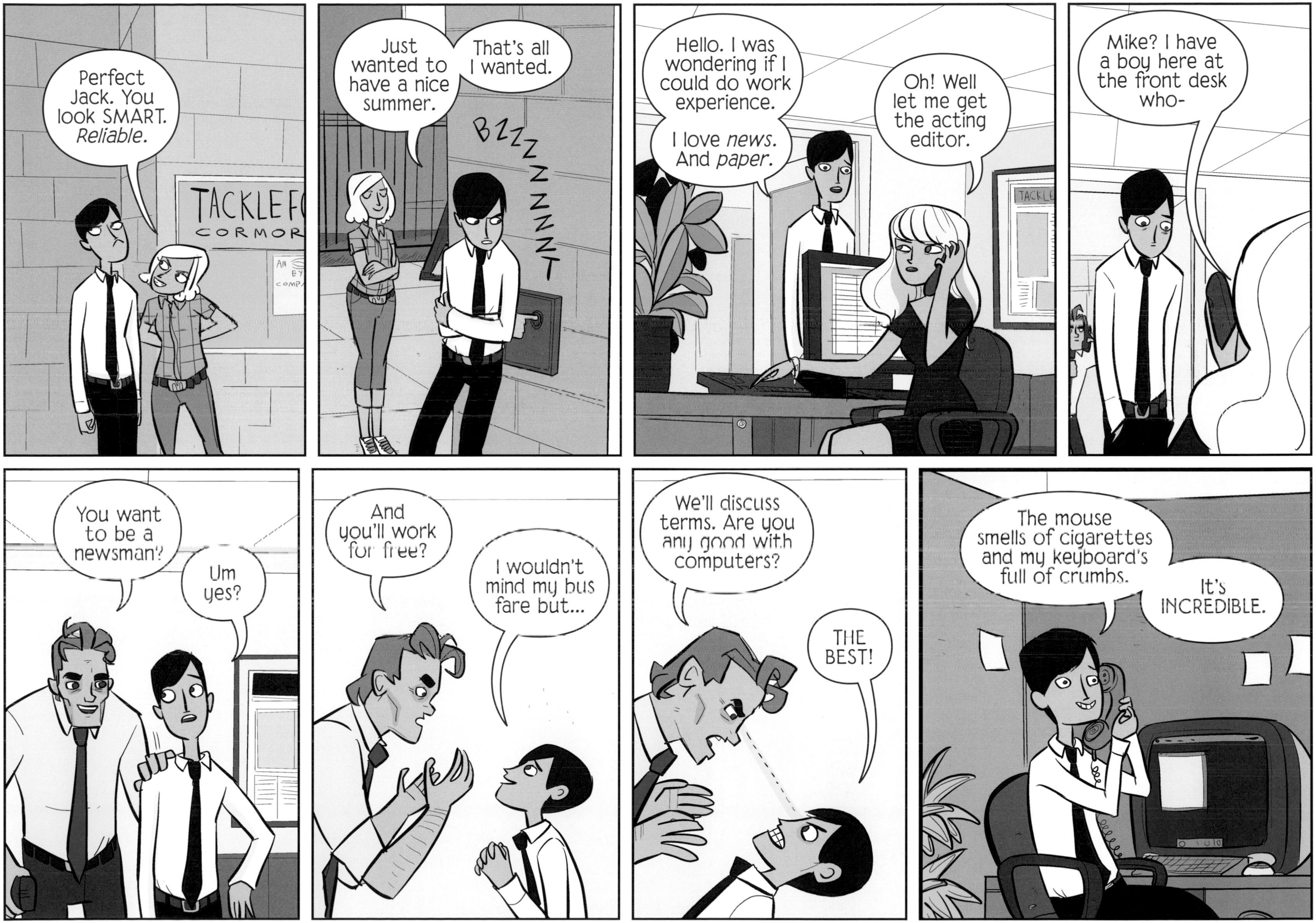

Perfect Jack. You look SMART. *Reliable.*
Just wanted to have a nice summer.
That's all I wanted.
Hello. I was wondering if I could do work experience.
I love *news.* And *paper.*
Oh! Well let me get the acting editor.
Mike? I have a boy here at the front desk who-
You want to be a newsman?
Um yes?
And you'll work for free?
I wouldn't mind my bus fare but...
We'll discuss terms. Are you any good with computers?
THE BEST!
The mouse smells of cigarettes and my keyboard's full of crumbs.
It's INCREDIBLE.

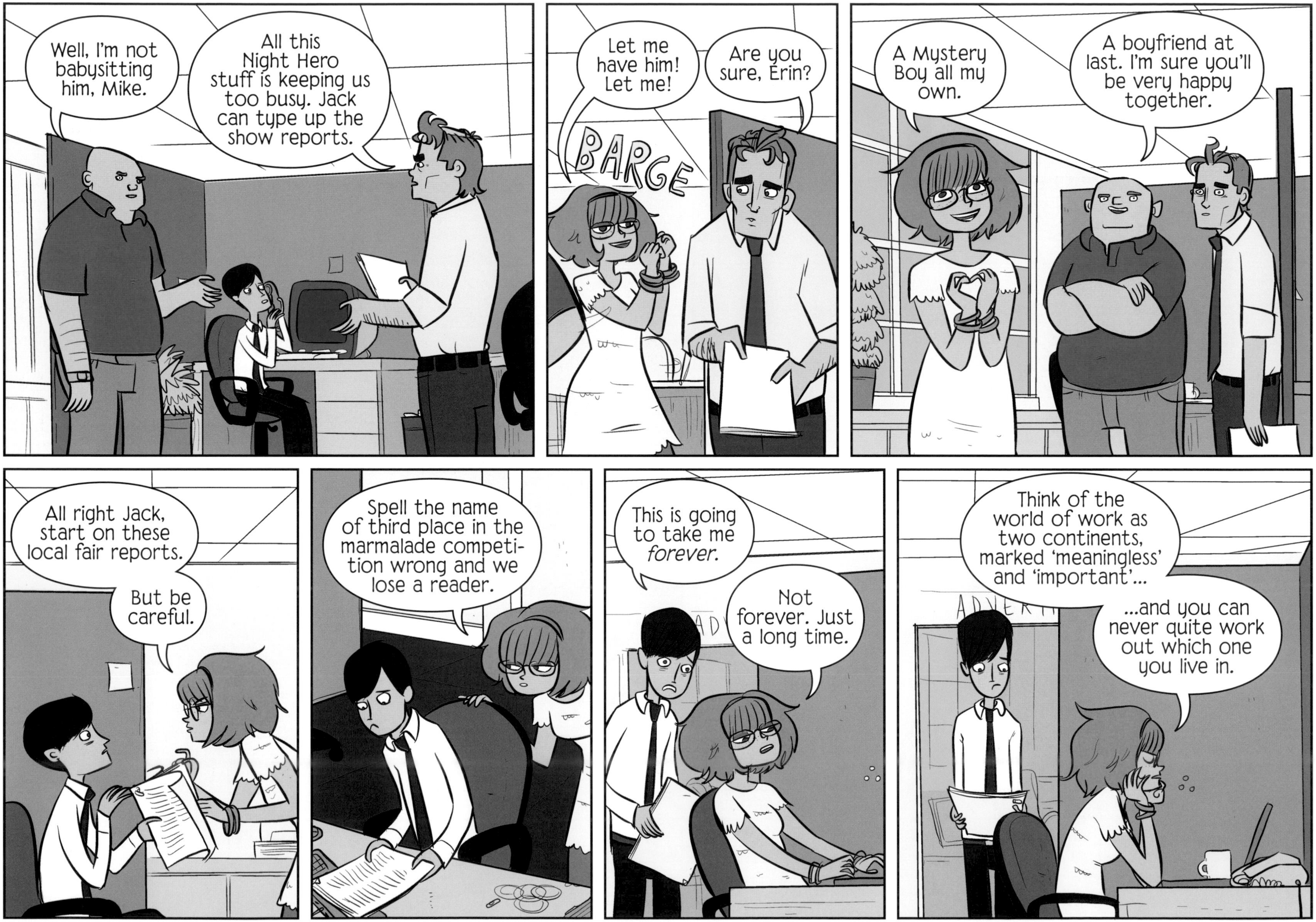
Well, I'm not babysitting him, Mike.
All this Night Hero stuff is keeping us too busy. Jack can type up the show reports.
Let me have him! Let me!
BARGE
Are you sure, Erin?
A Mystery Boy all my own.
A boyfriend at last. I'm sure you'll be very happy together.
All right Jack, start on these local fair reports.
But be careful.
Spell the name of third place in the marmalade competition wrong and we lose a reader.
This is going to take me *forever.*
Not forever. Just a long time.
Think of the world of work as two continents, marked 'meaningless' and 'important'...
...and you can never quite work out which one you live in.

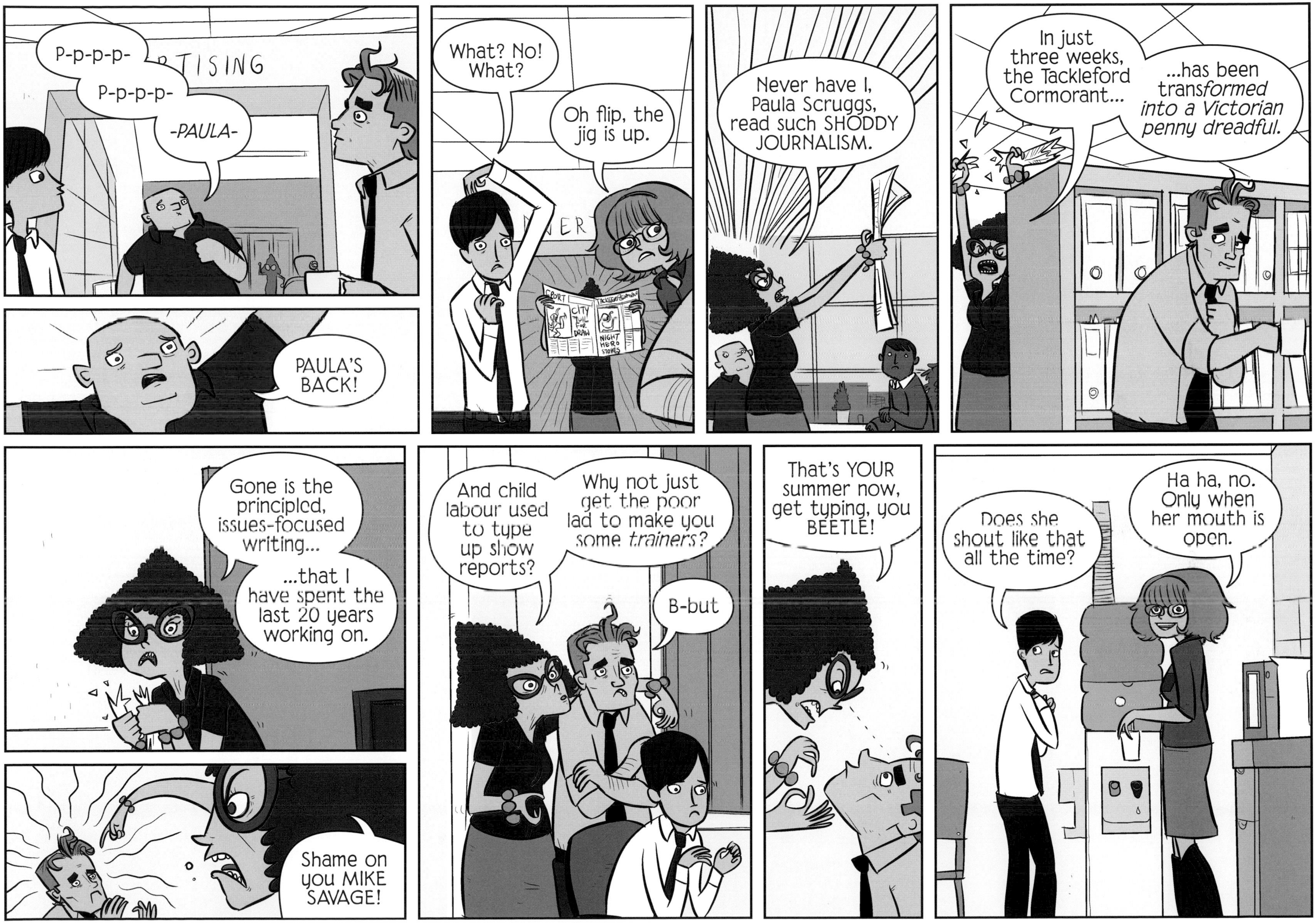
P-p-p-p-
P-p-p-p-
-PAULA-
RTISING
PAULA'S BACK!
What? No! What?
Oh flip, the jig is up.
Never have I, Paula Scruggs, read such SHODDY JOURNALISM.
In just three weeks, the Tackleford Cormorant...
...has been trans*formed into a Victorian penny dreadful.*
Gone is the principled, issues-focused writing...
...that I have spent the last 20 years working on.
Shame on you MIKE SAVAGE!
And child labour used to type up show reports?
Why not just get the poor lad to make you some *trainers?*
B-but
That's YOUR summer now, get typing, you BEETLE!
Does she shout like that all the time?
Ha ha, no. Only when her mouth is open.

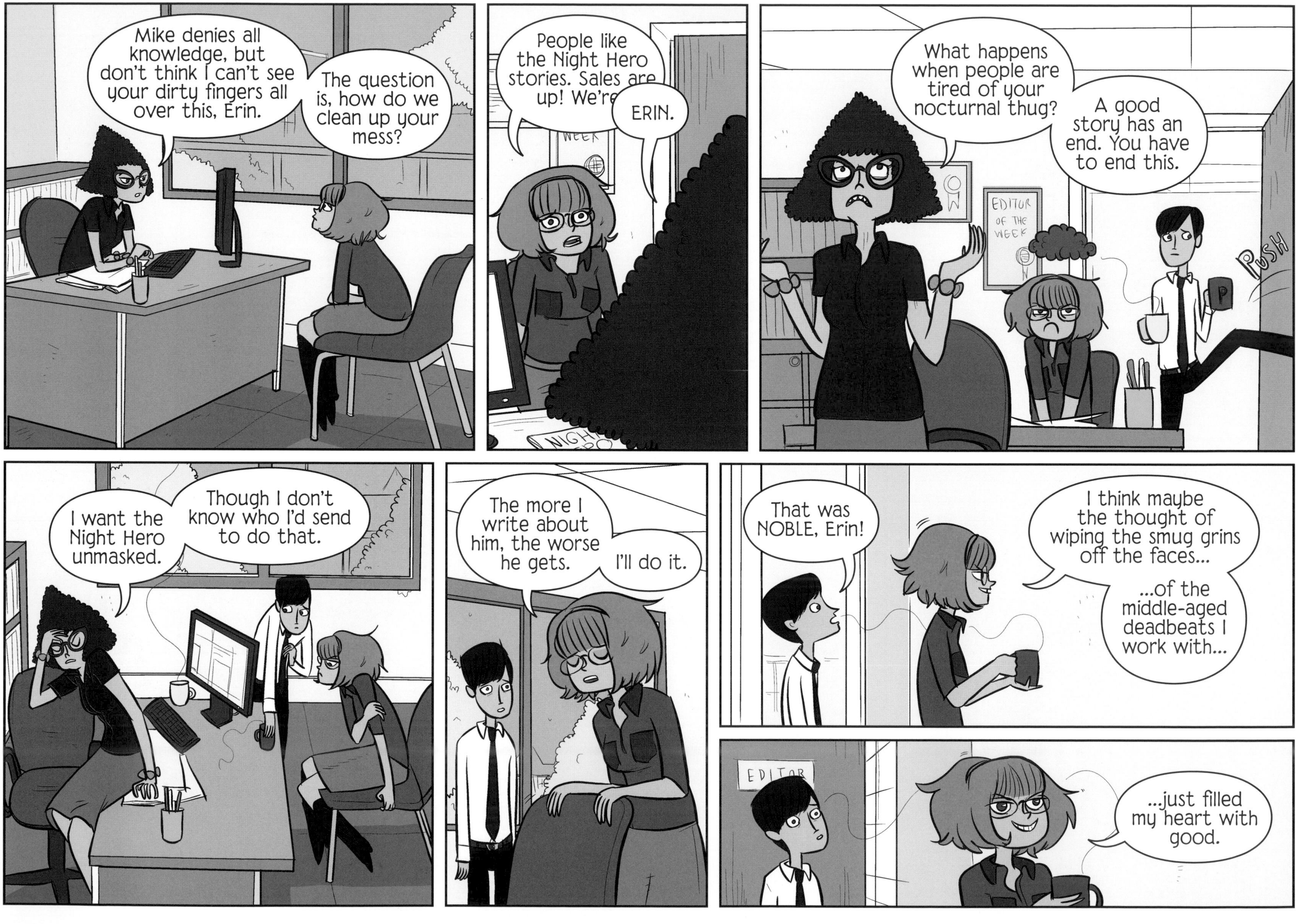
Mike denies all knowledge, but don't think I can't see your dirty fingers all over this, Erin.
The question is, how do we clean up your mess?
People like the Night Hero stories. Sales are up! We're
ERIN.
What happens when people are tired of your nocturnal thug?
A good story has an end. You have to end this.
EDITOR OF THE WEEK
PUSH
I want the Night Hero unmasked.
Though I don't know who I'd send to do that.
The more I write about him, the worse he gets.
I'll do it.
That was NOBLE, Erin!
I think maybe the thought of wiping the smug grins off the faces...
...of the middle-aged deadbeats I work with...
...just filled my heart with good.

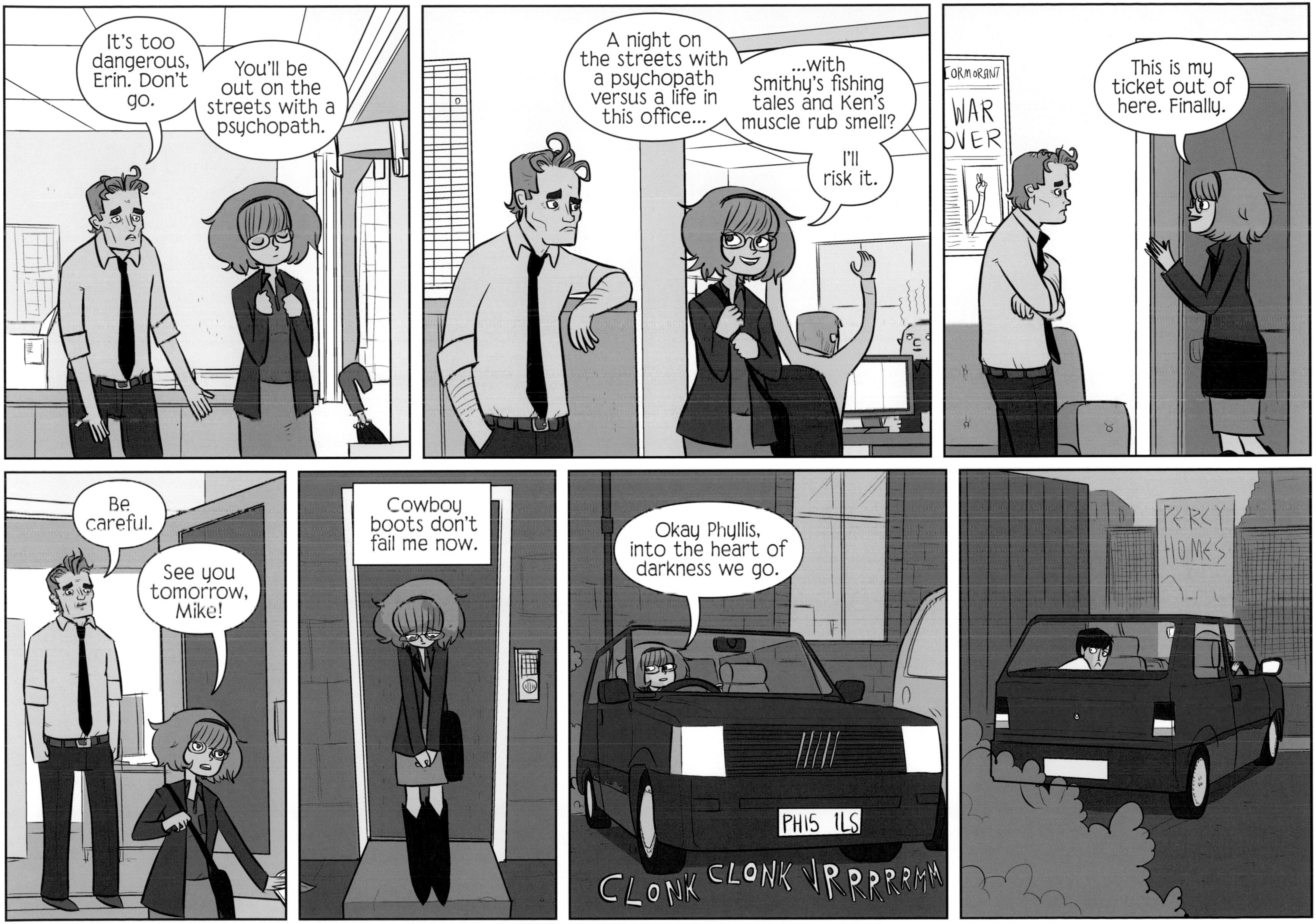
It's too dangerous, Erin. Don't go.
You'll be out on the streets with a psychopath.
A night on the streets with a psychopath versus a life in this office...
...with Smithy's fishing tales and Ken's muscle rub smell?
I'll risk it.
ORMORANT
WAR
OVER
This is my ticket out of here. Finally.
Be careful.
See you tomorrow, Mike!
Cowboy boots don't fail me now.
Okay Phyllis, into the heart of darkness we go.
PHI5 1LS
CLONK CLONK VRRRRRMM
PERCY HOMES

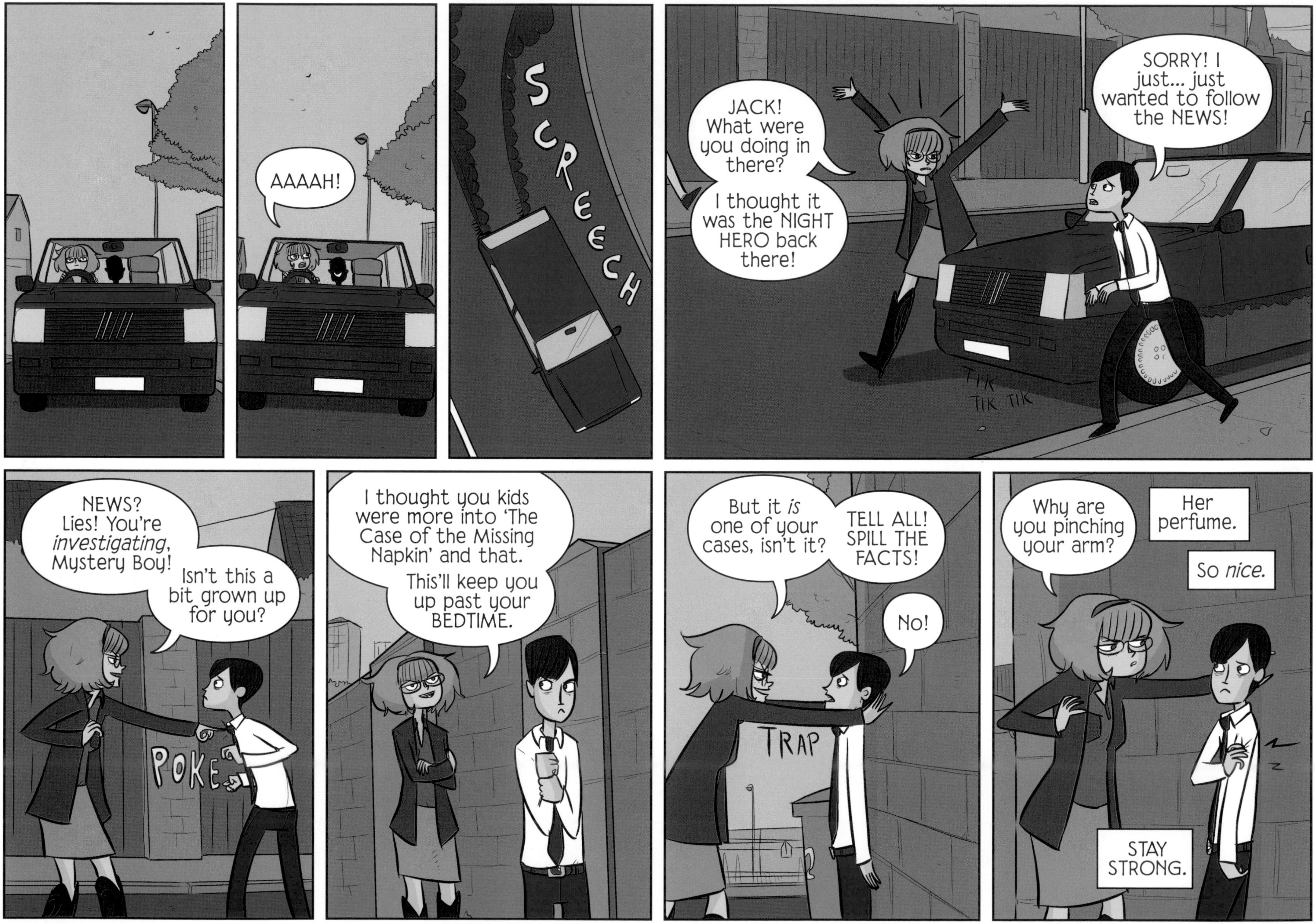
AAAAH!
SCREECH
JACK! What were you doing in there?
I thought it was the NIGHT HERO back there!
SORRY! I just... just wanted to follow the NEWS!
TIK TIK TIK
NEWS? Lies! You're *investigating*, Mystery Boy!
Isn't this a bit grown up for you?
POKE
I thought you kids were more into 'The Case of the Missing Napkin' and that.
This'll keep you up past your BEDTIME.
But it *is* one of your cases, isn't it?
TELL ALL! SPILL THE FACTS!
No!
TRAP
Why are you pinching your arm?
Her perfume.
So *nice*.
STAY STRONG.

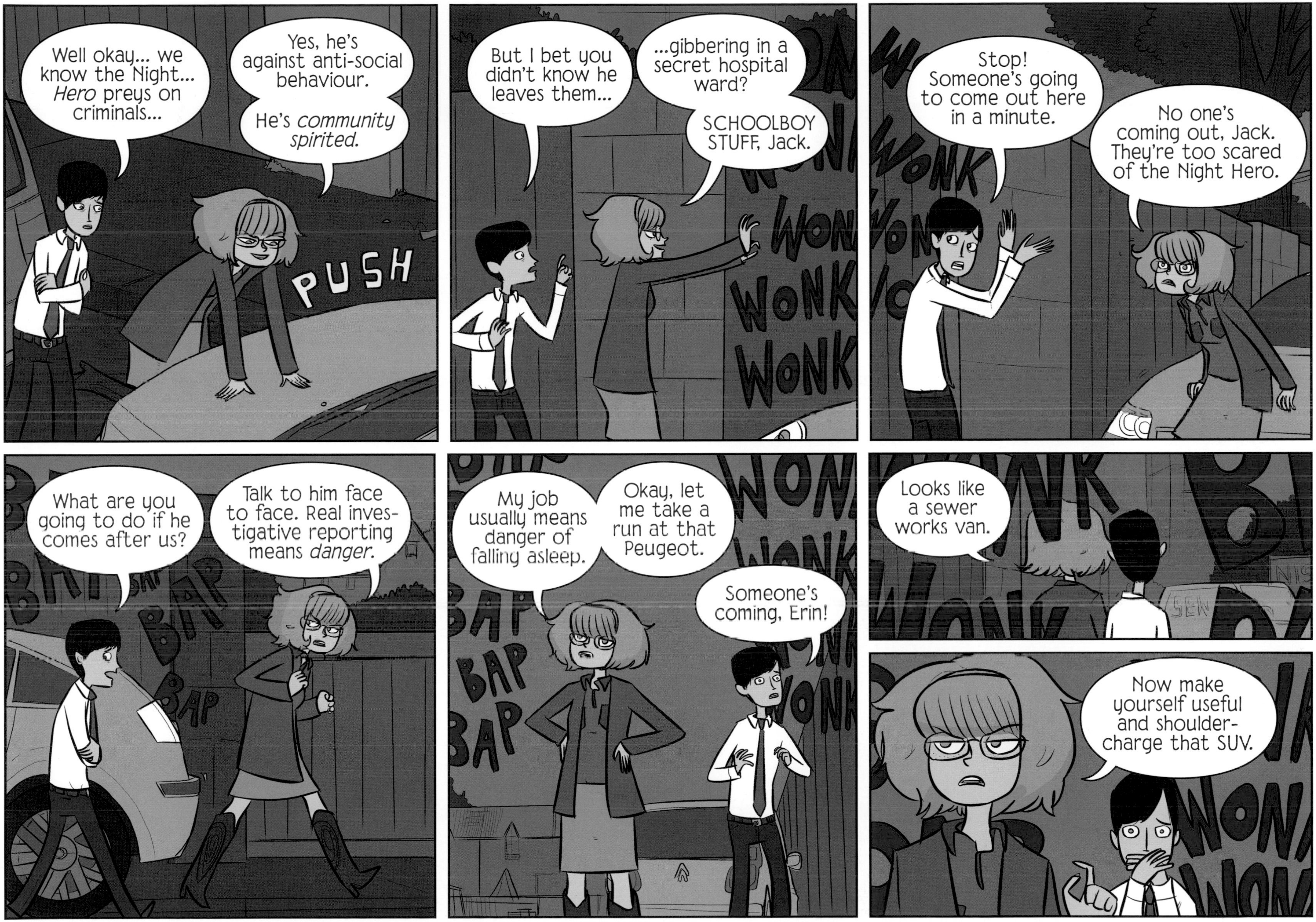
Well okay... we know the Night... *Hero* preys on criminals...
Yes, he's against anti-social behaviour.
He's *community spirited.*
PUSH
But I bet you didn't know he leaves them...
...gibbering in a secret hospital ward?
SCHOOLBOY STUFF, Jack.
WONK WONK WONK WONK
Stop! Someone's going to come out here in a minute.
No one's coming out, Jack. They're too scared of the Night Hero.
WONK
What are you going to do if he comes after us?
Talk to him face to face. Real investigative reporting means *danger.*
BAP BAP BAP
My job usually means danger of falling asleep.
Okay, let me take a run at that Peugeot.
Someone's coming, Erin!
BAP BAP BAP
WONK WONK
Looks like a sewer works van.
WONK
Now make yourself useful and shoulder-charge that SUV.
WONK

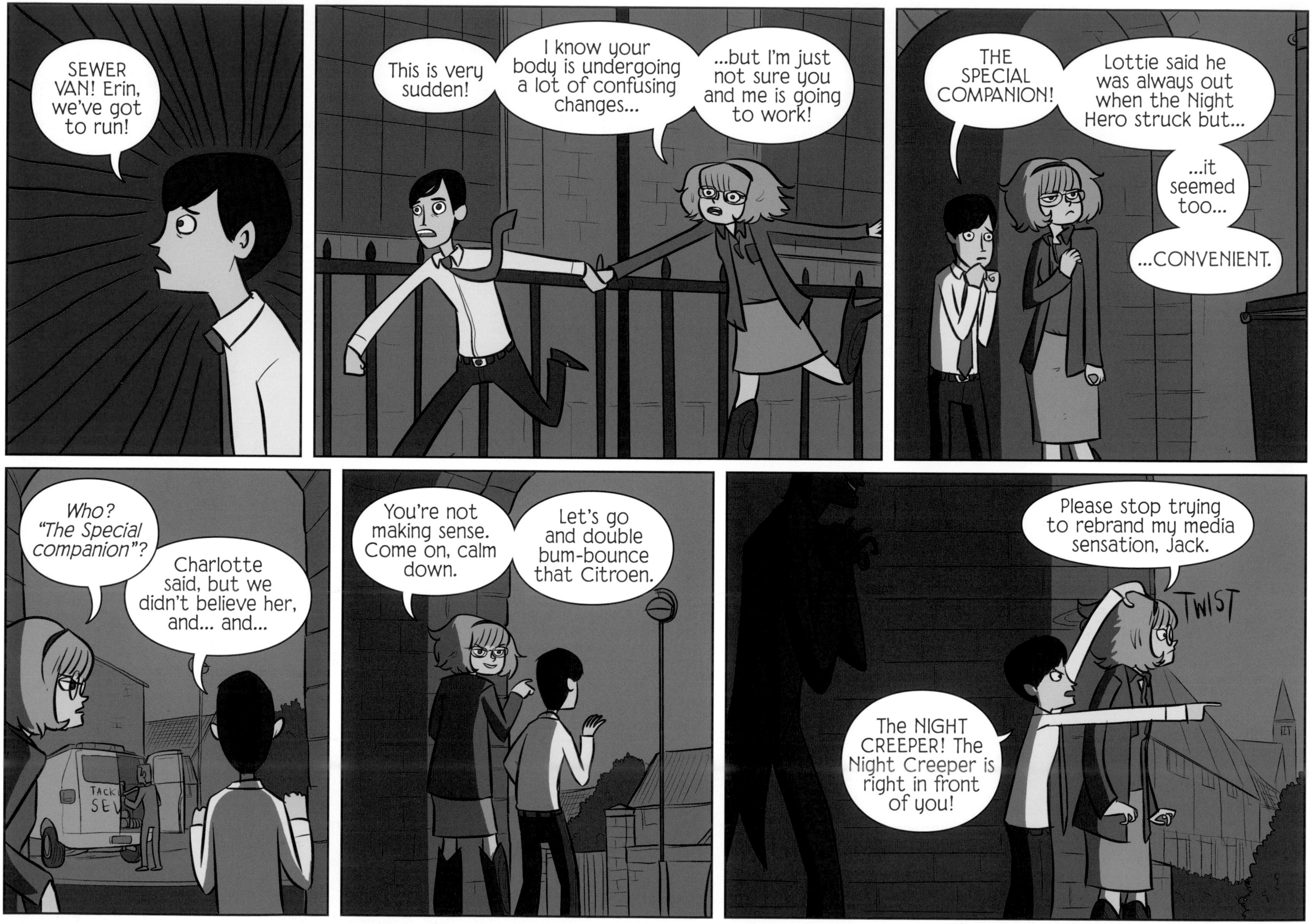
SEWER VAN! Erin, we've got to run!
This is very sudden!
I know your body is undergoing a lot of confusing changes...
...but I'm just not sure you and me is going to work!
THE SPECIAL COMPANION!
Lottie said he was always out when the Night Hero struck but...
...it seemed too...
...CONVENIENT.
Who? "The Special companion"?
Charlotte said, but we didn't believe her, and... and...
TACK SEV
You're not making sense. Come on, calm down.
Let's go and double bum-bounce that Citroen.
Please stop trying to rebrand my media sensation, Jack.
TWIST
The NIGHT CREEPER! The Night Creeper is right in front of you!

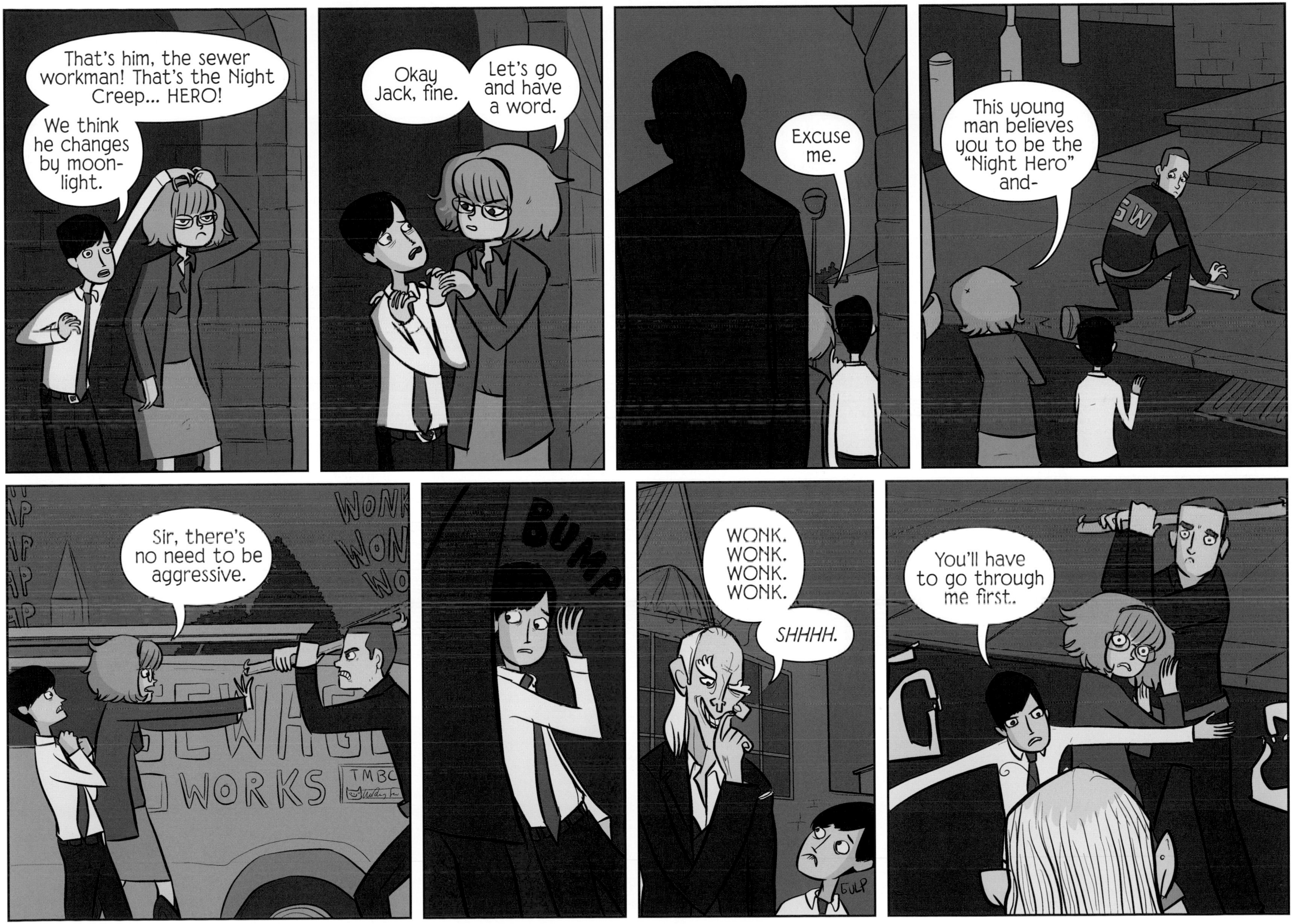
That's him, the sewer workman! That's the Night Creep... HERO!
We think he changes by moon-light.
Okay Jack, fine.
Let's go and have a word.
Excuse me.
This young man believes you to be the "Night Hero" and-
SW
WONK
WONK
WO
Sir, there's no need to be aggressive.
WORKS
TMBC
BUMP
WONK. WONK. WONK. WONK.
SHHHH.
GULP
You'll have to go through me first.

Bad Machinery, Volume Six

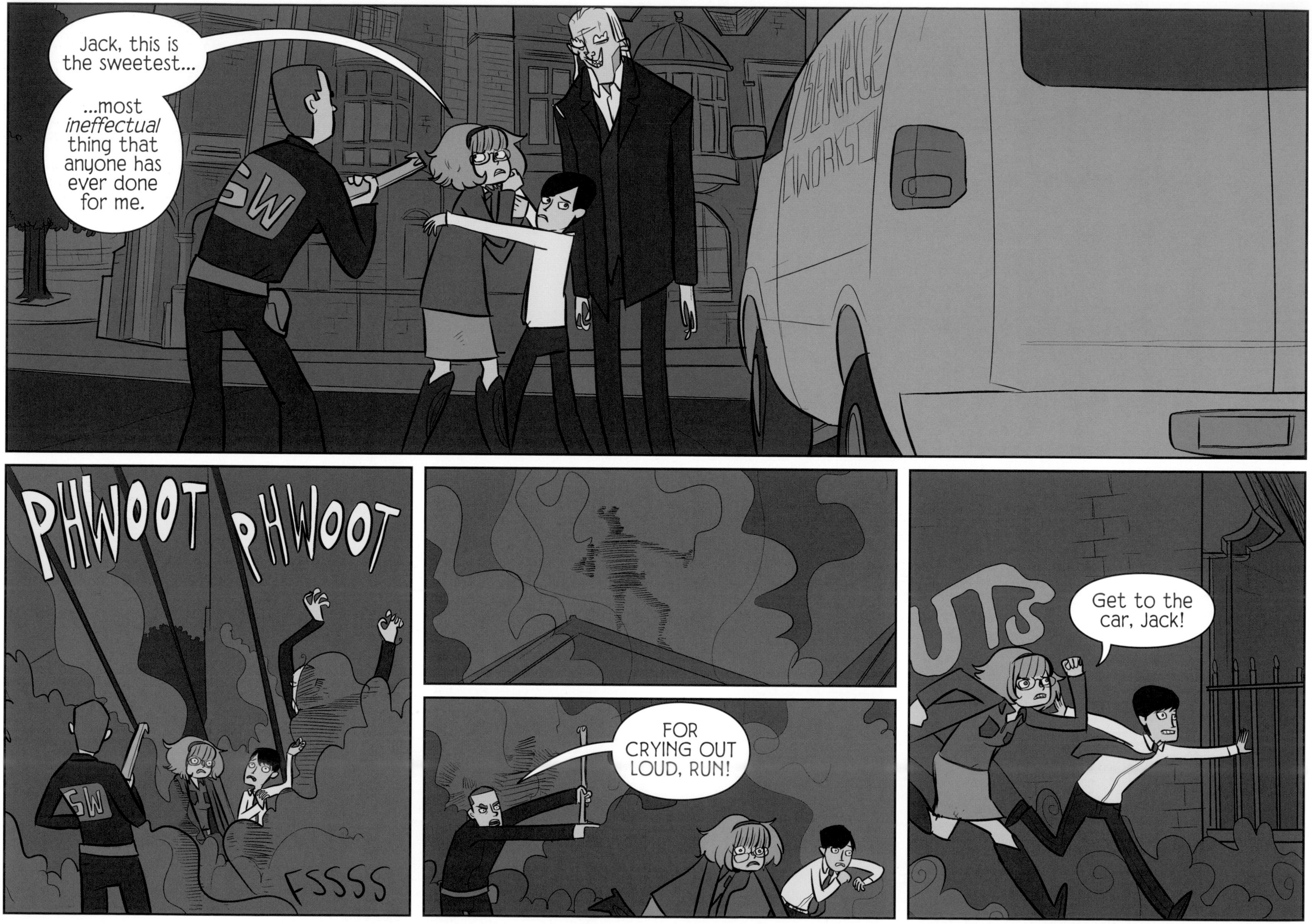

Jack, this is the sweetest...
...most *ineffectual* thing that anyone has ever done for me.
SEWAGE WORKS
SW
PHWOOT PHWOOT
FSSSS
FOR CRYING OUT LOUD, RUN!
Get to the car, Jack!

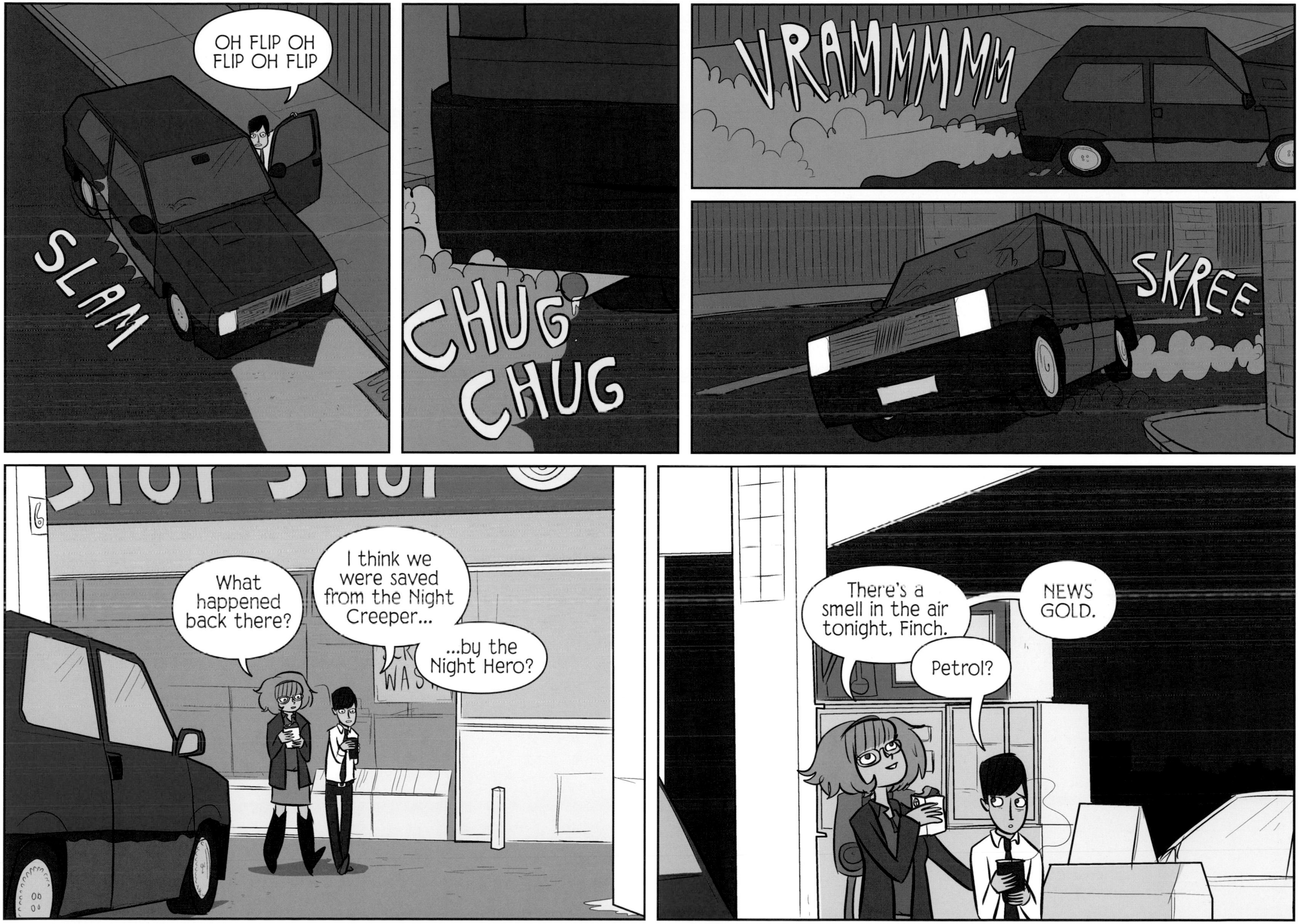
OH FLIP OH FLIP OH FLIP
SLAM
CHUG CHUG
VRAMMMMM
SKREE
What happened back there?
I think we were saved from the Night Creeper...
...by the Night Hero?
There's a smell in the air tonight, Finch.
Petrol?
NEWS GOLD.

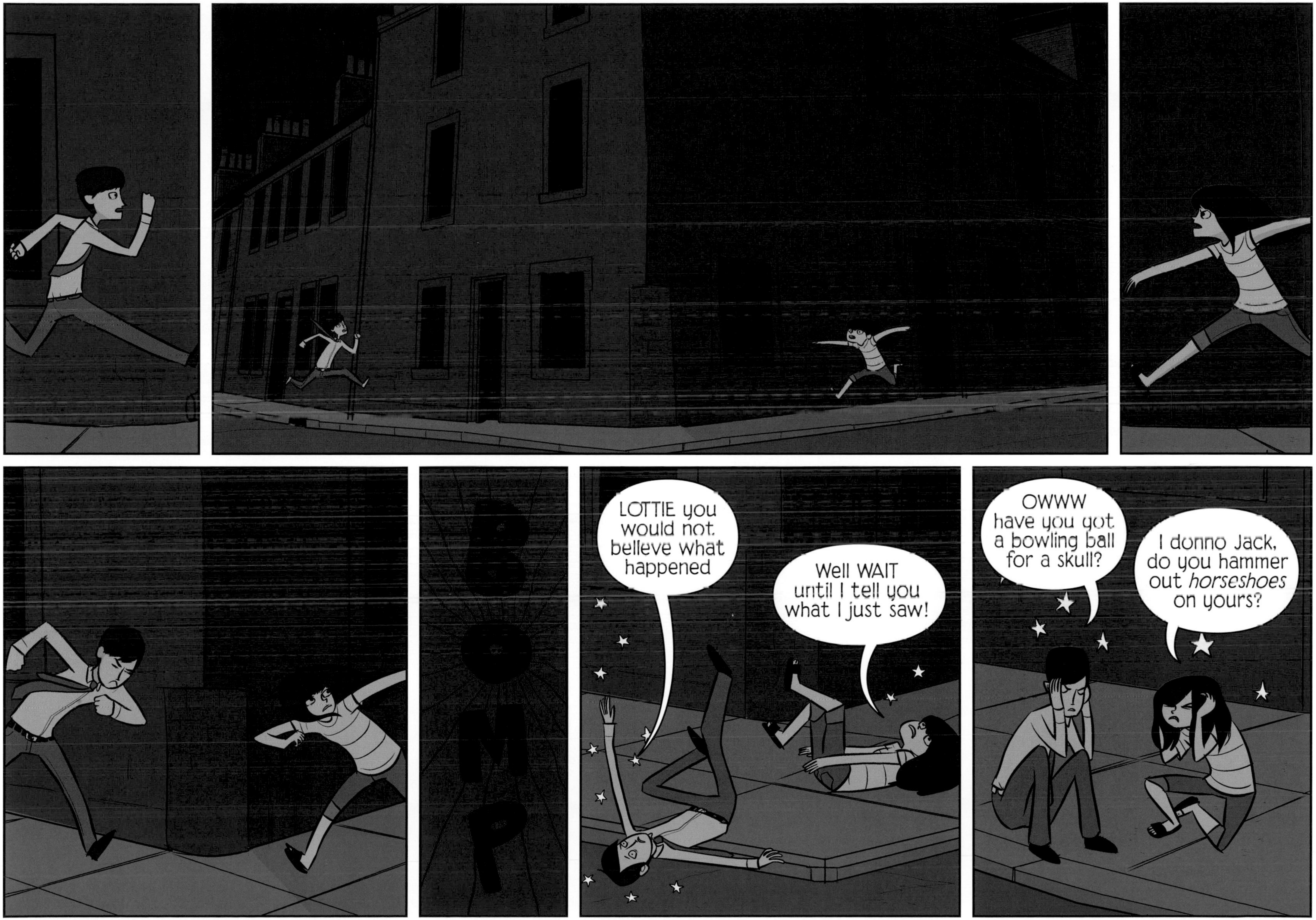
BOMP
LOTTIE you would not believe what happened
Well WAIT until I tell you what I just saw!
OWWW have you got a bowling ball for a skull?
I donno Jack, do you hammer out *horseshoes* on yours?

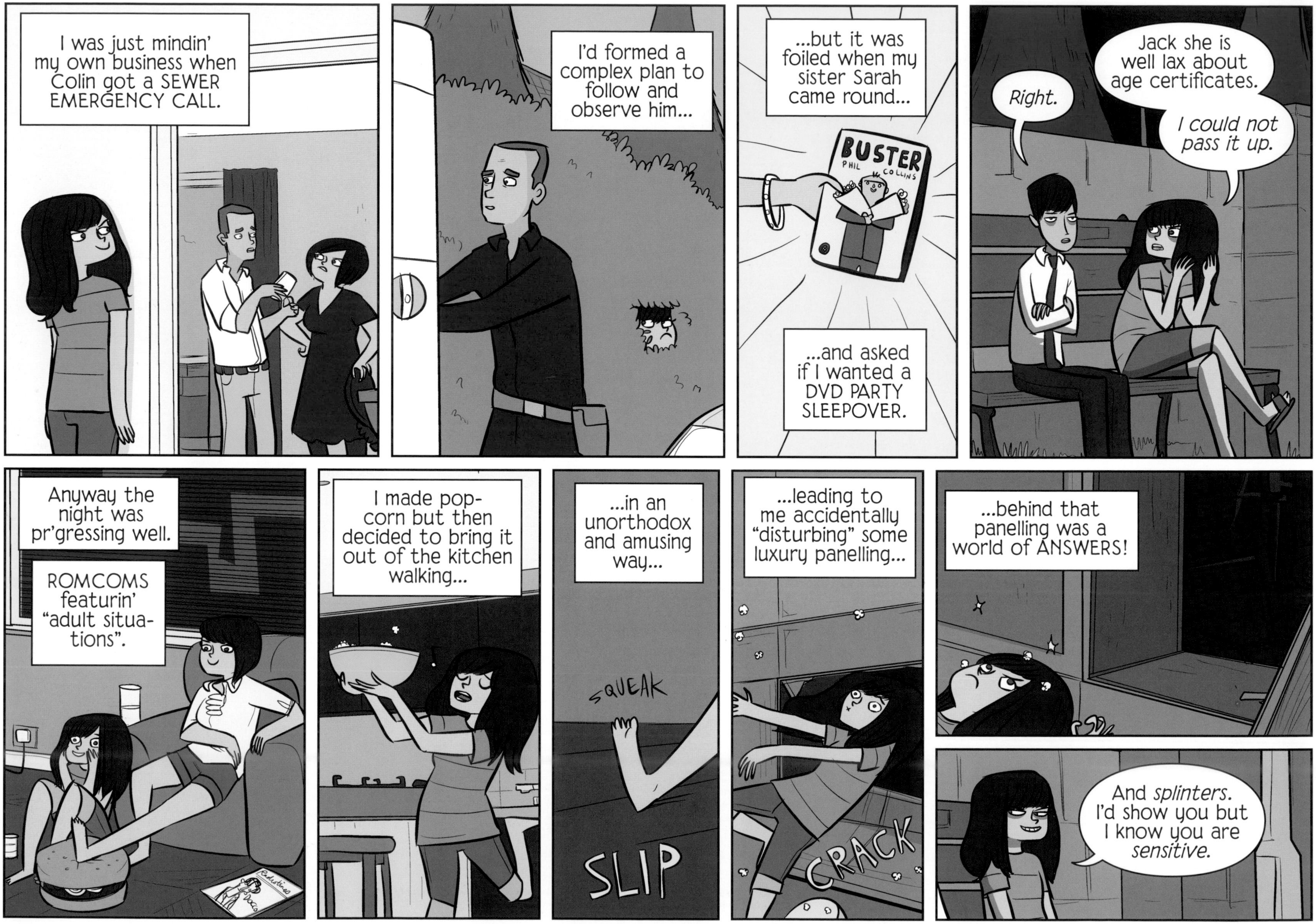
I was just mindin' my own business when Colin got a SEWER EMERGENCY CALL.
I'd formed a complex plan to follow and observe him...
...but it was foiled when my sister Sarah came round...
BUSTER
PHIL COLLINS
...and asked if I wanted a DVD PARTY SLEEPOVER.
Right.
Jack she is well lax about age certificates.
I could not pass it up.
Anyway the night was pr'gressing well.
ROMCOMS featurin' "adult situations".
I made pop-corn but then decided to bring it out of the kitchen walking...
...in an unorthodox and amusing way...
SQUEAK
SLIP
...leading to me accidentally "disturbing" some luxury panelling...
CRACK
...behind that panelling was a world of ANSWERS!
And splinters. I'd show you but I know you are sensitive.

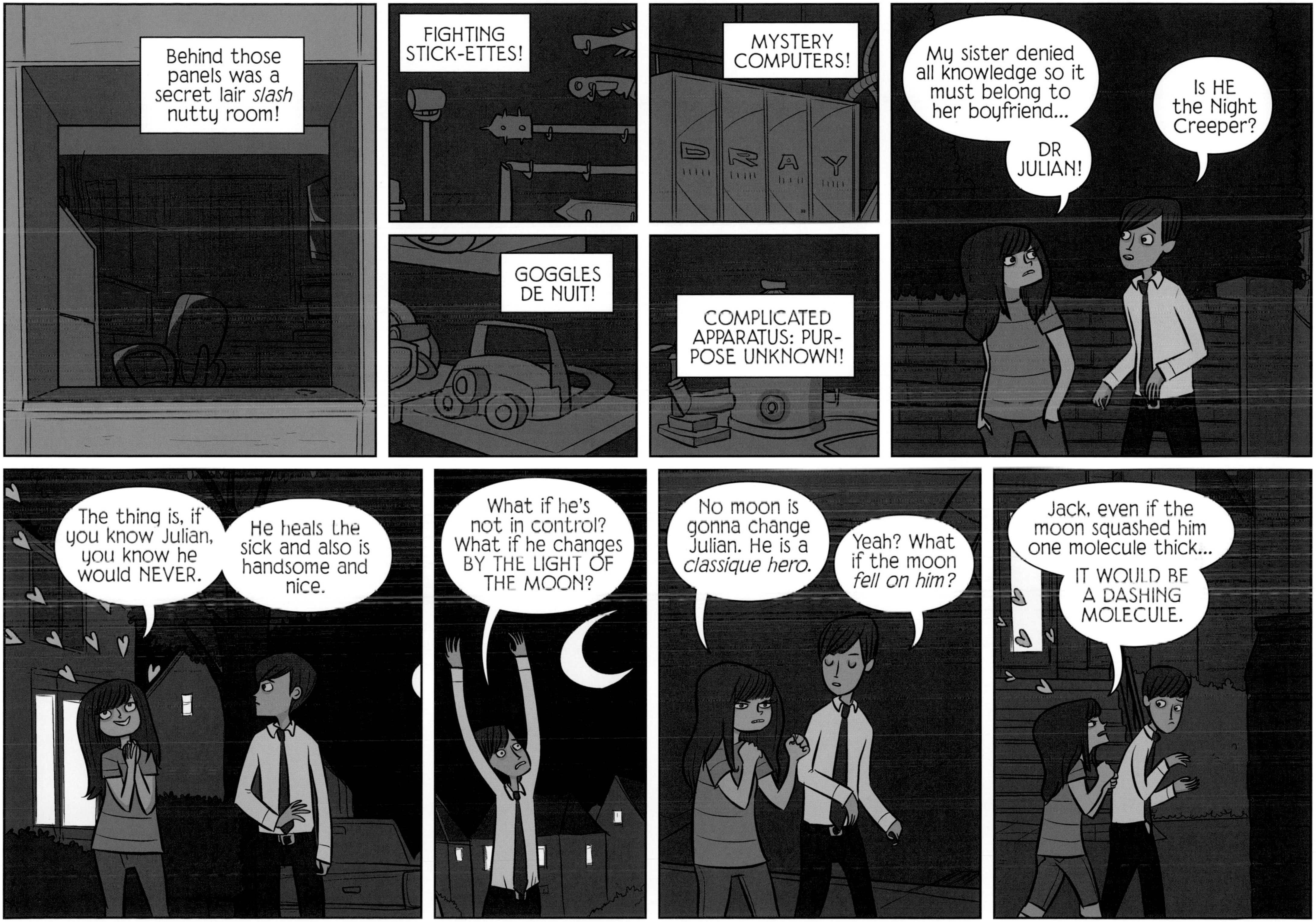
Behind those panels was a secret lair *slash* nutty room!
FIGHTING STICK-ETTES!
MYSTERY COMPUTERS!
DRAY
My sister denied all knowledge so it must belong to her boyfriend...
DR JULIAN!
Is HE the Night Creeper?
GOGGLES DE NUIT!
COMPLICATED APPARATUS: PURPOSE UNKNOWN!
The thing is, if you know Julian, you know he would NEVER.
He heals the sick and also is handsome and nice.
What if he's not in control? What if he changes BY THE LIGHT OF THE MOON?
No moon is gonna change Julian. He is a *classique hero.*
Yeah? What if the moon *fell on him?*
Jack, even if the moon squashed him one molecule thick...
IT WOULD BE A DASHING MOLECULE.

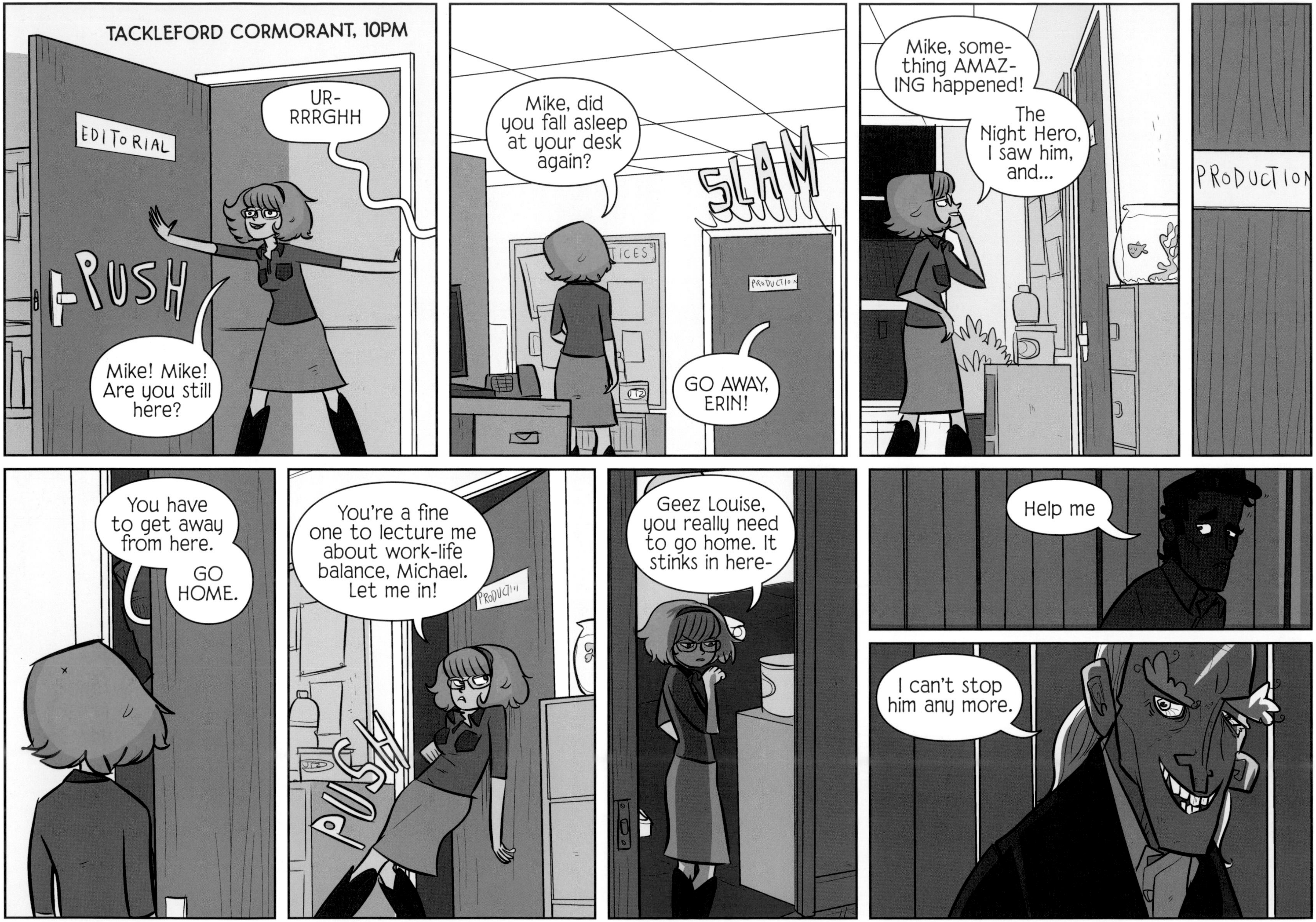
TACKLEFORD CORMORANT, 10PM
EDITORIAL
UR-RRRGHH
PUSH
Mike! Mike! Are you still here?
Mike, did you fall asleep at your desk again?
SLAM
PRODUCTION
GO AWAY, ERIN!
Mike, something AMAZING happened!
The Night Hero, I saw him, and...
PRODUCTION
You have to get away from here.
GO HOME.
You're a fine one to lecture me about work-life balance, Michael. Let me in!
PUSH
Geez Louise, you really need to go home. It stinks in here-
Help me
I can't stop him any more.

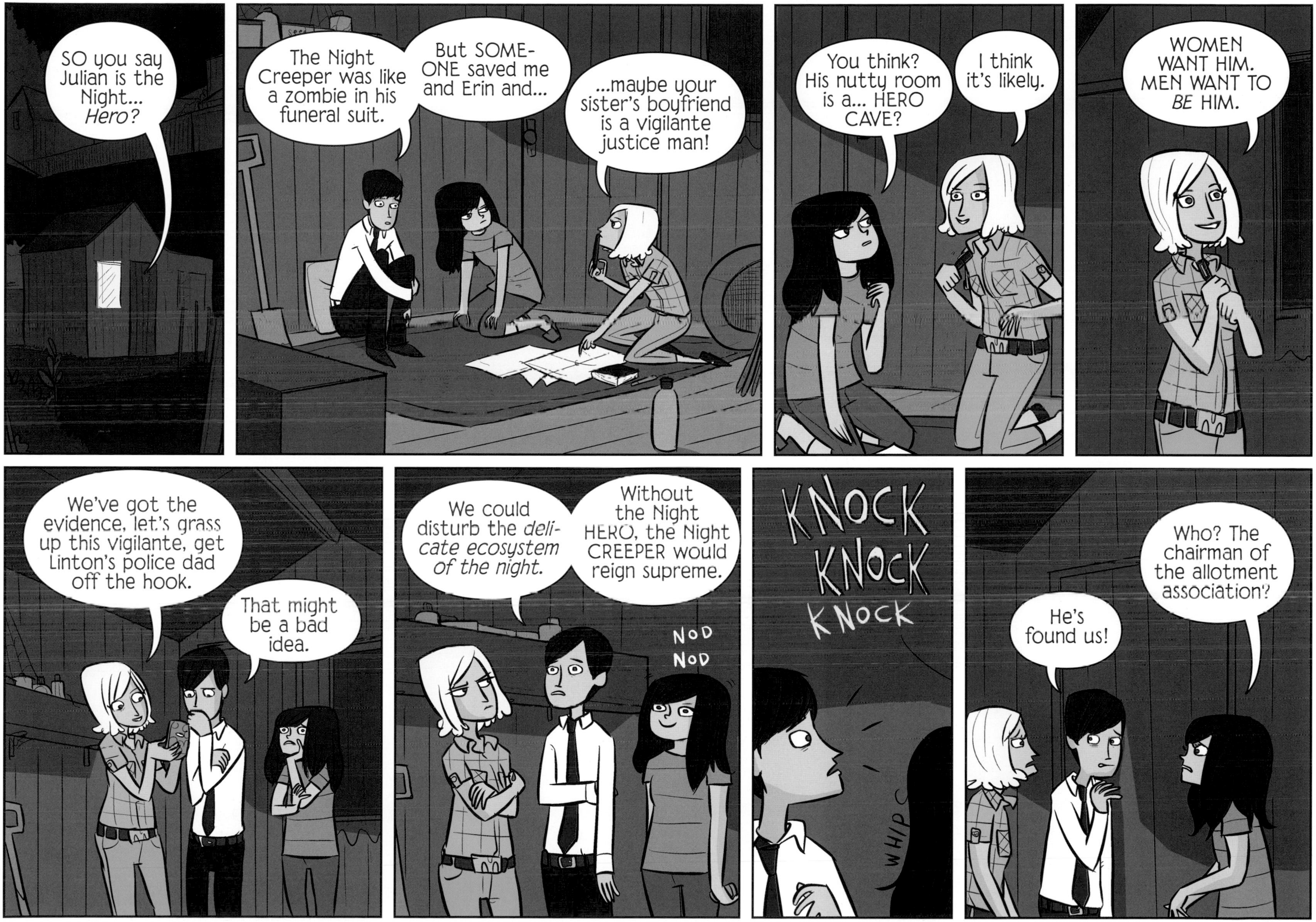
SO you say Julian is the Night... *Hero?*
The Night Creeper was like a zombie in his funeral suit.
But SOME-ONE saved me and Erin and...
...maybe your sister's boyfriend is a vigilante justice man!
You think? His nutty room is a... HERO CAVE?
I think it's likely.
WOMEN WANT HIM. MEN WANT TO *BE* HIM.
We've got the evidence, let's grass up this vigilante, get Linton's police dad off the hook.
That might be a bad idea.
We could disturb the *delicate ecosystem of the night.*
Without the Night HERO, the Night CREEPER would reign supreme.
NOD NOD
KNOCK KNOCK KNOCK
WHIP
He's found us!
Who? The chairman of the allotment association?

Bad Machinery, Volume Six

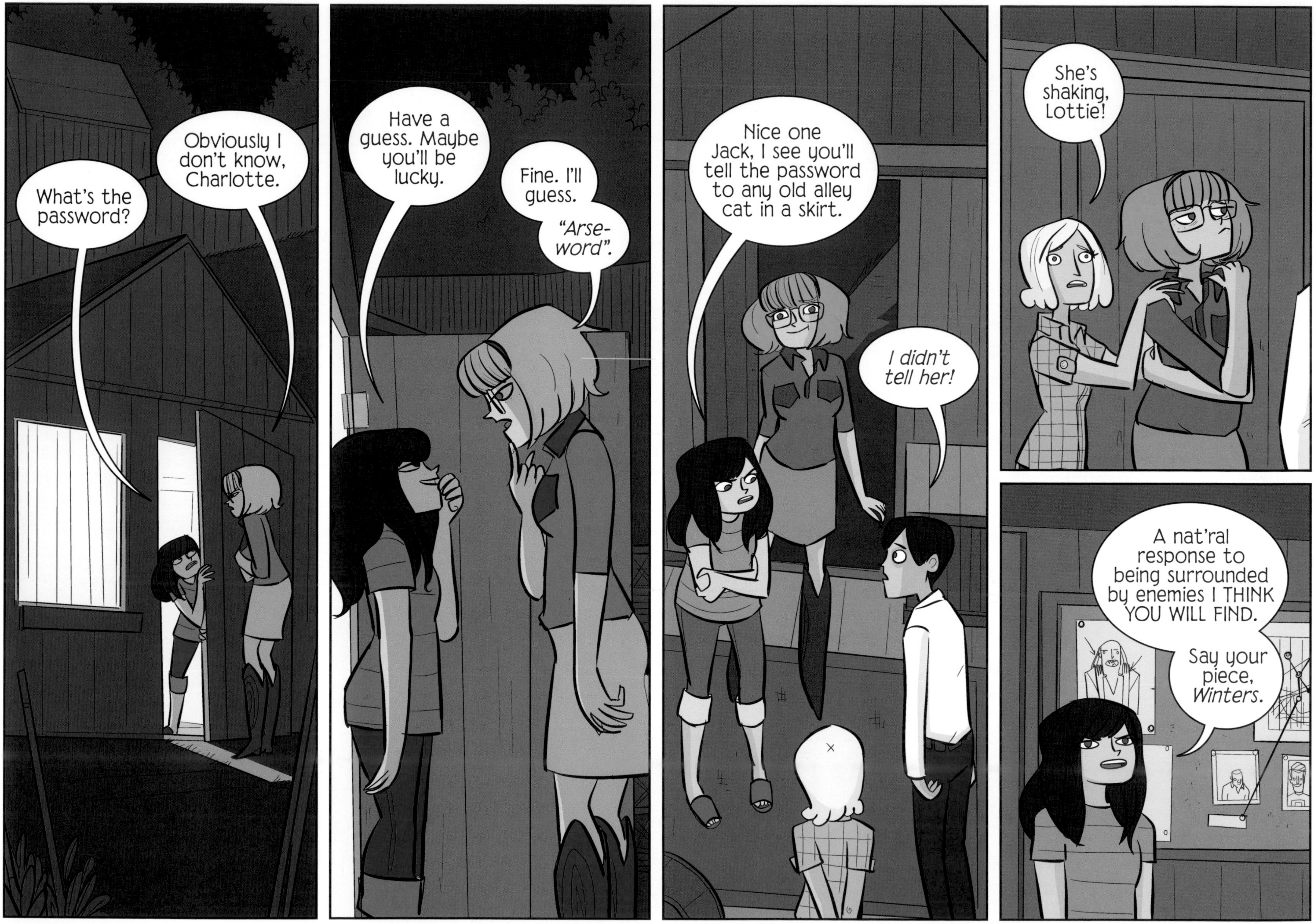
What's the password?
Obviously I don't know, Charlotte.
Have a guess. Maybe you'll be lucky.
Fine. I'll guess.
"Arse-word".
Nice one Jack, I see you'll tell the password to any old alley cat in a skirt.
I didn't tell her!
She's shaking, Lottie!
A nat'ral response to being surrounded by enemies I THINK YOU WILL FIND.
Say your piece, *Winters.*

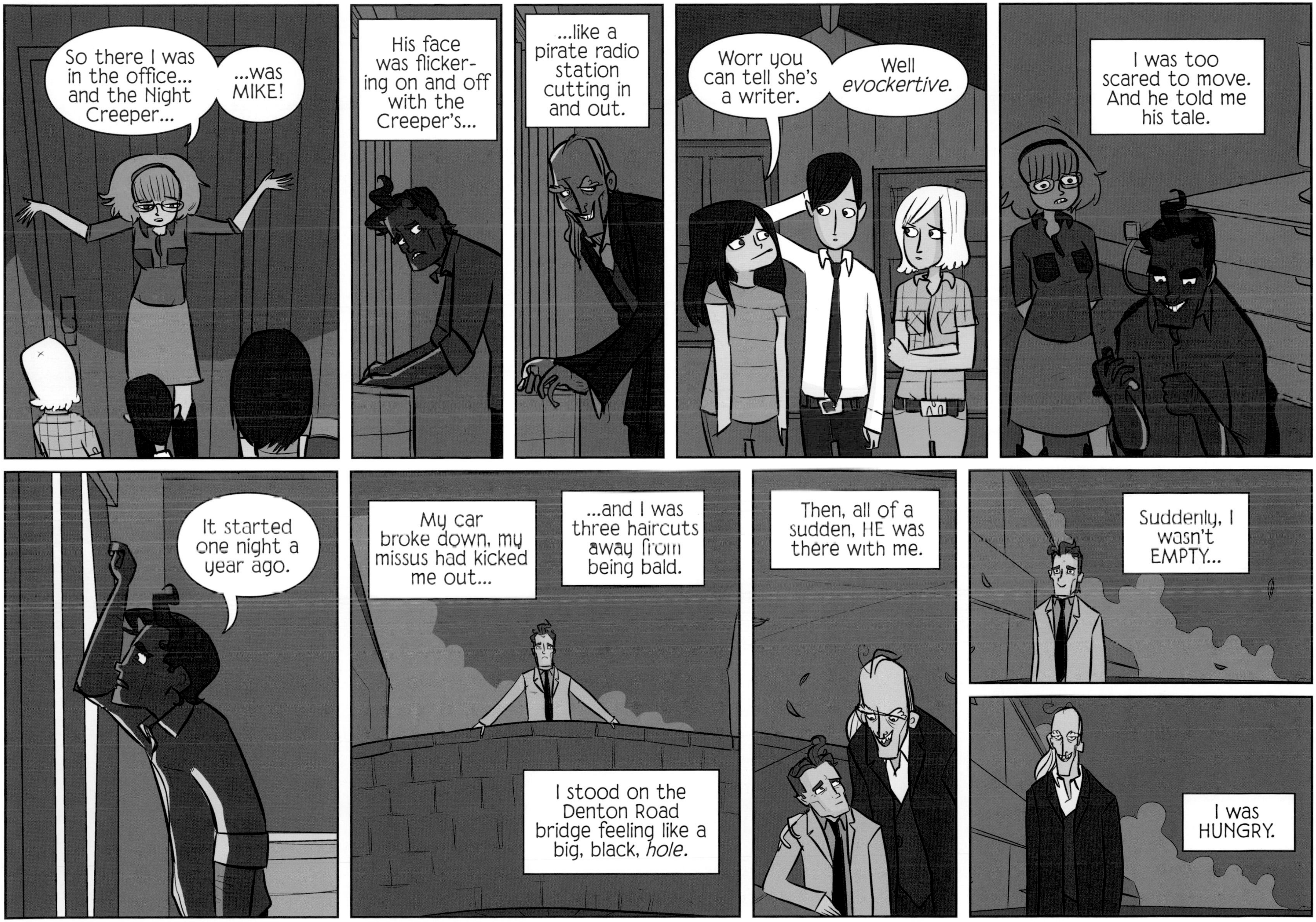

So there I was in the office... and the Night Creeper...
...was MIKE!
His face was flicker-ing on and off with the Creeper's...
...like a pirate radio station cutting in and out.
Worr you can tell she's a writer.
Well *evockertive.*
I was too scared to move. And he told me his tale.
It started one night a year ago.
My car broke down, my missus had kicked me out...
...and I was three haircuts away from being bald.
I stood on the Denton Road bridge feeling like a big, black, *hole.*
Then, all of a sudden, HE was there with me.
Suddenly, I wasn't EMPTY...
I was HUNGRY.

Bad Machinery, Volume Six

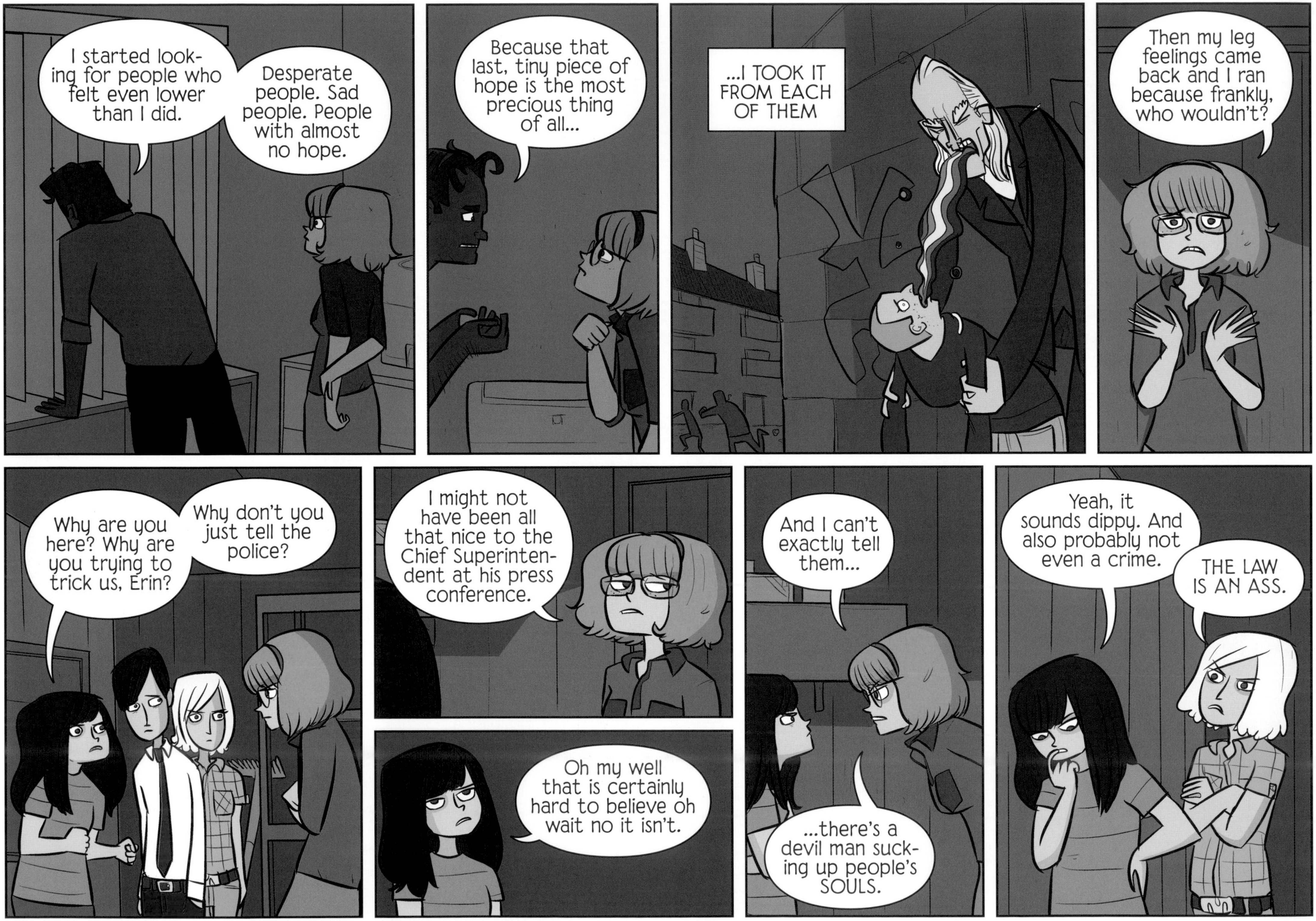

I started looking for people who felt even lower than I did.
Desperate people. Sad people. People with almost no hope.
Because that last, tiny piece of hope is the most precious thing of all...
...I TOOK IT FROM EACH OF THEM
Then my leg feelings came back and I ran because frankly, who wouldn't?
Why are you here? Why are you trying to trick us, Erin?
Why don't you just tell the police?
I might not have been all that nice to the Chief Superintendent at his press conference.
Oh my well that is certainly hard to believe oh wait no it isn't.
And I can't exactly tell them...
...there's a devil man sucking up people's SOULS.
Yeah, it sounds dippy. And also probably not even a crime.
THE LAW IS AN ASS.

The Case of the Unwelcome Visitor

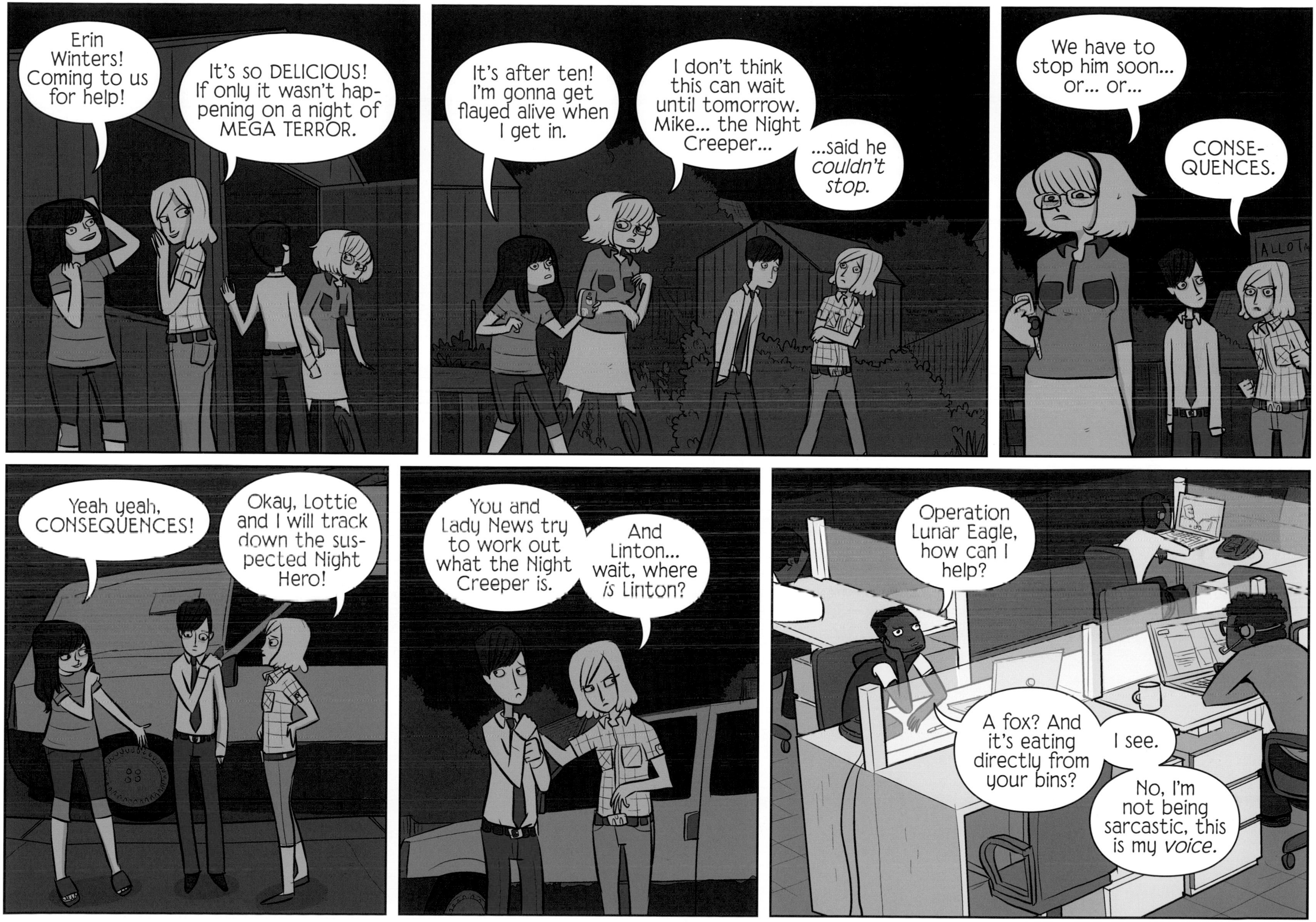

Erin Winters! Coming to us for help!
It's so DELICIOUS! If only it wasn't happening on a night of MEGA TERROR.
It's after ten! I'm gonna get flayed alive when I get in.
I don't think this can wait until tomorrow. Mike... the Night Creeper...
...said he *couldn't stop.*
We have to stop him soon... or... or...
CONSEQUENCES.
Yeah yeah, CONSEQUENCES!
Okay, Lottie and I will track down the suspected Night Hero!
You and Lady News try to work out what the Night Creeper is.
And Linton... wait, where *is* Linton?
Operation Lunar Eagle, how can I help?
A fox? And it's eating directly from your bins?
I see.
No, I'm not being sarcastic, this is my *voice.*

Bad Machinery, Volume Six

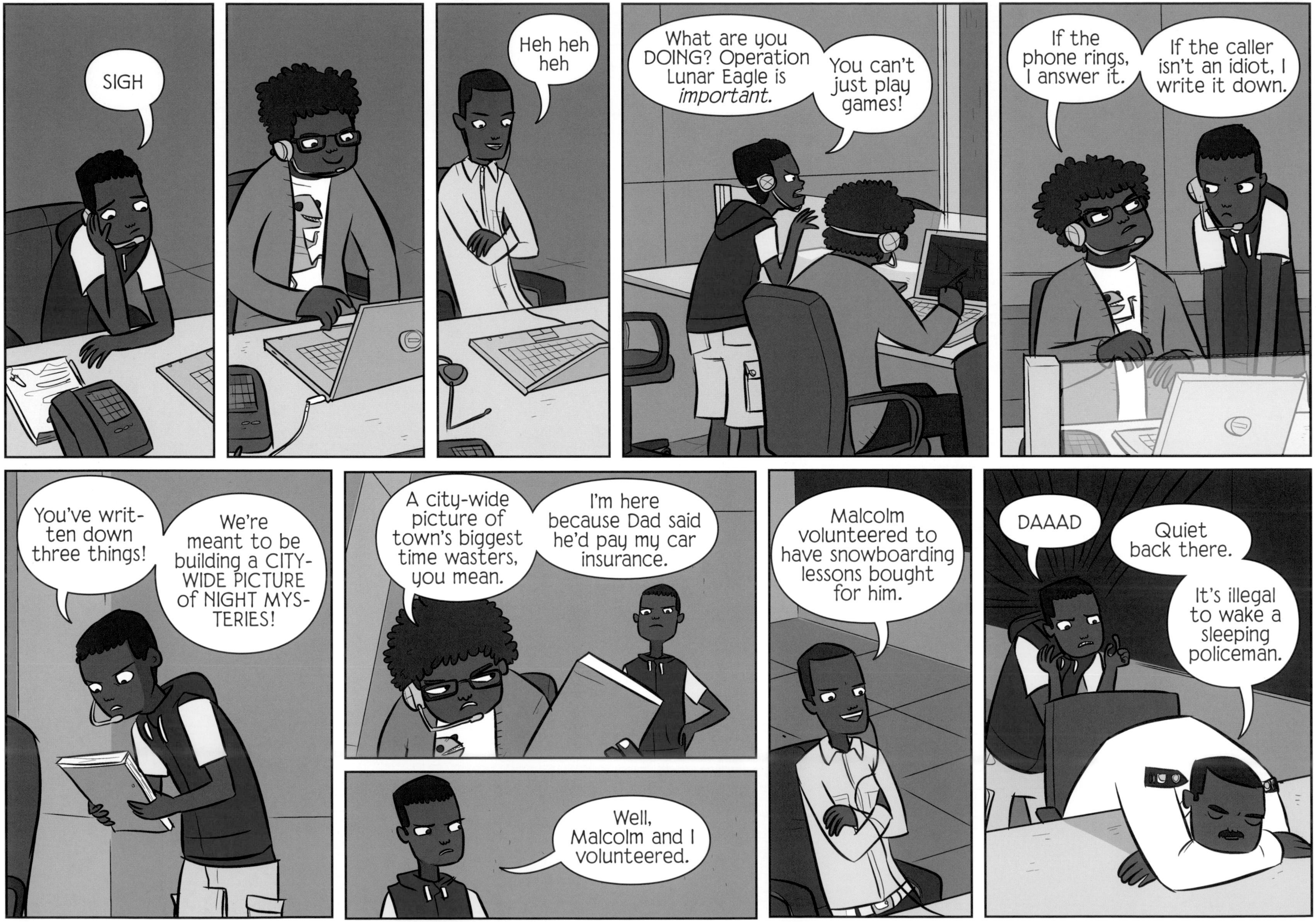
SIGH
Heh heh heh
What are you DOING? Operation Lunar Eagle is *important.*
You can't just play games!
If the phone rings, I answer it.
If the caller isn't an idiot, I write it down.
You've writ-ten down three things!
We're meant to be building a CITY-WIDE PICTURE of NIGHT MYS-TERIES!
A city-wide picture of town's biggest time wasters, you mean.
I'm here because Dad said he'd pay my car insurance.
Well, Malcolm and I volunteered.
Malcolm volunteered to have snowboarding lessons bought for him.
DAAAD
Quiet back there.
It's illegal to wake a sleeping policeman.

The Case of the Unwelcome Visitor

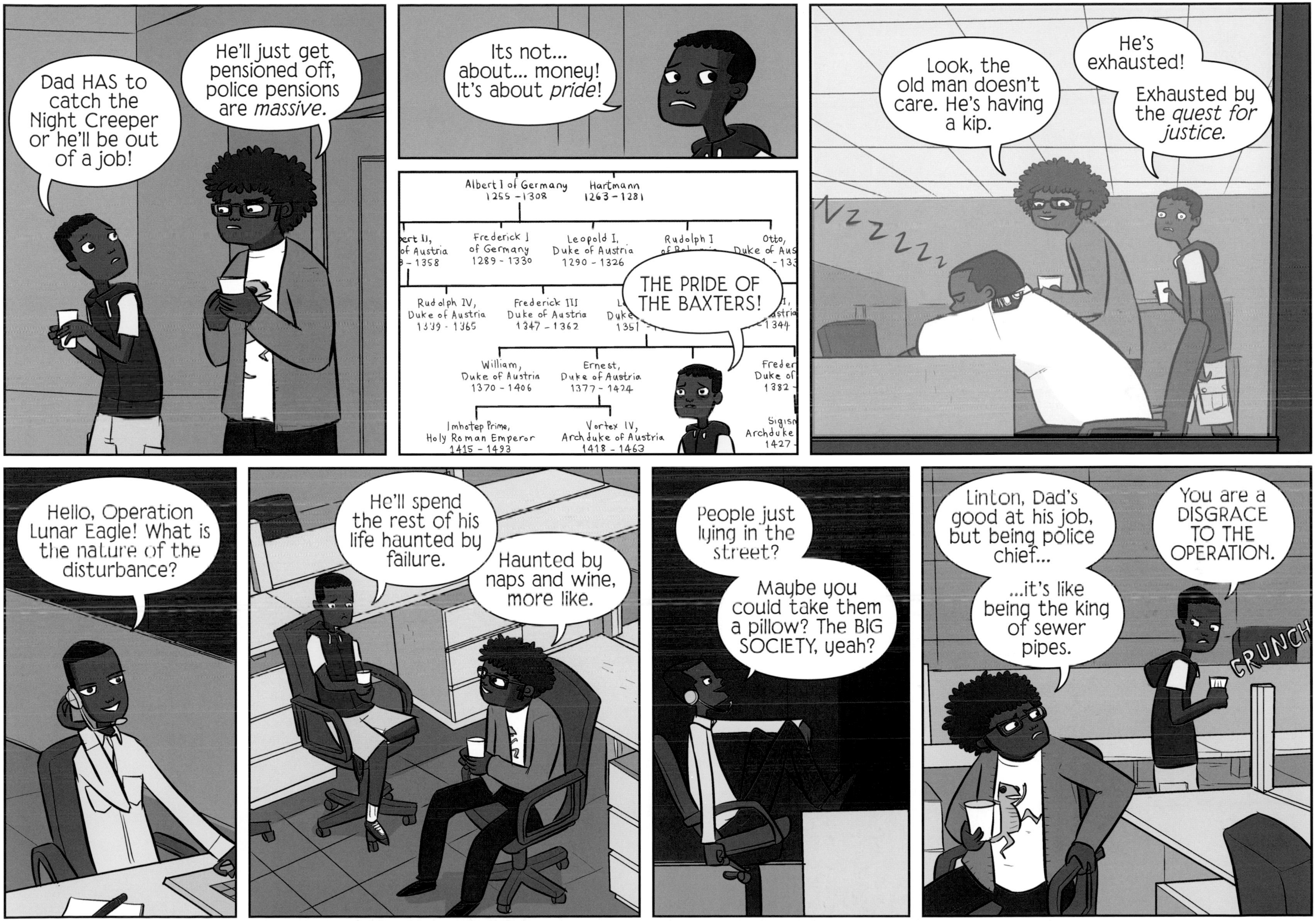
Dad HAS to catch the Night Creeper or he'll be out of a job!
He'll just get pensioned off, police pensions are *massive.*
Its not... about... money! It's about *pride*!
Albert I of Germany 1255 - 1308
Hartmann 1263 - 1281
Frederick I of Germany 1289 - 1330
Leopold I, Duke of Austria 1290 - 1326
Rudolph IV, Duke of Austria 1339 - 1365
Frederick III Duke of Austria 1347 - 1362
William, Duke of Austria 1370 - 1406
Ernest, Duke of Austria 1377 - 1424
Imhotep Prime, Holy Roman Emperor 1415 - 1493
Vortex IV, Archduke of Austria 1418 - 1463
THE PRIDE OF THE BAXTERS!
Look, the old man doesn't care. He's having a kip.
He's exhausted!
Exhausted by the *quest for justice.*
NZZZZZz
Hello, Operation Lunar Eagle! What is the nature of the disturbance?
He'll spend the rest of his life haunted by failure.
Haunted by naps and wine, more like.
People just lying in the street?
Maybe you could take them a pillow? The BIG SOCIETY, yeah?
Linton, Dad's good at his job, but being police chief...
...it's like being the king of sewer pipes.
You are a DISGRACE TO THE OPERATION.
CRUNCH

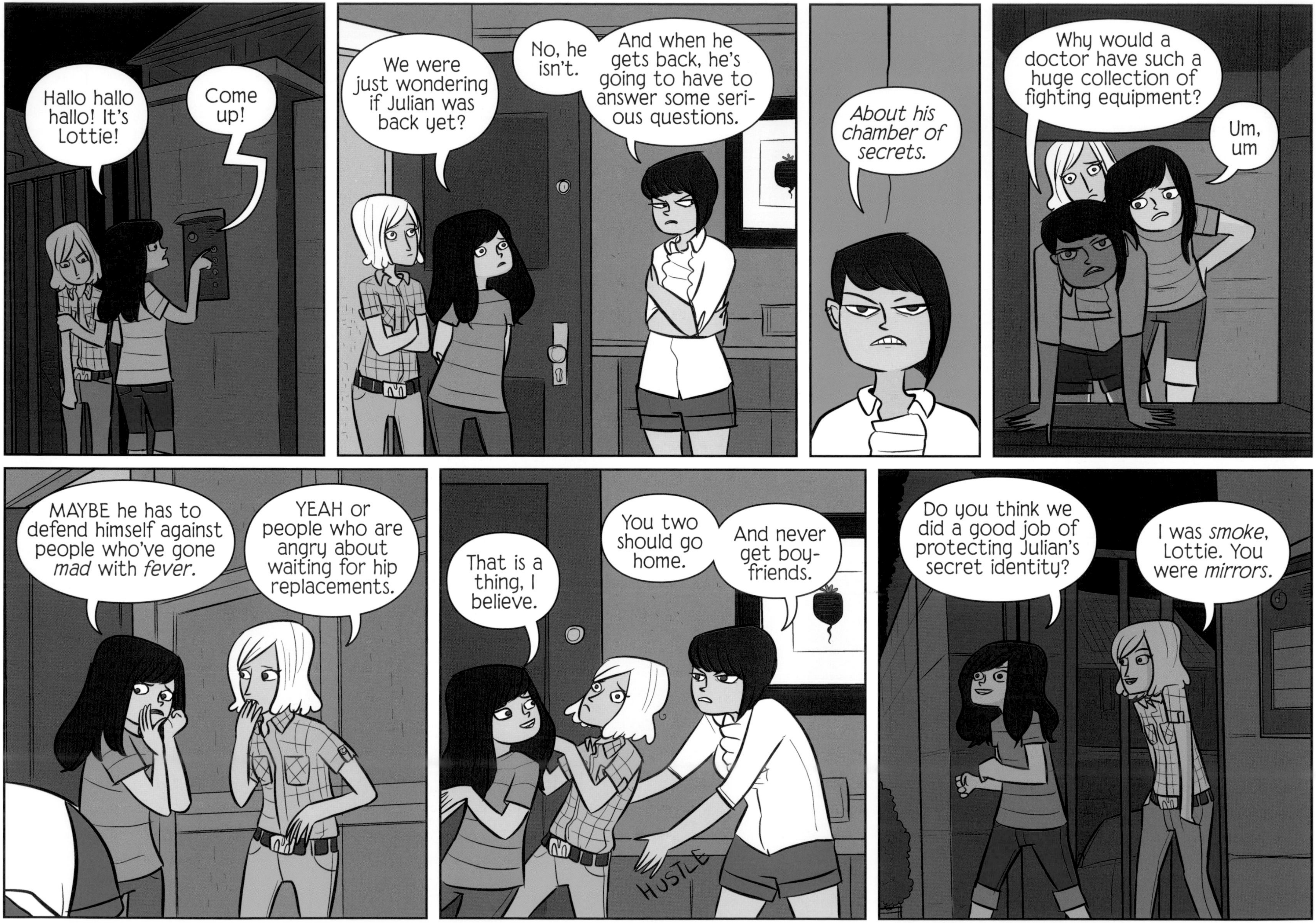

Hallo hallo hallo! It's Lottie!
Come up!
We were just wondering if Julian was back yet?
No, he isn't.
And when he gets back, he's going to have to answer some serious questions.
About his chamber of secrets.
Why would a doctor have such a huge collection of fighting equipment?
Um, um
MAYBE he has to defend himself against people who've gone *mad* with *fever*.
YEAH or people who are angry about waiting for hip replacements.
That is a thing, I believe.
You two should go home.
And never get boyfriends.
HUSTLE
Do you think we did a good job of protecting Julian's secret identity?
I was *smoke*, Lottie. You were *mirrors*.

The Case of the Unwelcome Visitor

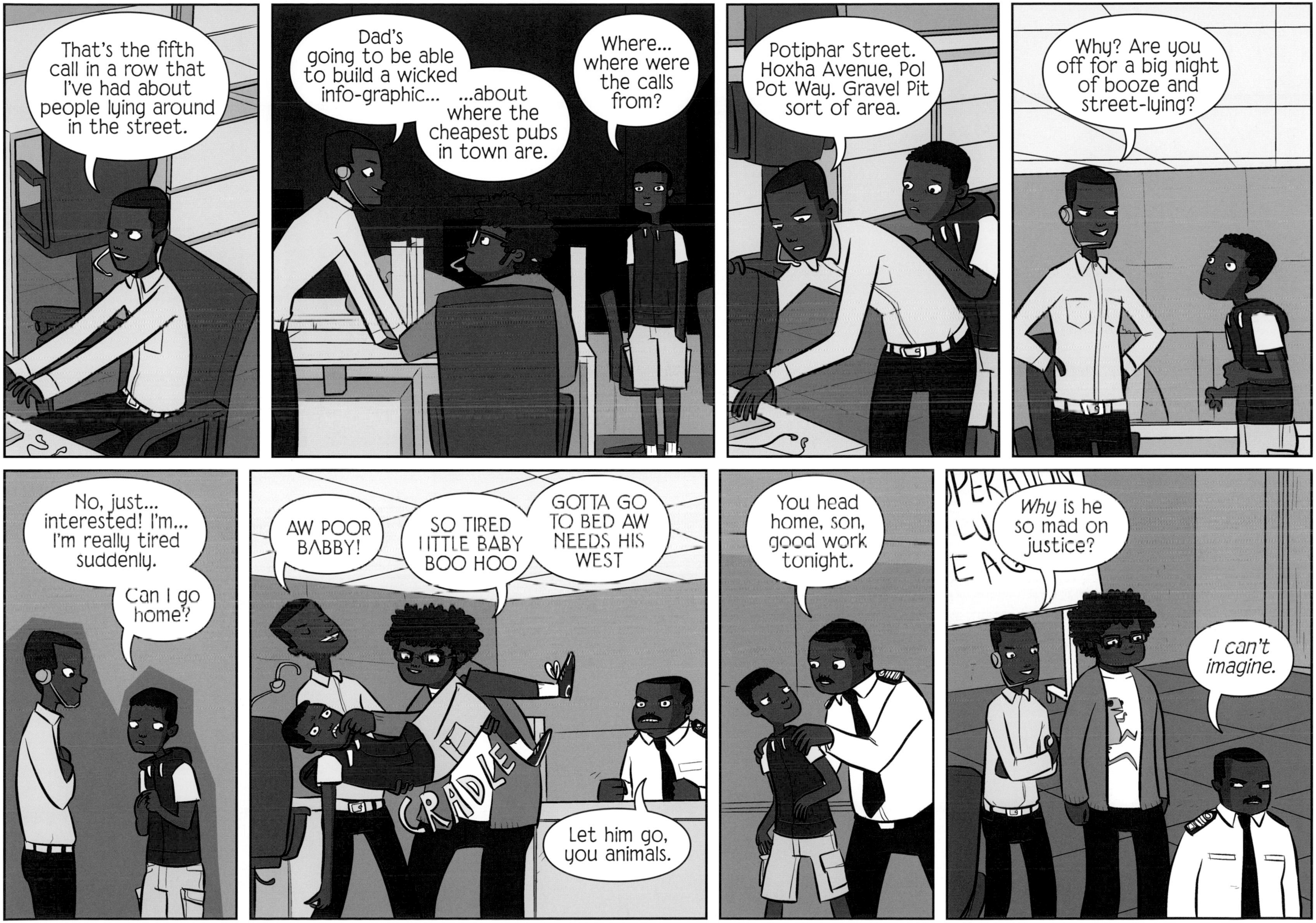
That's the fifth call in a row that I've had about people lying around in the street.
Dad's going to be able to build a wicked info-graphic...
...about where the cheapest pubs in town are.
Where... where were the calls from?
Potiphar Street. Hoxha Avenue, Pol Pot Way. Gravel Pit sort of area.
Why? Are you off for a big night of booze and street-lying?
No, just... interested! I'm... I'm really tired suddenly.
Can I go home?
AW POOR BABBY!
SO TIRED LITTLE BABY BOO HOO
GOTTA GO TO BED AW NEEDS HIS WEST
CRADLE
Let him go, you animals.
You head home, son, good work tonight.
Why is he so mad on justice?
I can't imagine.

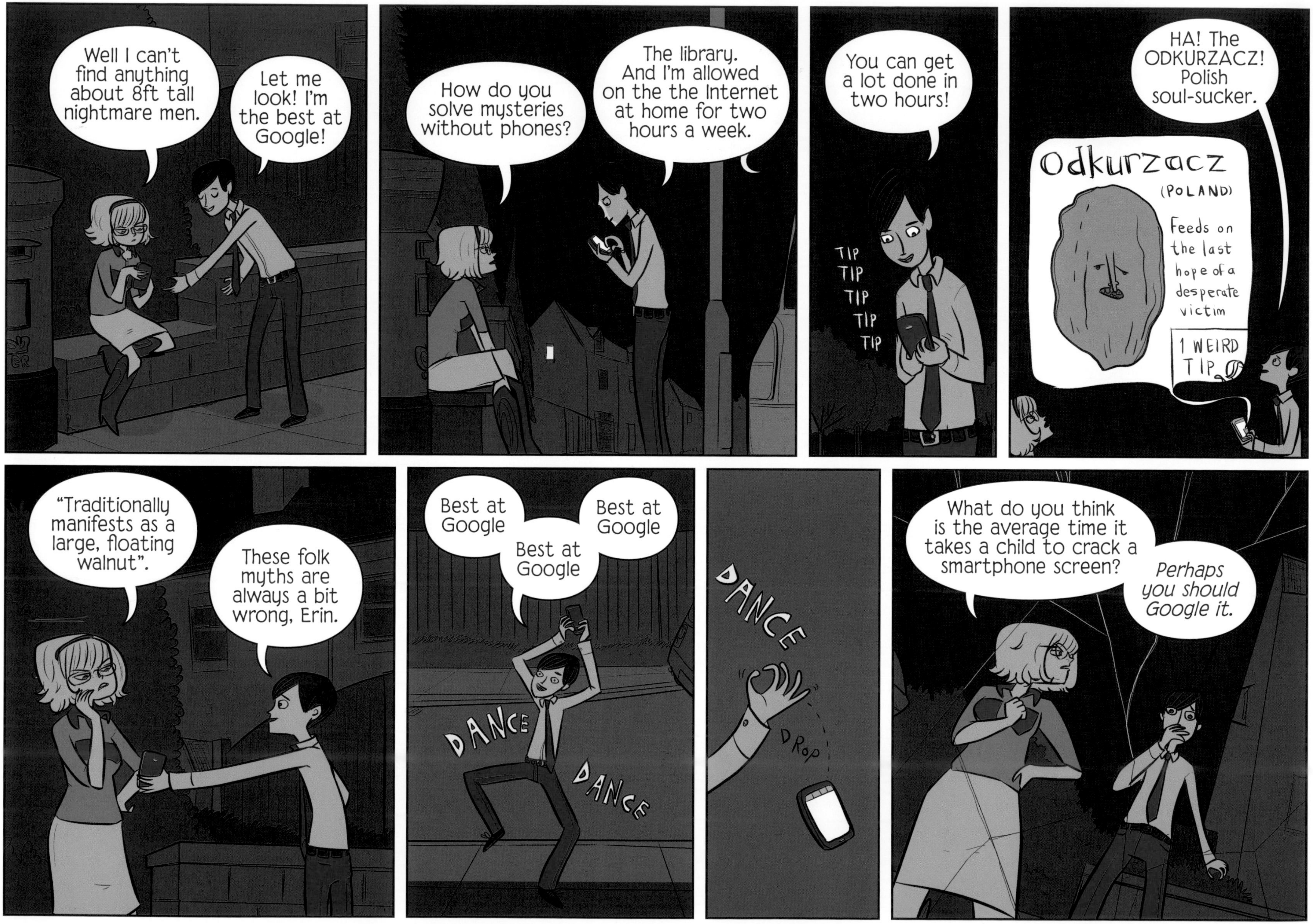
Well I can't find anything about 8ft tall nightmare men.
Let me look! I'm the best at Google!
How do you solve mysteries without phones?
The library. And I'm allowed on the the Internet at home for two hours a week.
You can get a lot done in two hours!
TIP TIP TIP TIP TIP
HA! The ODKURZACZ! Polish soul-sucker.
Odkurzacz
(POLAND)
Feeds on the last hope of a desperate victim
1 WEIRD TIP
"Traditionally manifests as a large, floating walnut".
These folk myths are always a bit wrong, Erin.
Best at Google
Best at Google
Best at Google
DANCE
DANCE
DANCE
DROP
What do you think is the average time it takes a child to crack a smartphone screen?
Perhaps you should Google it.

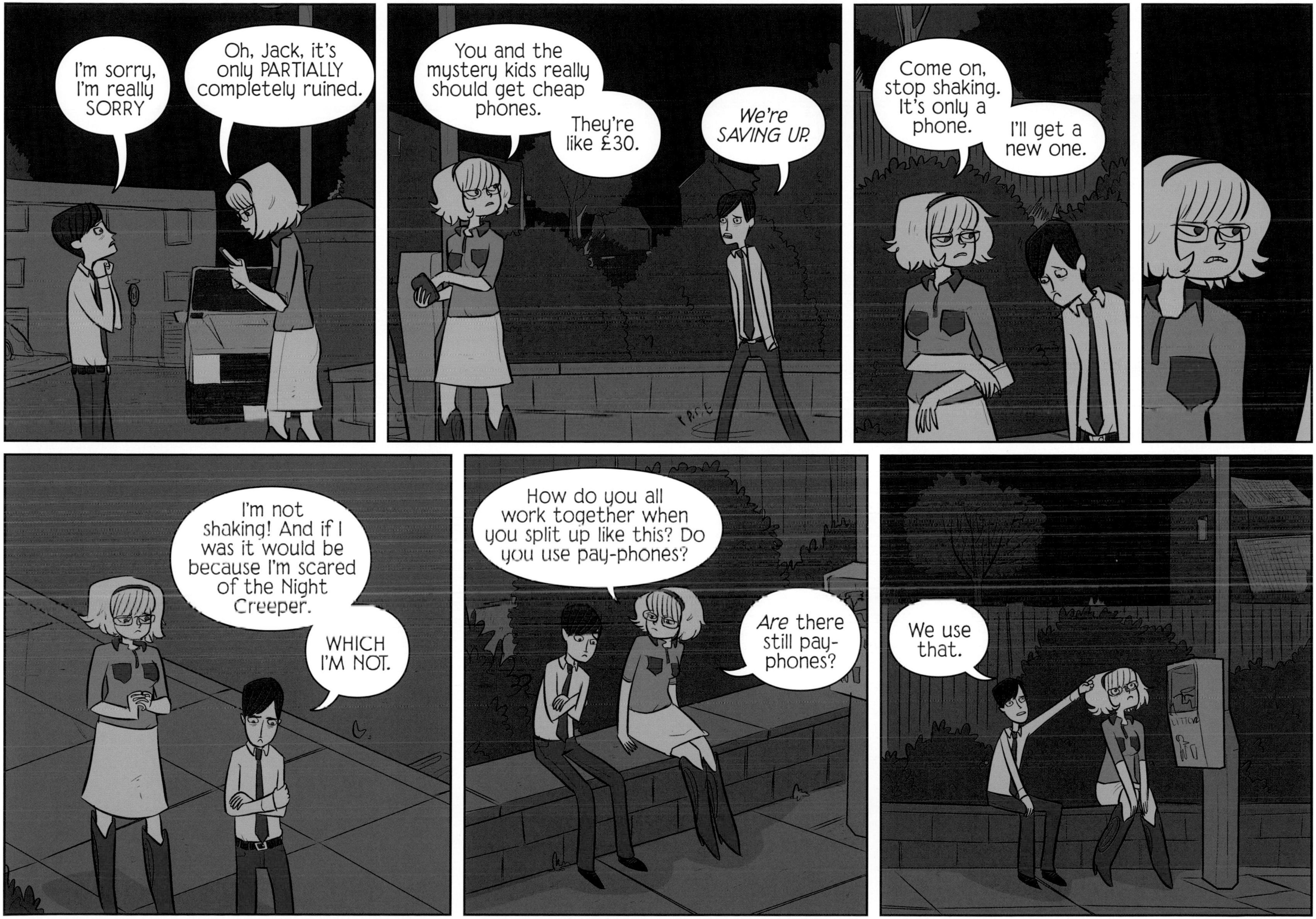
I'm sorry, I'm really SORRY
Oh, Jack, it's only PARTIALLY completely ruined.
You and the mystery kids really should get cheap phones.
They're like £30.
We're SAVING UP.
Come on, stop shaking. It's only a phone.
I'll get a new one.
I'm not shaking! And if I was it would be because I'm scared of the Night Creeper.
WHICH I'M NOT.
How do you all work together when you split up like this? Do you use pay-phones?
Are there still pay-phones?
We use that.

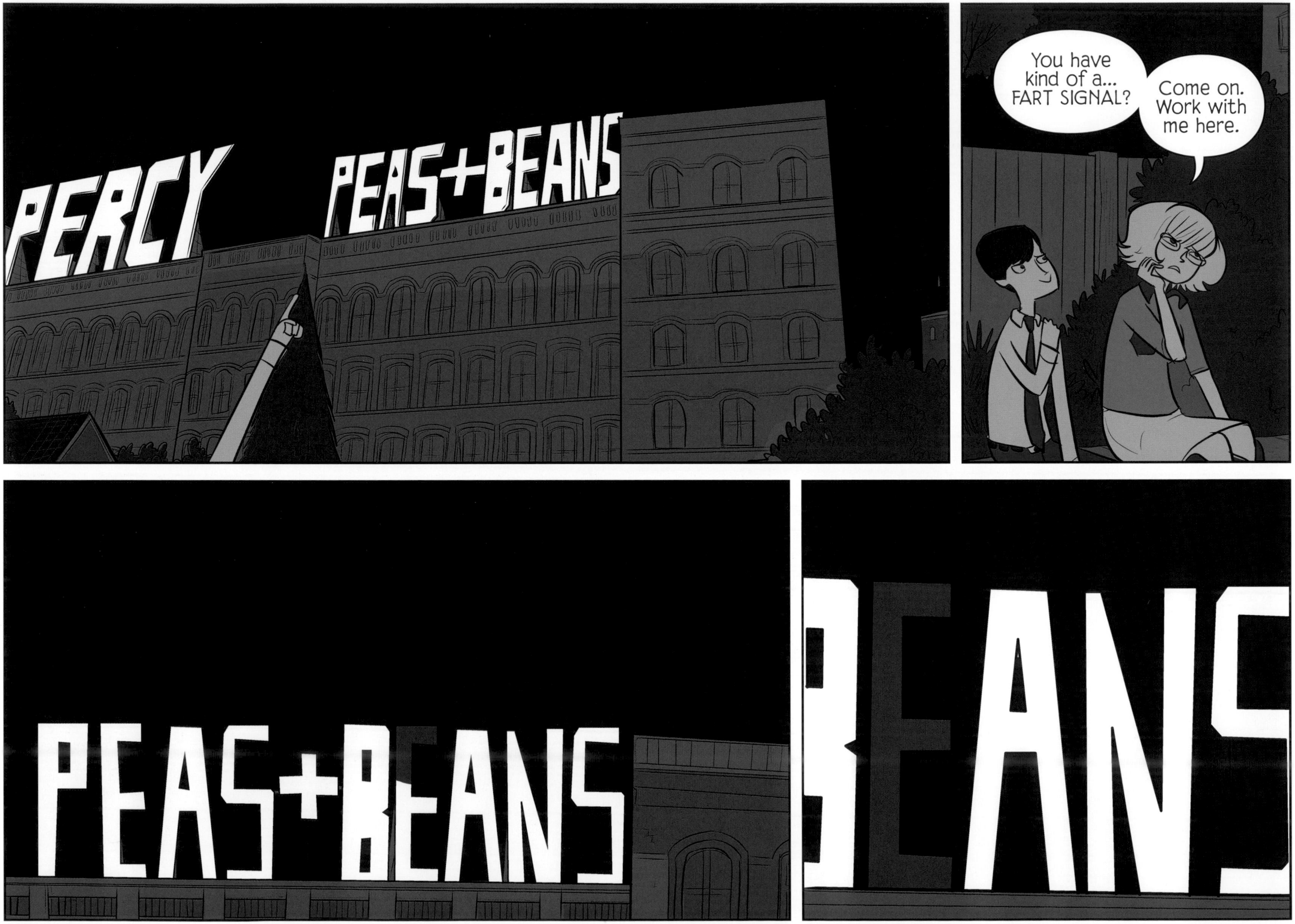
PERCY
PEAS+BEANS
You have kind of a... FART SIGNAL?
Come on. Work with me here.
PEAS+BEANS
BEANS

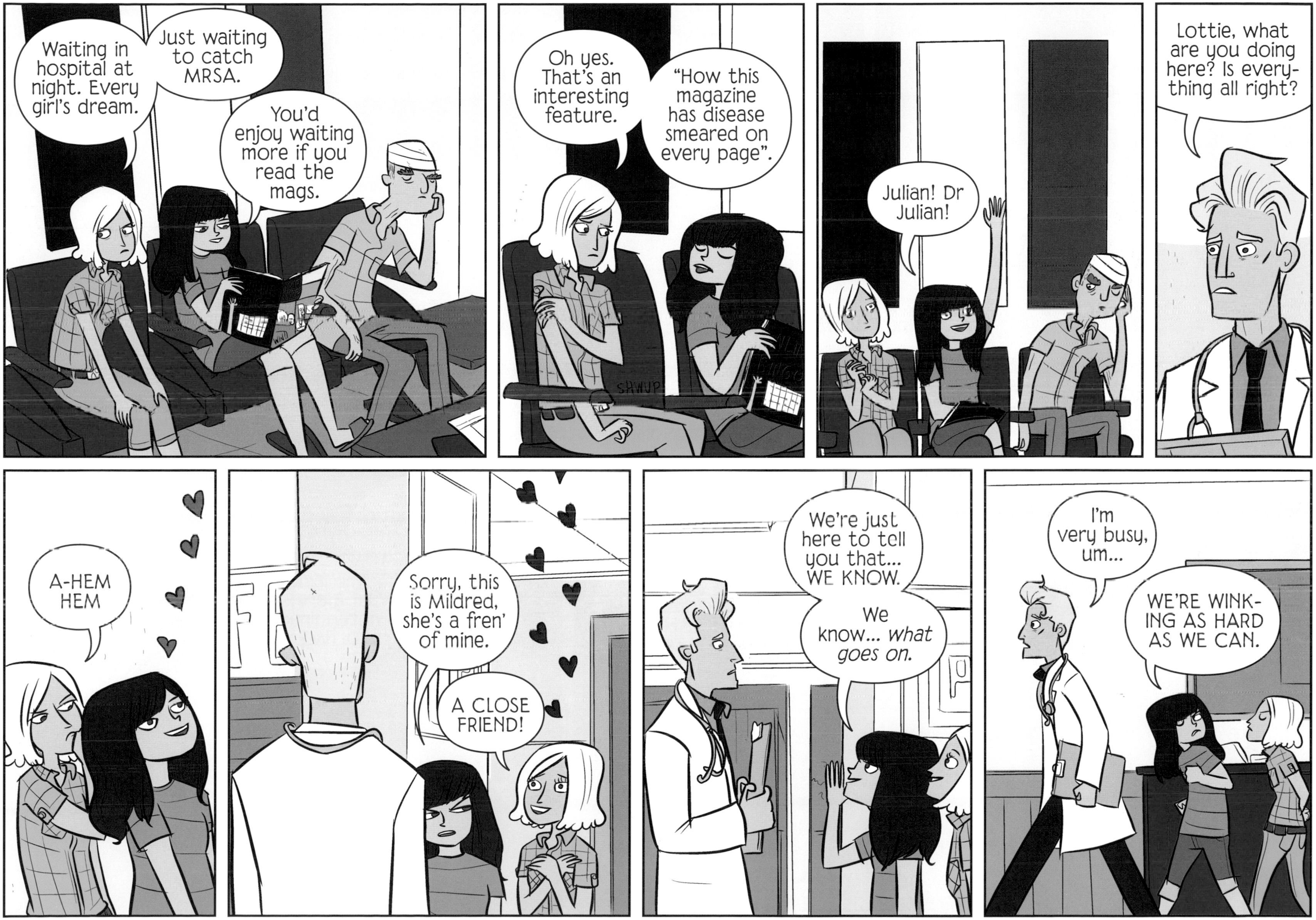
Waiting in hospital at night. Every girl's dream.
Just waiting to catch MRSA.
You'd enjoy waiting more if you read the mags.
Oh yes. That's an interesting feature.
"How this magazine has disease smeared on every page".
SHWUP!
Julian! Dr Julian!
Lottie, what are you doing here? Is everything all right?
A-HEM HEM
Sorry, this is Mildred, she's a fren' of mine.
A CLOSE FRIEND!
We're just here to tell you that... WE KNOW.
We know... *what goes on.*
I'm very busy, um...
WE'RE WINKING AS HARD AS WE CAN.

Bad Machinery, Volume Six

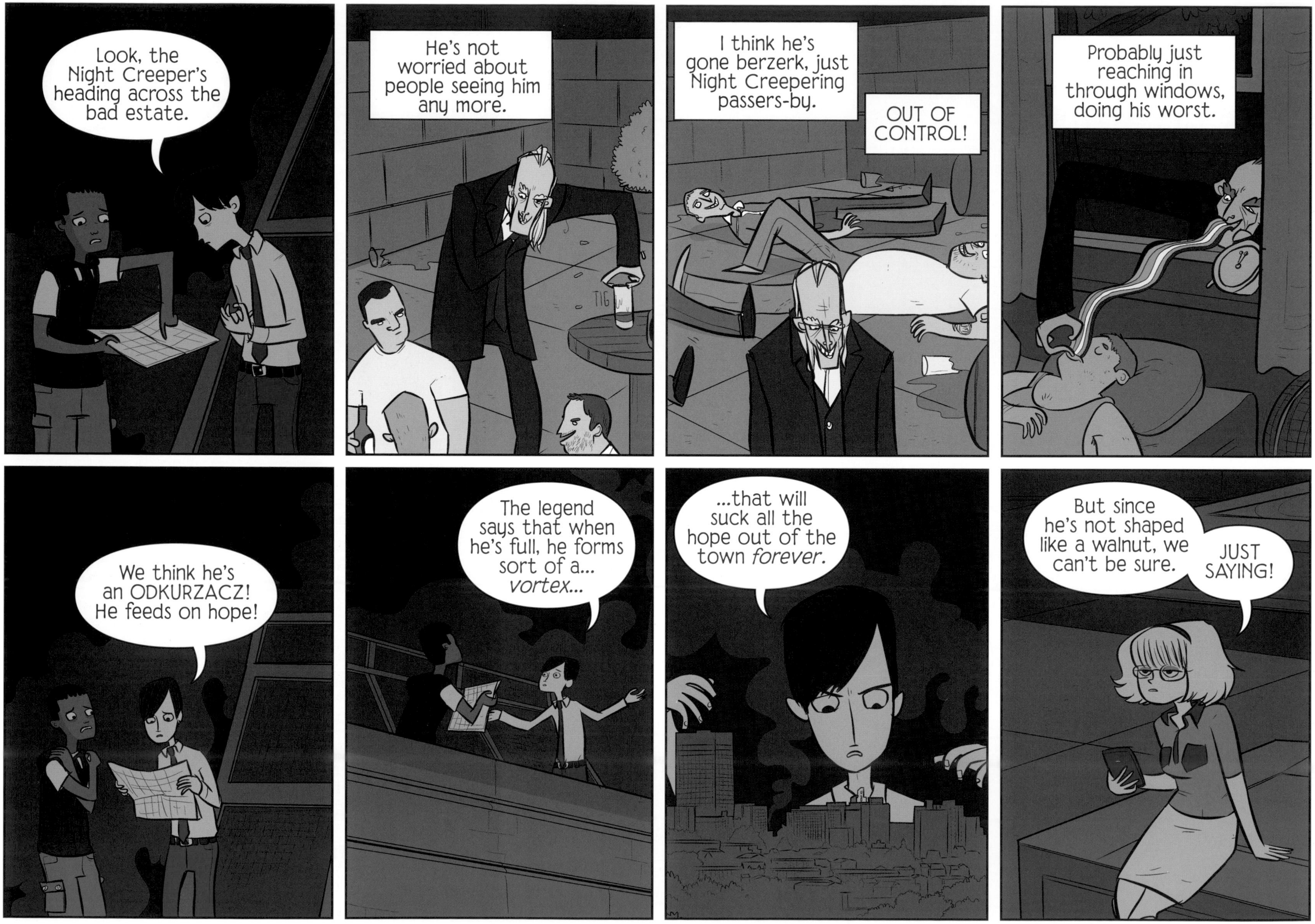
Look, the Night Creeper's heading across the bad estate.
He's not worried about people seeing him any more.
I think he's gone berzerk, just Night Creepering passers-by.
OUT OF CONTROL!
Probably just reaching in through windows, doing his worst.
We think he's an ODKURZACZ! He feeds on hope!
The legend says that when he's full, he forms sort of a... *vortex*...
...that will suck all the hope out of the town *forever.*
But since he's not shaped like a walnut, we can't be sure.
JUST SAYING!

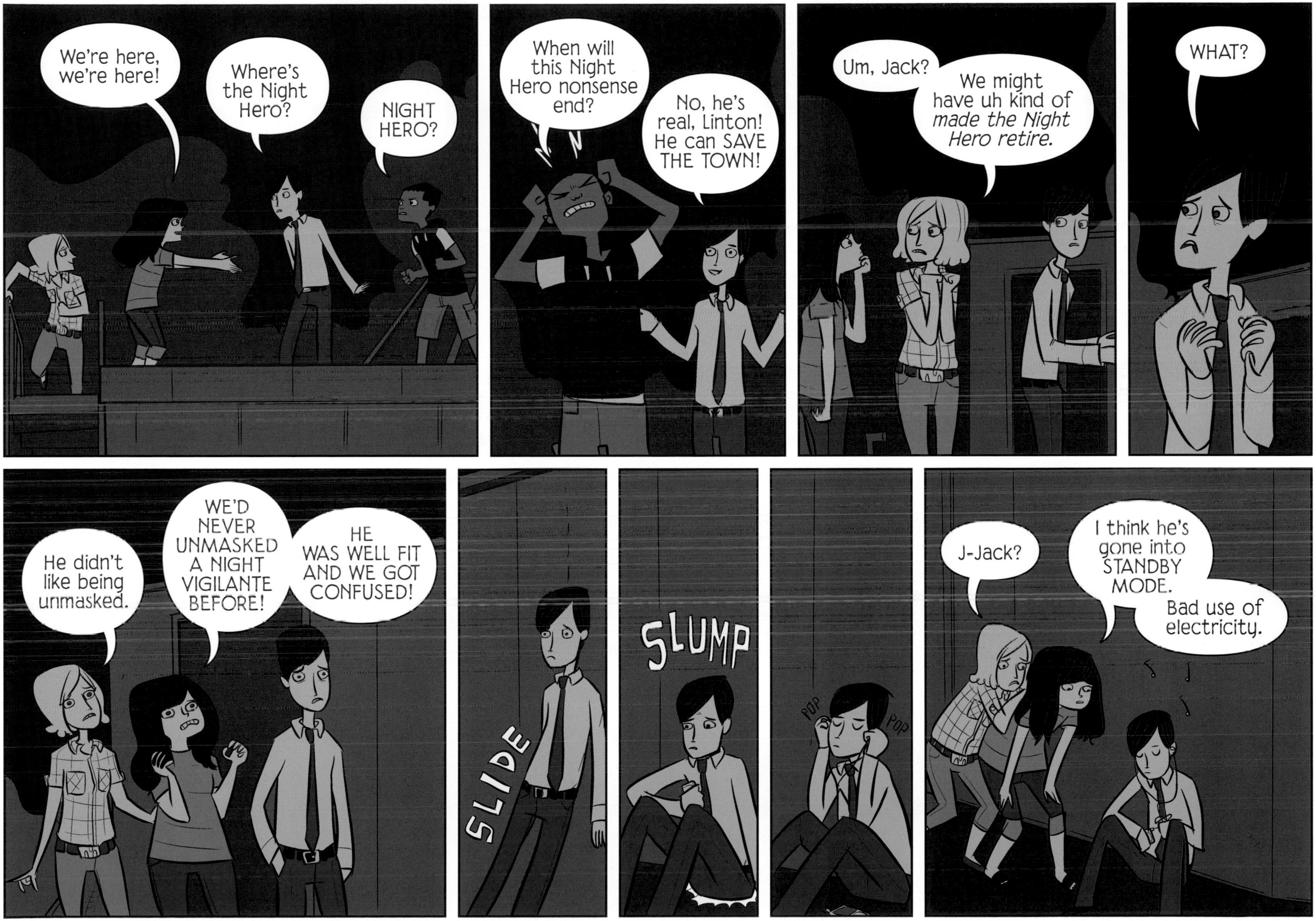
We're here, we're here!
Where's the Night Hero?
NIGHT HERO?
When will this Night Hero nonsense end?
No, he's real, Linton! He can SAVE THE TOWN!
Um, Jack?
We might have uh kind of *made the Night Hero retire.*
WHAT?
He didn't like being unmasked.
WE'D NEVER UNMASKED A NIGHT VIGILANTE BEFORE!
HE WAS WELL FIT AND WE GOT CONFUSED!
SLIDE
SLUMP
POP
POP
J-Jack?
I think he's gone into STANDBY MODE.
Bad use of electricity.

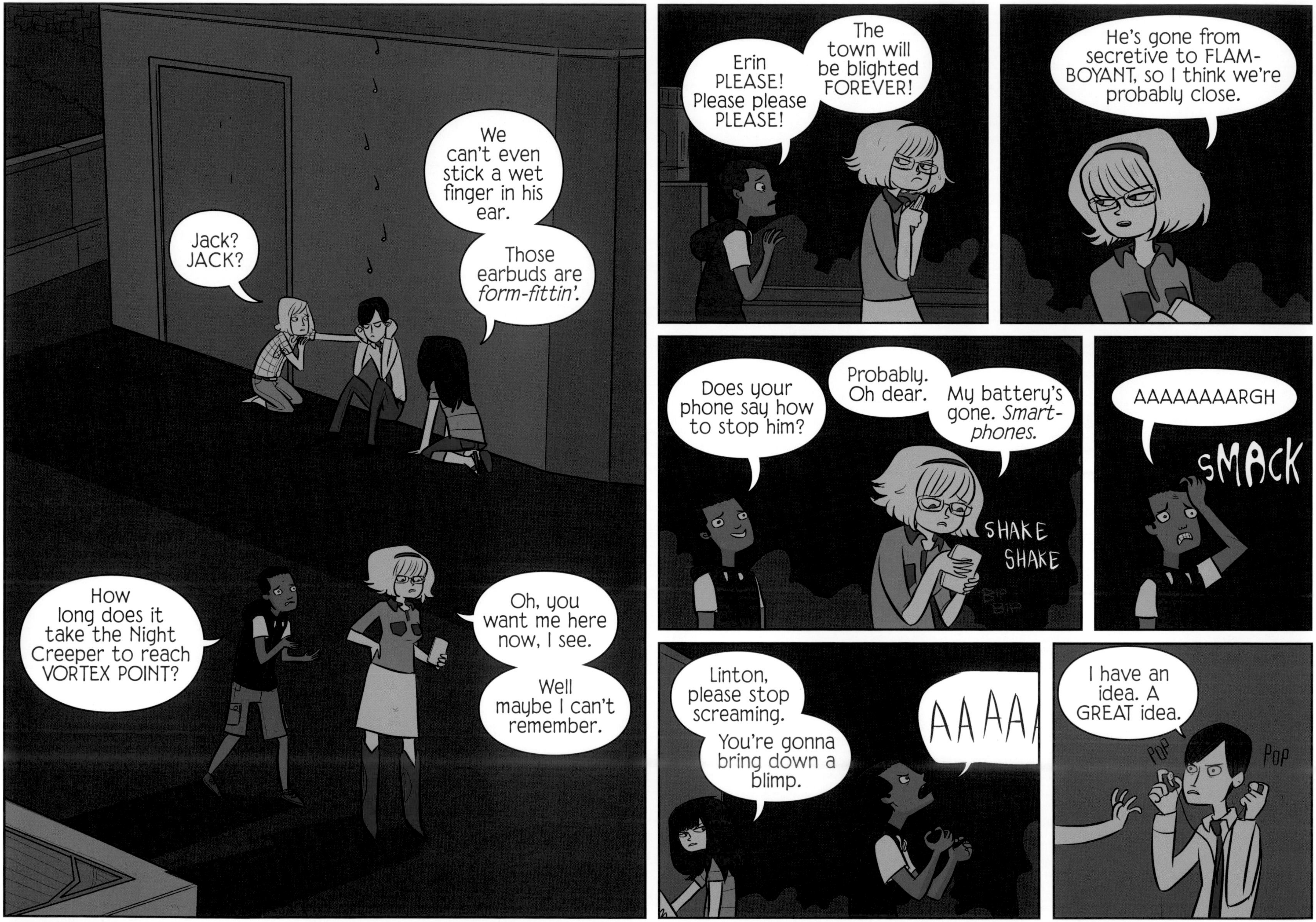
Jack? JACK?
We can't even stick a wet finger in his ear.
Those earbuds are *form-fittin'*.
How long does it take the Night Creeper to reach VORTEX POINT?
Oh, you want me here now, I see.
Well maybe I can't remember.
Erin PLEASE! Please please PLEASE!
The town will be blighted FOREVER!
He's gone from secretive to FLAM-BOYANT, so I think we're probably close.
Does your phone say how to stop him?
Probably. Oh dear.
My battery's gone. *Smart-phones.*
SHAKE
SHAKE
AAAAAAAARGH
SMACK
Linton, please stop screaming.
You're gonna bring down a blimp.
AAAA
I have an idea. A GREAT idea.
POP
POP

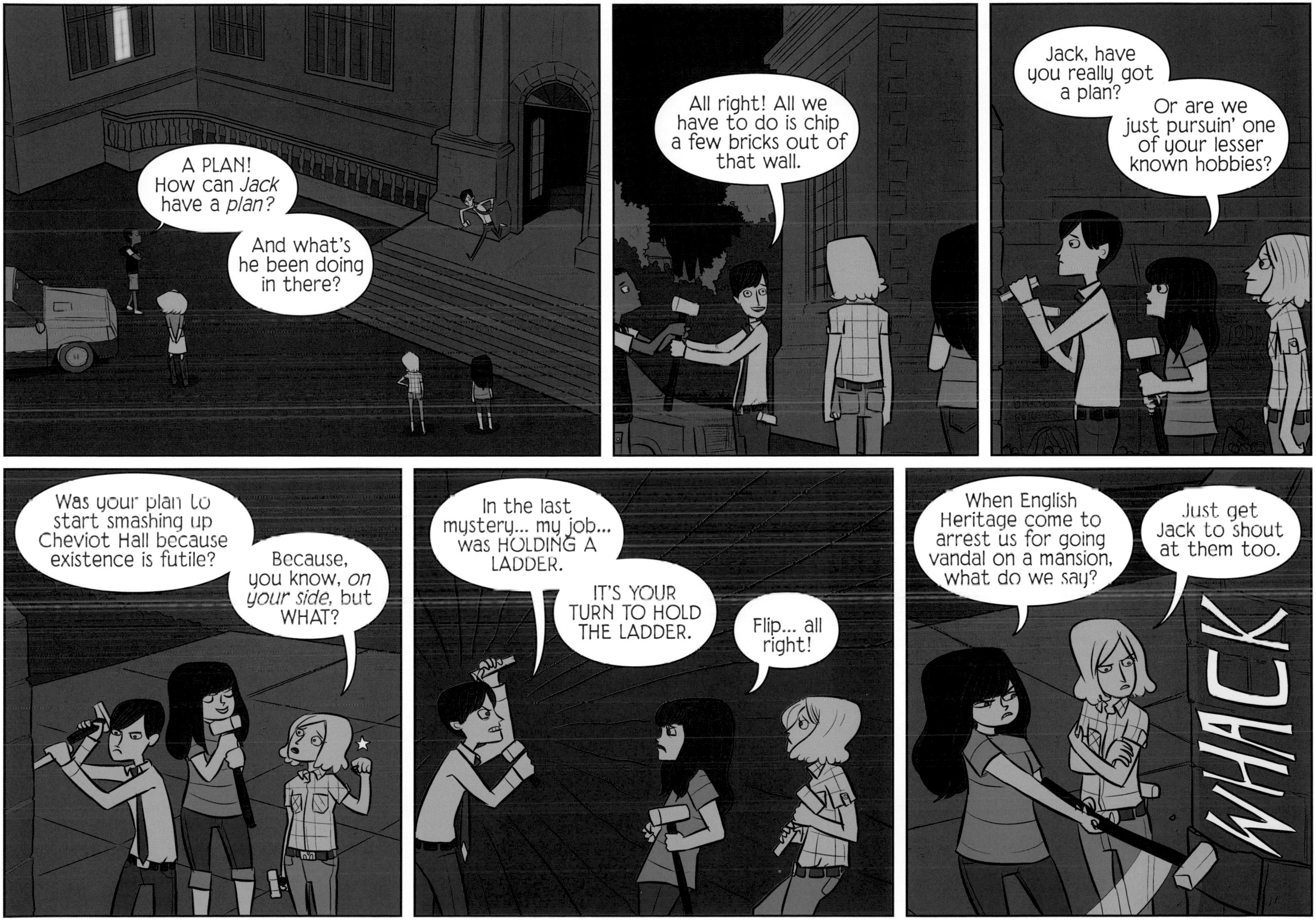
A PLAN! How can *Jack* have a *plan?*
And what's he been doing in there?
All right! All we have to do is chip a few bricks out of that wall.
Jack, have you really got a plan?
Or are we just pursuin' one of your lesser known hobbies?
Was your plan to start smashing up Cheviot Hall because existence is futile?
Because, you know, *on your side*, but WHAT?
In the last mystery... my job... was HOLDING A LADDER.
IT'S YOUR TURN TO HOLD THE LADDER.
Flip... all right!
When English Heritage come to arrest us for going vandal on a mansion, what do we say?
Just get Jack to shout at them too.
WHACK

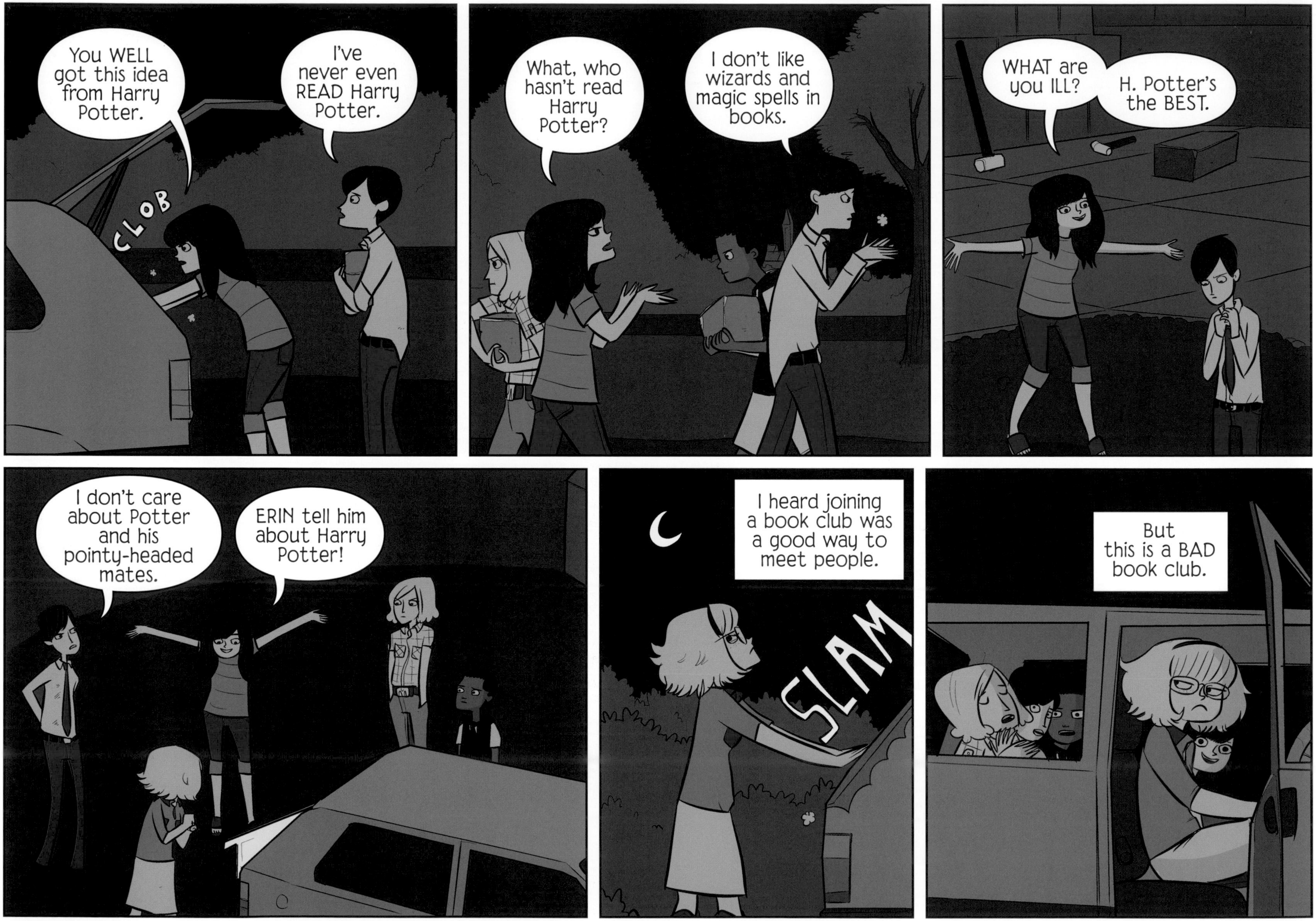
You WELL got this idea from Harry Potter.
I've never even READ Harry Potter.
CLOB
What, who hasn't read Harry Potter?
I don't like wizards and magic spells in books.
WHAT are you ILL?
H. Potter's the BEST.
I don't care about Potter and his pointy-headed mates.
ERIN tell him about Harry Potter!
I heard joining a book club was a good way to meet people.
SLAM
But this is a BAD book club.

The Case of the Unwelcome Visitor

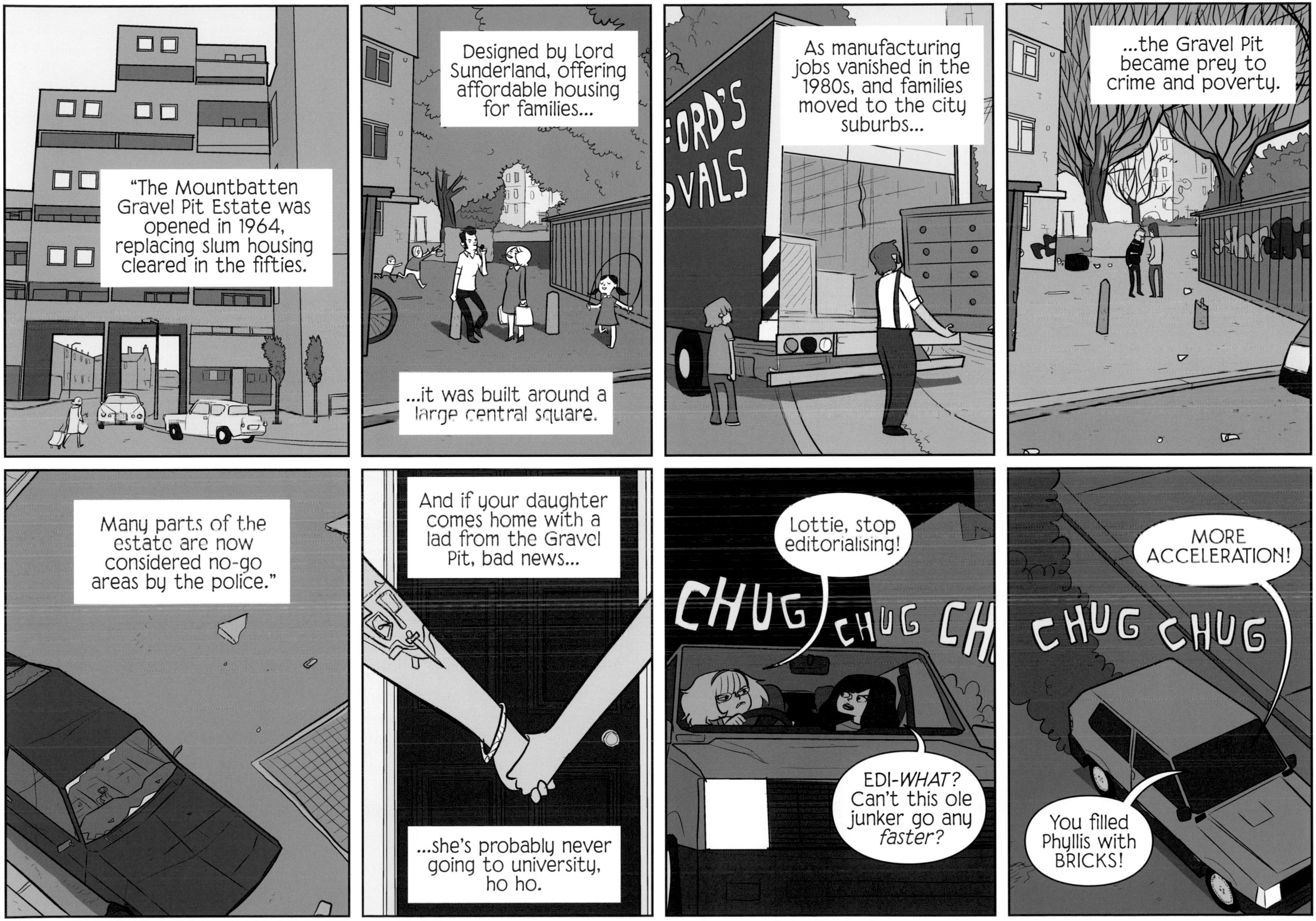
"The Mountbatten Gravel Pit Estate was opened in 1964, replacing slum housing cleared in the fifties.
Designed by Lord Sunderland, offering affordable housing for families...
...it was built around a large central square.
As manufacturing jobs vanished in the 1980s, and families moved to the city suburbs...
...the Gravel Pit became prey to crime and poverty.
Many parts of the estate are now considered no-go areas by the police."
And if your daughter comes home with a lad from the Gravel Pit, bad news...
...she's probably never going to university, ho ho.
Lottie, stop editorialising!
CHUG
CHUG CH
EDI-*WHAT?* Can't this ole junker go any *faster?*
MORE ACCELERATION!
CHUG CHUG
You filled Phyllis with BRICKS!

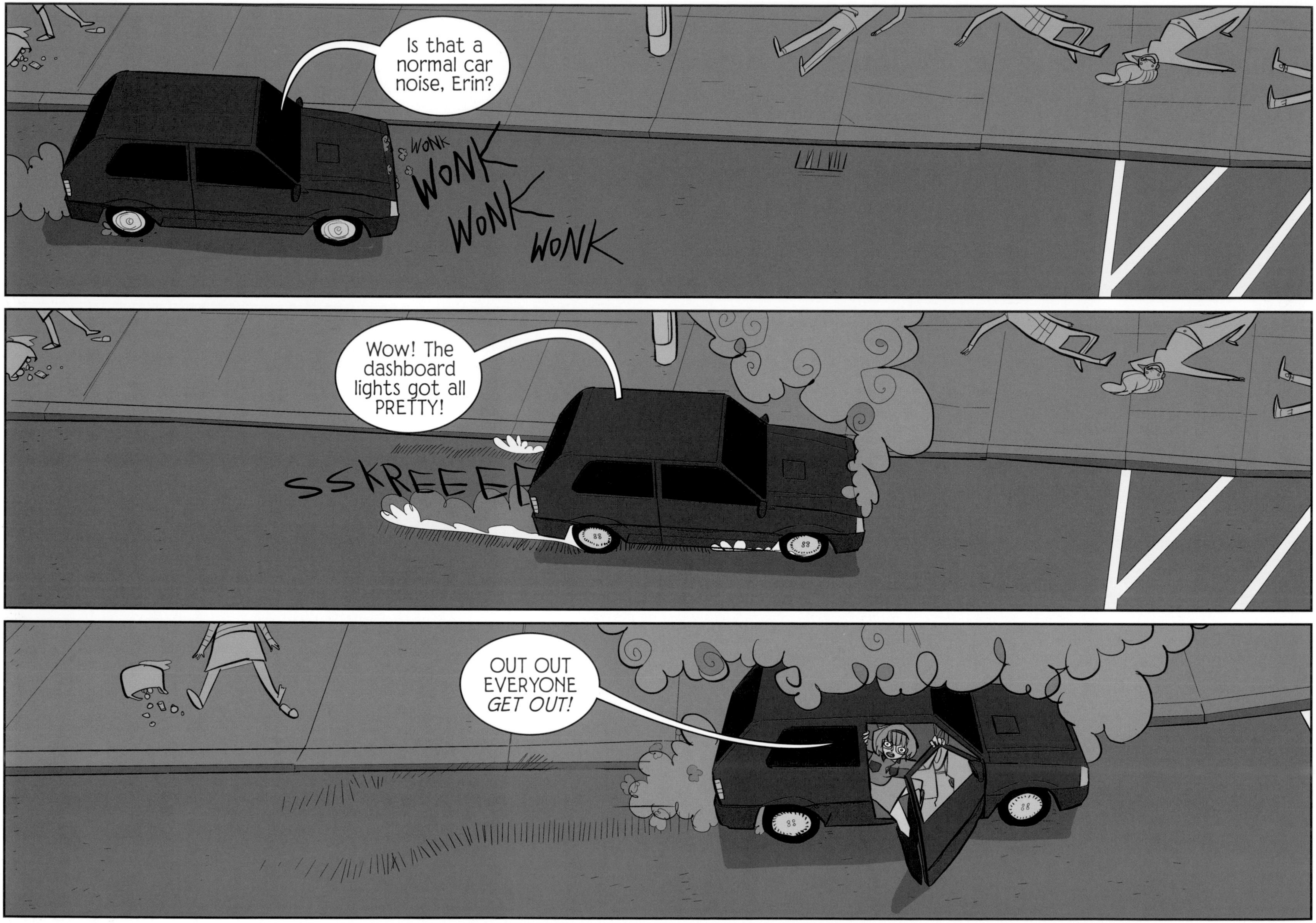
Is that a normal car noise, Erin?
WONK
WONK
WONK
WONK
Wow! The dashboard lights got all PRETTY!
SSKREEEE
OUT OUT EVERYONE *GET OUT!*

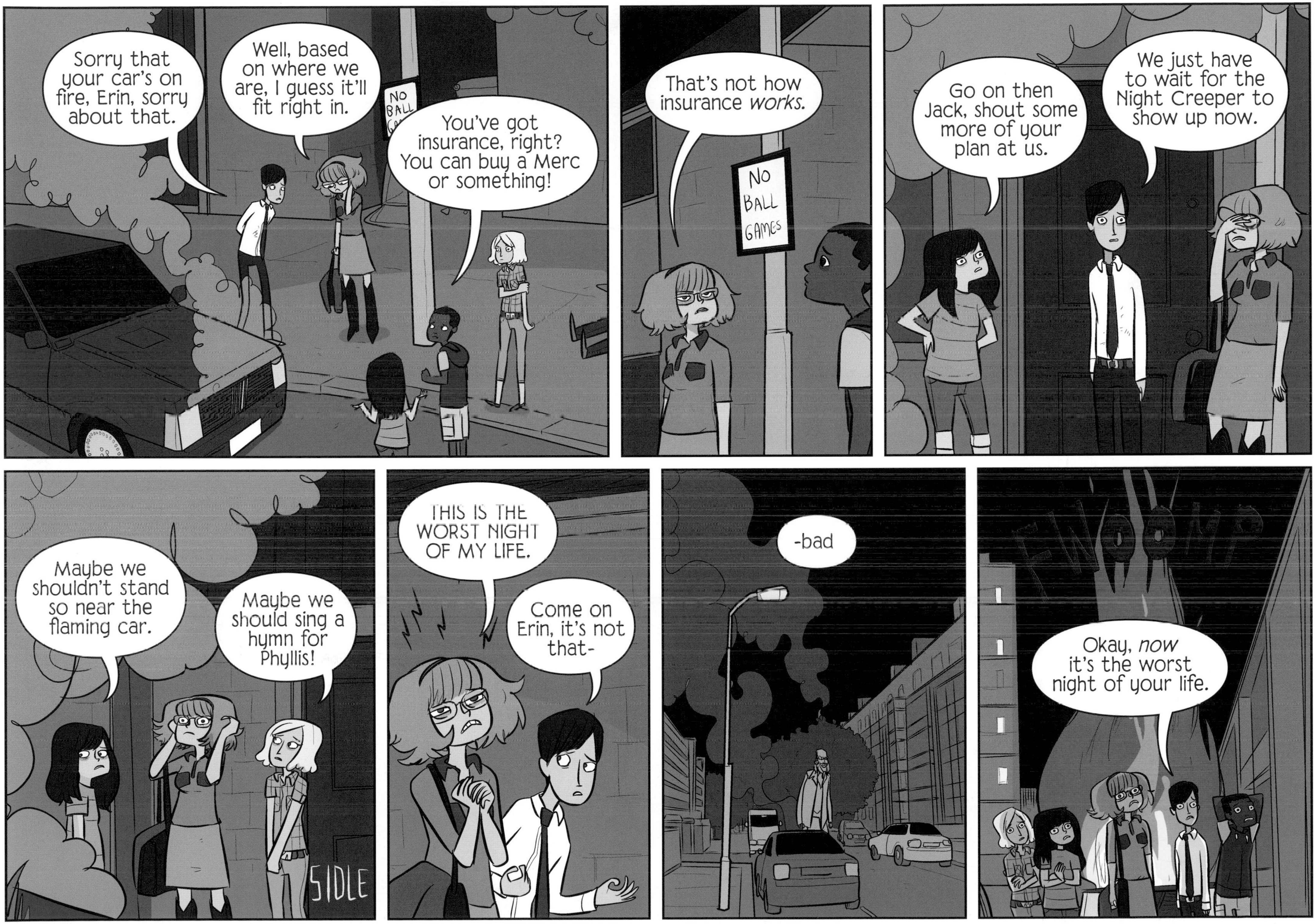
Sorry that your car's on fire, Erin, sorry about that.
Well, based on where we are, I guess it'll fit right in.
NO BALL GAMES
You've got insurance, right? You can buy a Merc or something!
That's not how insurance *works*.
NO BALL GAMES
Go on then Jack, shout some more of your plan at us.
We just have to wait for the Night Creeper to show up now.
Maybe we shouldn't stand so near the flaming car.
Maybe we should sing a hymn for Phyllis!
SIDLE
THIS IS THE WORST NIGHT OF MY LIFE.
Come on Erin, it's not that-
-bad
FWOOMP
Okay, *now* it's the worst night of your life.

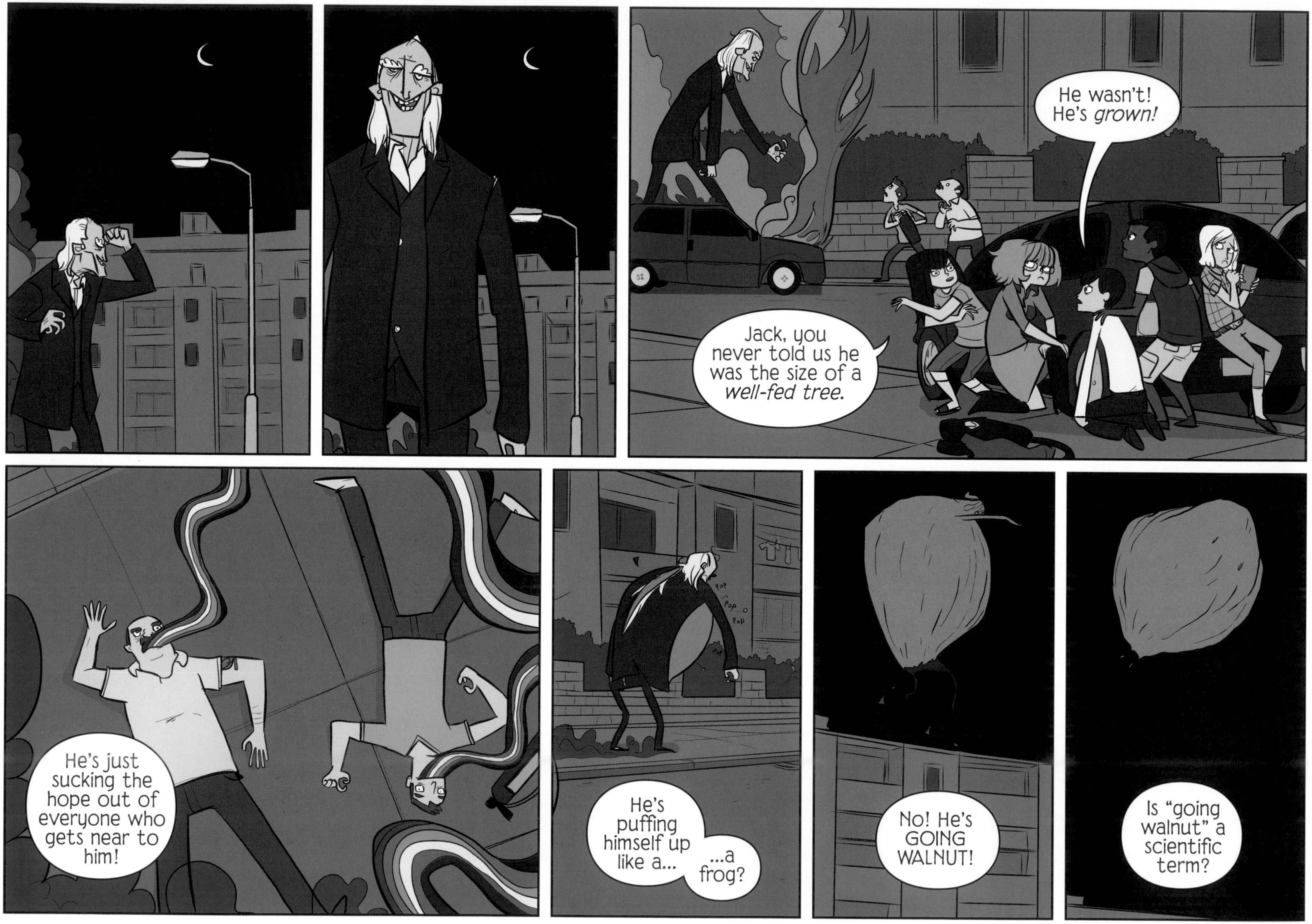
Jack, you never told us he was the size of a *well-fed tree.*
He wasn't! He's *grown!*
He's just sucking the hope out of everyone who gets near to him!
He's puffing himself up like a...
...a frog?
No! He's GOING WALNUT!
Is "going walnut" a scientific term?

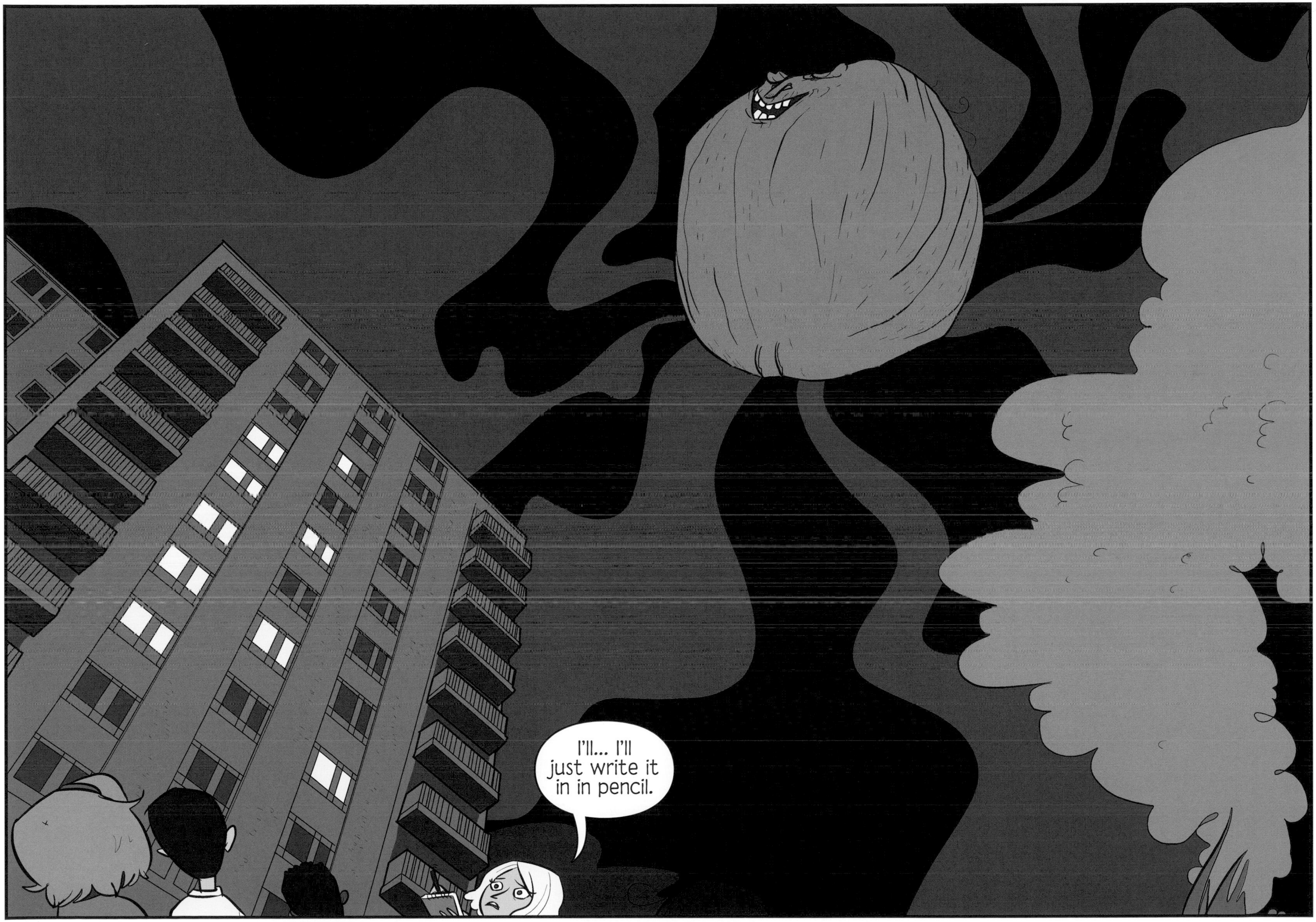
I'll... I'll just write it in in pencil.

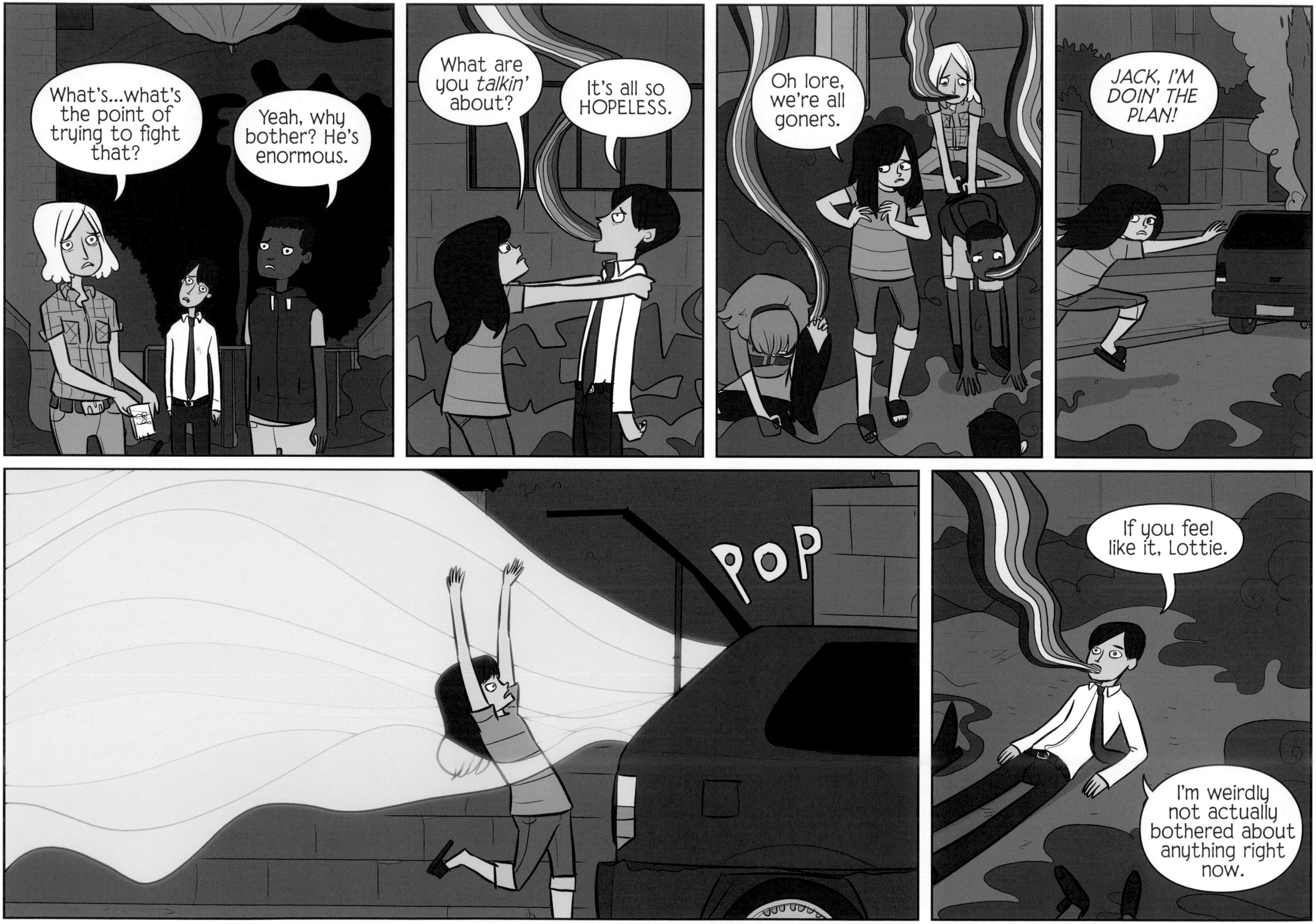

What's...what's the point of trying to fight that?
Yeah, why bother? He's enormous.
What are you *talkin'* about?
It's all so HOPELESS.
Oh lore, we're all goners.
JACK, I'M DOIN' THE PLAN!
POP
If you feel like it, Lottie.
I'm weirdly not actually bothered about anything right now.

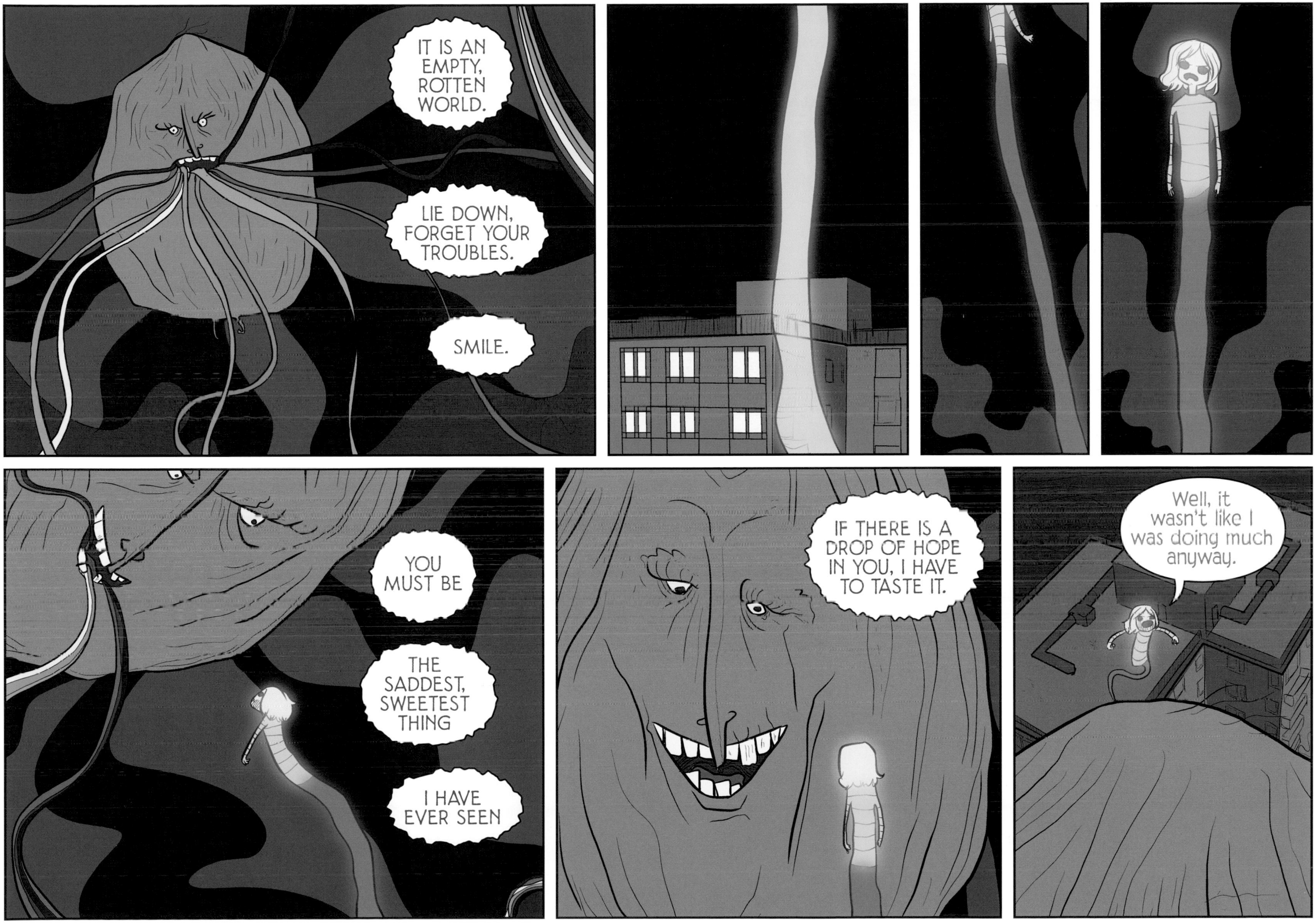
IT IS AN EMPTY, ROTTEN WORLD.
LIE DOWN, FORGET YOUR TROUBLES.
SMILE.
YOU MUST BE
THE SADDEST, SWEETEST THING
I HAVE EVER SEEN
IF THERE IS A DROP OF HOPE IN YOU, I HAVE TO TASTE IT.
Well, it wasn't like I was doing much anyway.

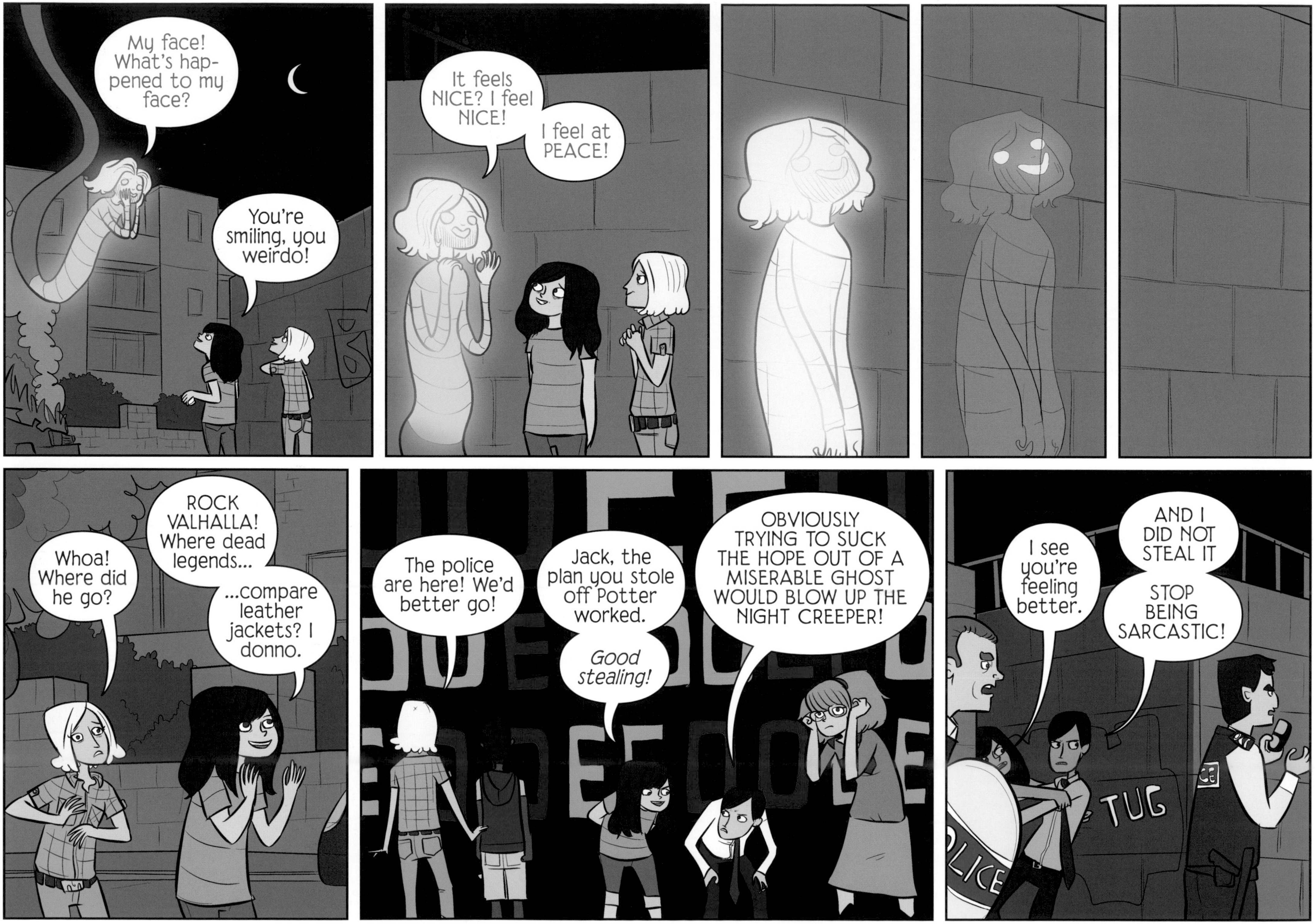
My face! What's hap-pened to my face?
You're smiling, you weirdo!
It feels NICE? I feel NICE!
I feel at PEACE!
Whoa! Where did he go?
ROCK VALHALLA! Where dead legends...
...compare leather jackets? I donno.
The police are here! We'd better go!
Jack, the plan you stole off Potter worked.
Good stealing!
OBVIOUSLY TRYING TO SUCK THE HOPE OUT OF A MISERABLE GHOST WOULD BLOW UP THE NIGHT CREEPER!
I see you're feeling better.
AND I DID NOT STEAL IT
STOP BEING SARCASTIC!
TUG
POLICE

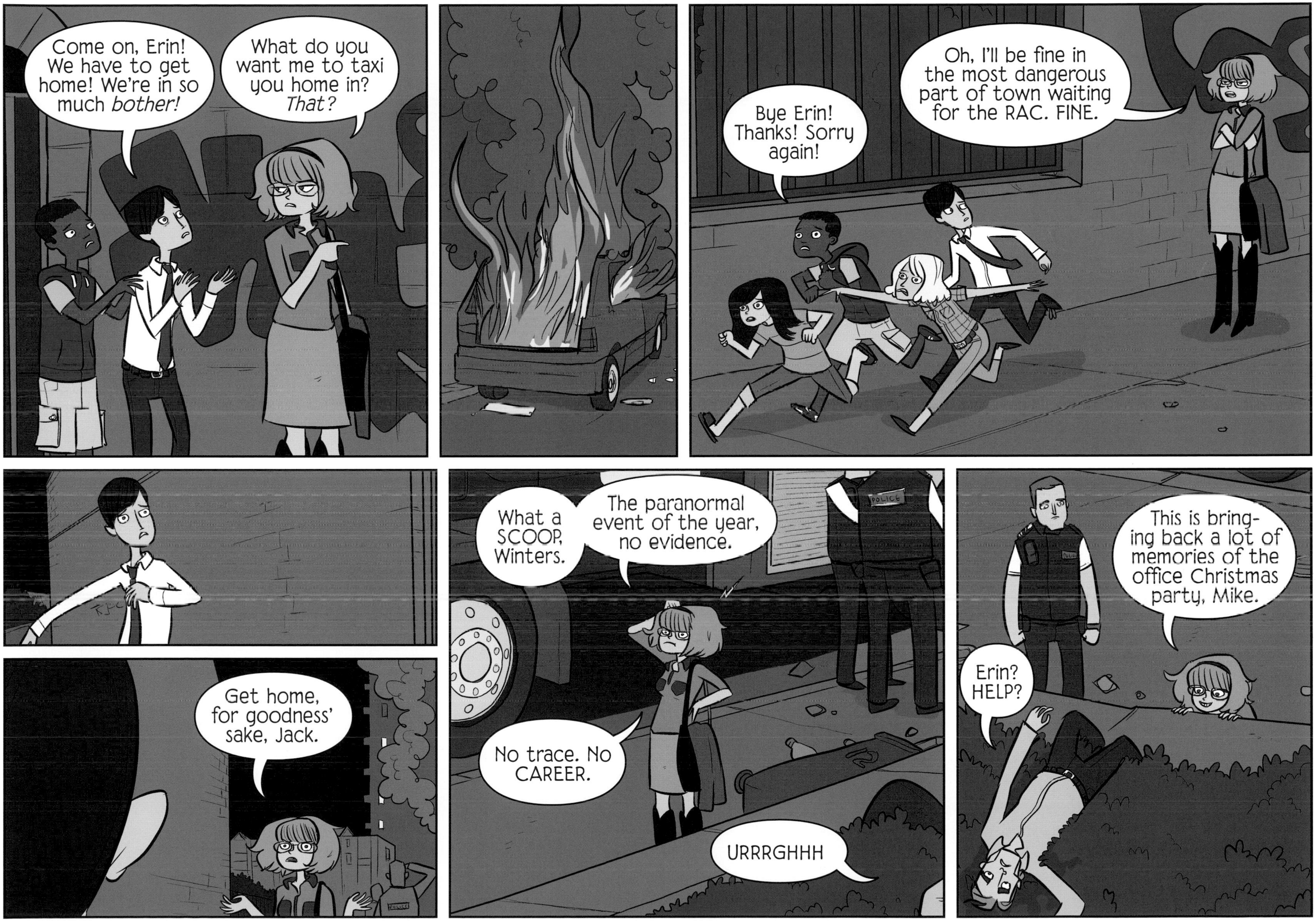
Come on, Erin! We have to get home! We're in so much *bother!*
What do you want me to taxi you home in? *That?*
Oh, I'll be fine in the most dangerous part of town waiting for the RAC. FINE.
Bye Erin! Thanks! Sorry again!
What a SCOOP, Winters.
The paranormal event of the year, no evidence.
No trace. No CAREER.
URRRGHHH
This is bringing back a lot of memories of the office Christmas party, Mike.
Erin? HELP?
Get home, for goodness' sake, Jack.

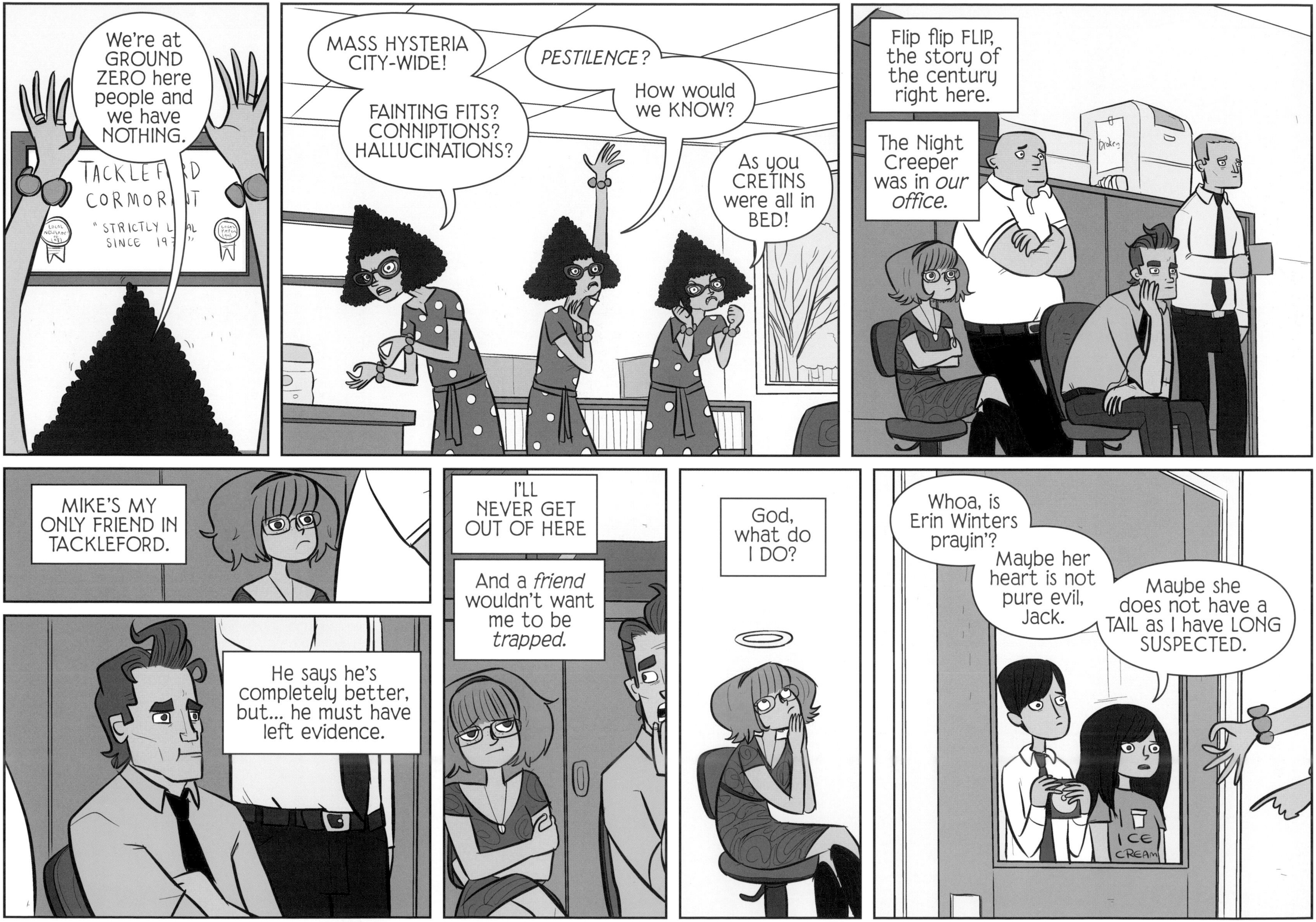
We're at GROUND ZERO here people and we have NOTHING.
TACKLEFORD CORMORANT "STRICTLY LOCAL SINCE 197"
MASS HYSTERIA CITY-WIDE!
FAINTING FITS? CONNIPTIONS? HALLUCINATIONS?
PESTILENCE?
How would we KNOW?
As you CRETINS were all in BED!
Flip flip FLIP, the story of the century right here.
The Night Creeper was in our office.
MIKE'S MY ONLY FRIEND IN TACKLEFORD.
He says he's completely better, but... he must have left evidence.
I'LL NEVER GET OUT OF HERE
And a friend wouldn't want me to be trapped.
God, what do I DO?
Whoa, is Erin Winters prayin'?
Maybe her heart is not pure evil, Jack.
Maybe she does not have a TAIL as I have LONG SUSPECTED.
ICE CREAM

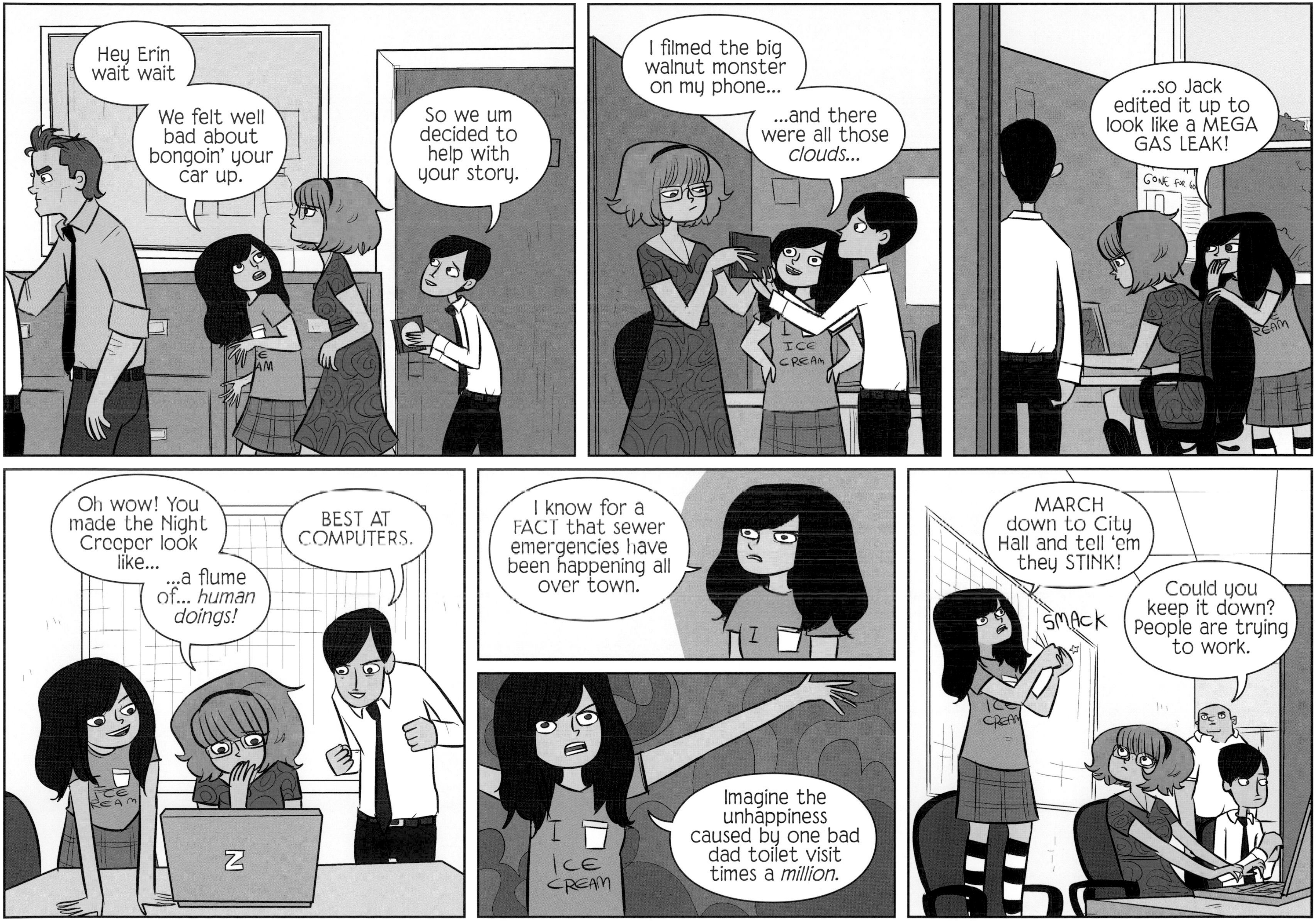
Hey Erin wait wait
We felt well bad about bongoin' your car up.
So we um decided to help with your story.
I filmed the big walnut monster on my phone...
...and there were all those *clouds*...
...so Jack edited it up to look like a MEGA GAS LEAK!
GONE FOR GO
Oh wow! You made the Night Creeper look like...
...a flume of... *human doings!*
BEST AT COMPUTERS.
I know for a FACT that sewer emergencies have been happening all over town.
Imagine the unhappiness caused by one bad dad toilet visit times a *million.*
MARCH down to City Hall and tell 'em they STINK!
SMACK
Could you keep it down? People are trying to work.

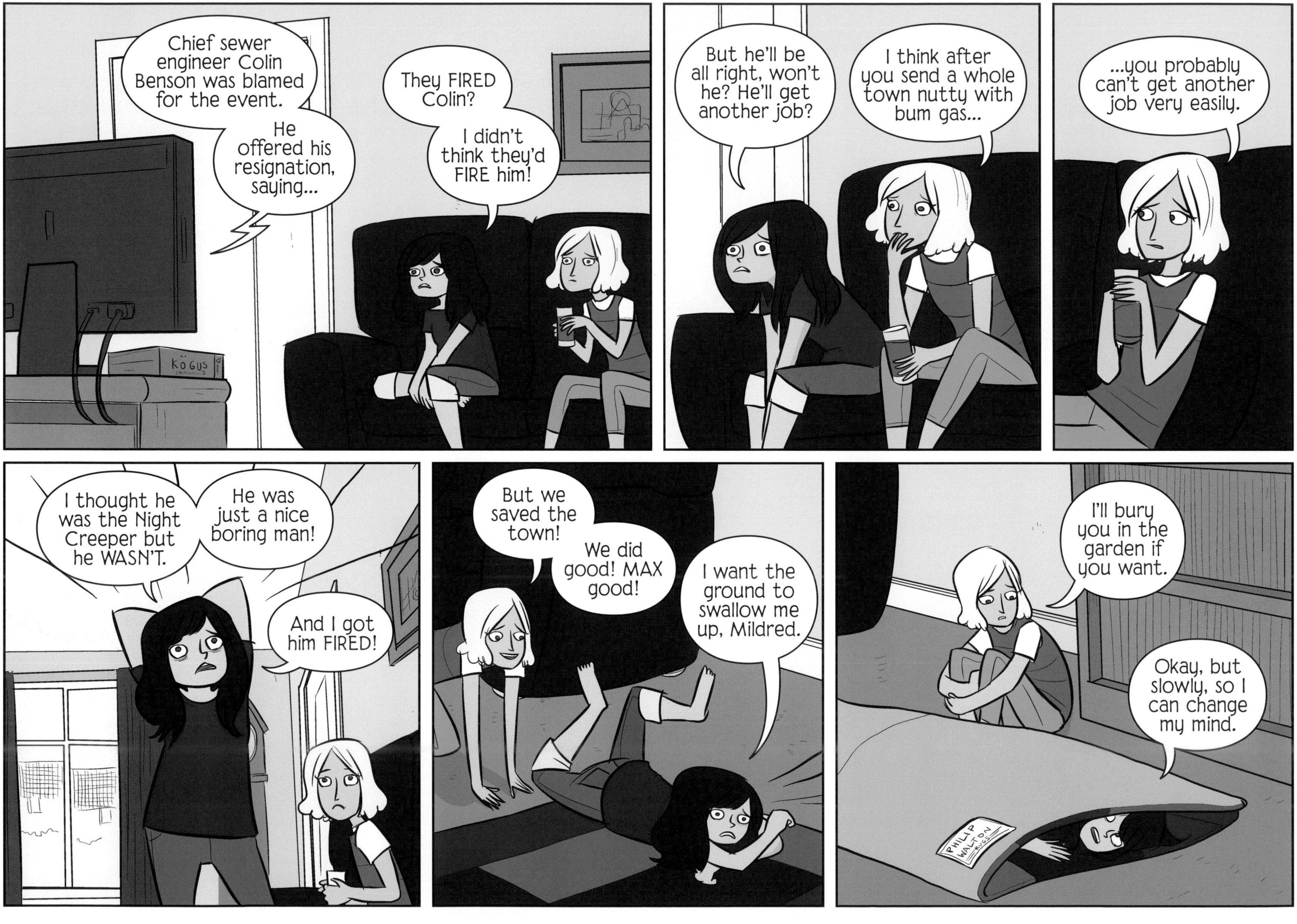

Chief sewer engineer Colin Benson was blamed for the event.
He offered his resignation, saying...
They FIRED Colin?
I didn't think they'd FIRE him!
But he'll be all right, won't he? He'll get another job?
I think after you send a whole town nutty with bum gas...
...you probably can't get another job very easily.
I thought he was the Night Creeper but he WASN'T.
He was just a nice boring man!
And I got him FIRED!
But we saved the town!
We did good! MAX good!
I want the ground to swallow me up, Mildred.
I'll bury you in the garden if you want.
Okay, but slowly, so I can change my mind.
PHILIP WALTON RUGS

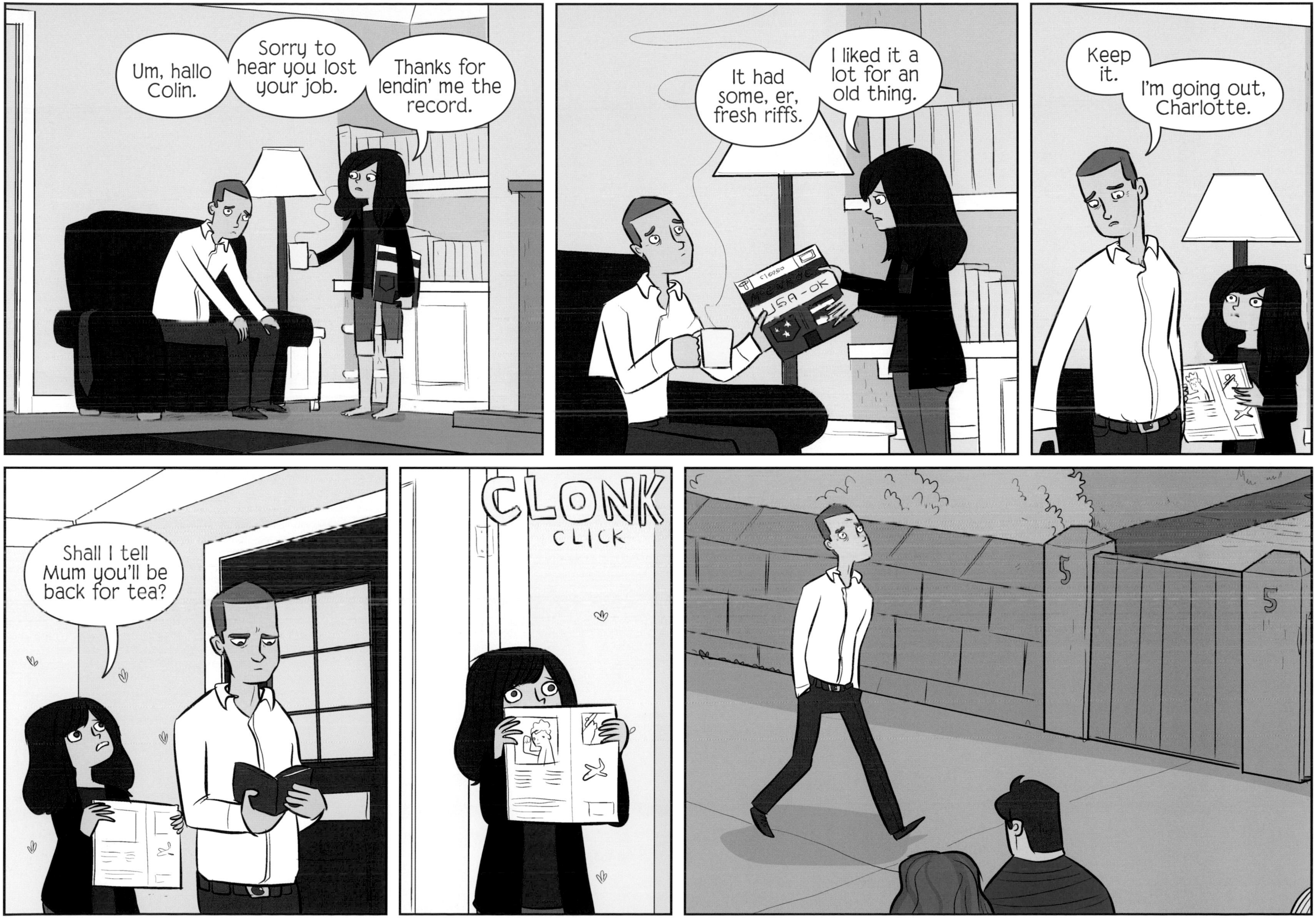
Um, hallo Colin.
Sorry to hear you lost your job.
Thanks for lendin' me the record.
It had some, er, fresh riffs.
I liked it a lot for an old thing.
Keep it.
I'm going out, Charlotte.
Shall I tell Mum you'll be back for tea?
CLONK
CLICK

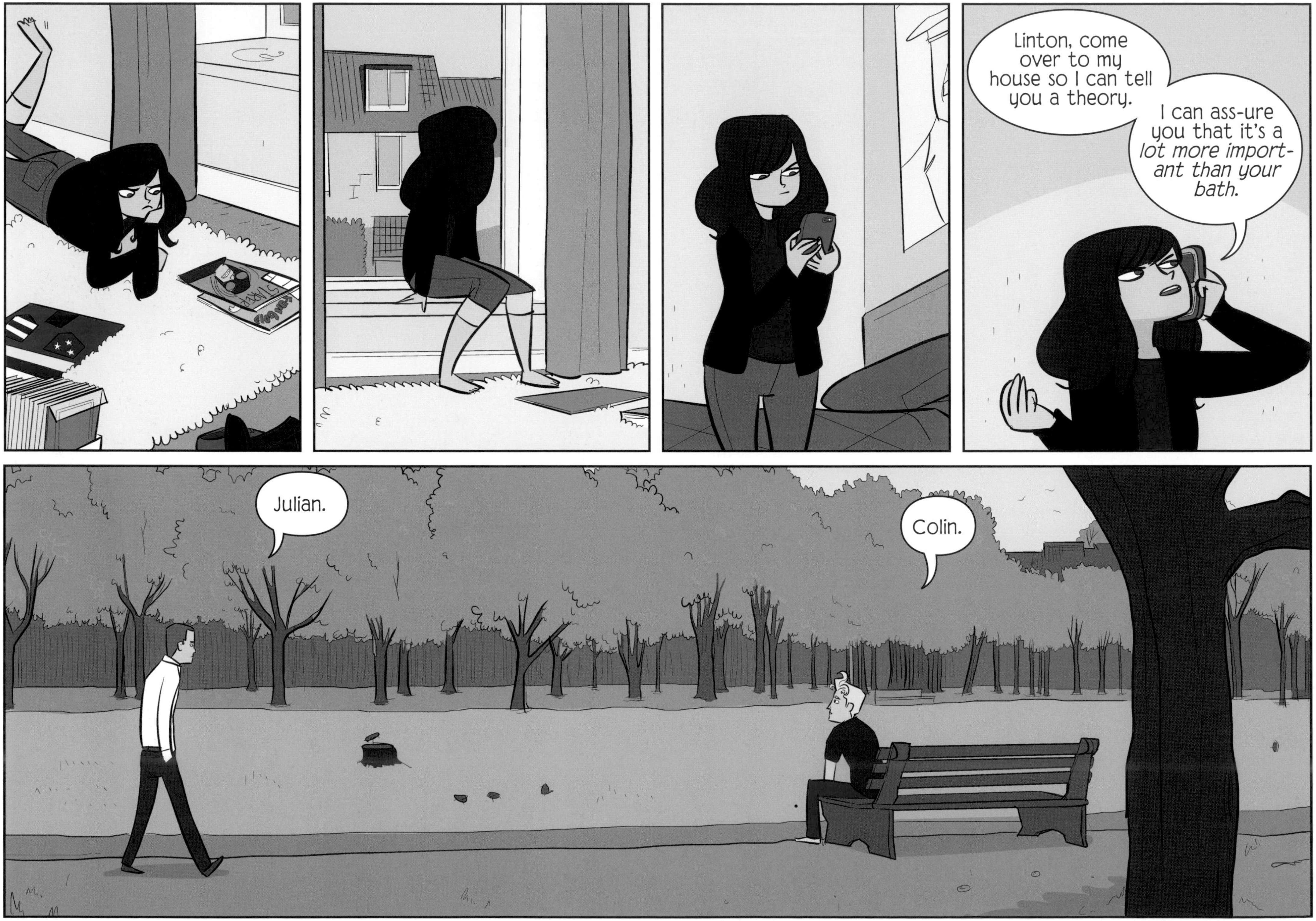
Linton, come over to my house so I can tell you a theory.
I can ass-ure you that it's a *lot more import-ant than your bath.*
Julian.
Colin.

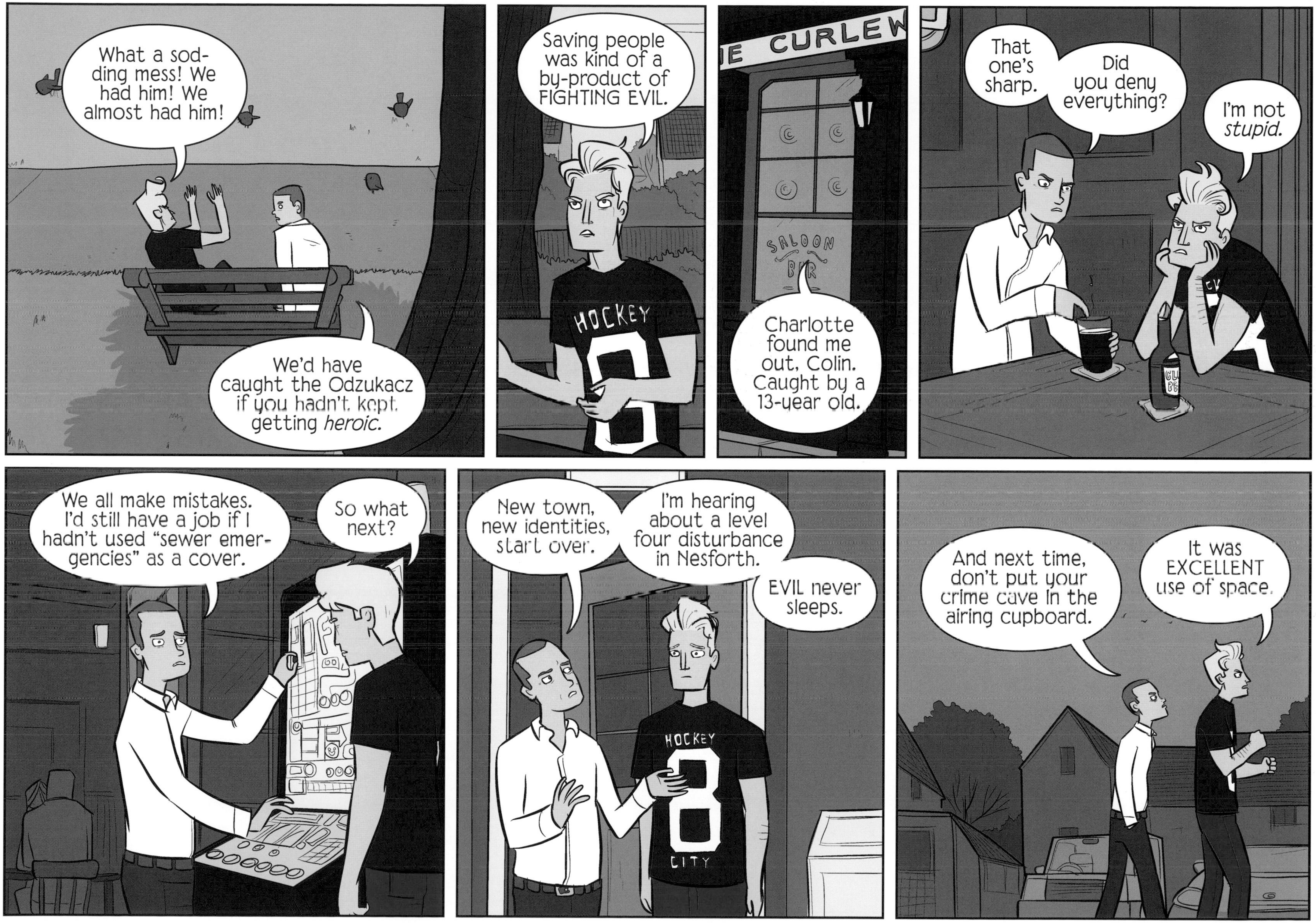
What a sodding mess! We had him! We almost had him!
We'd have caught the Odzukacz if you hadn't kept getting *heroic.*
Saving people was kind of a by-product of FIGHTING EVIL.
CURLEW
SALOON BAR
Charlotte found me out, Colin. Caught by a 13-year old.
That one's sharp.
Did you deny everything?
I'm not *stupid.*
We all make mistakes. I'd still have a job if I hadn't used "sewer emergencies" as a cover.
So what next?
New town, new identities, start over.
I'm hearing about a level four disturbance in Nesforth.
EVIL never sleeps.
And next time, don't put your crime cave in the airing cupboard.
It was EXCELLENT use of space.

Bad Machinery, Volume Six

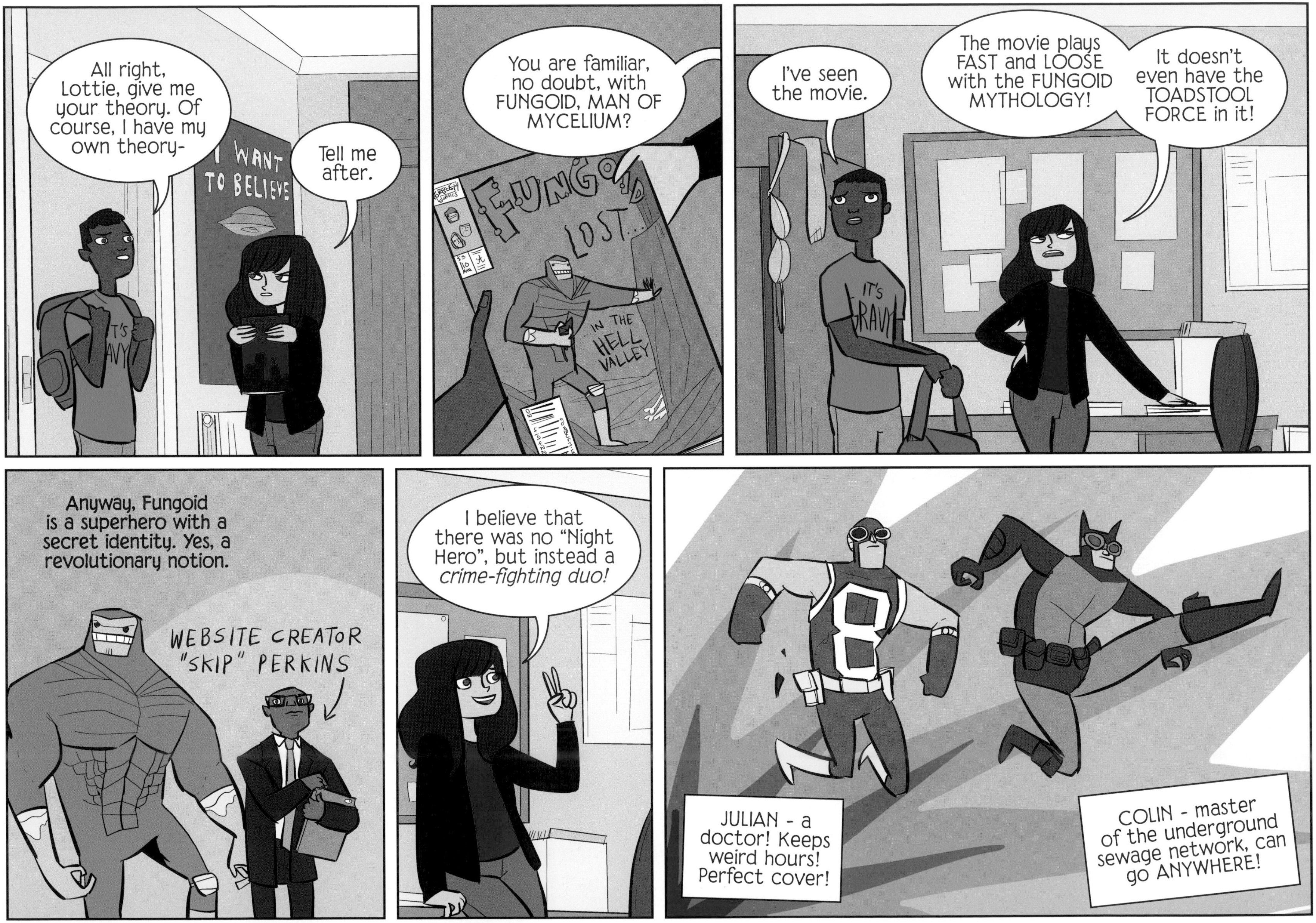
All right, Lottie, give me your theory. Of course, I have my own theory-
I WANT TO BELIEVE
Tell me after.
You are familiar, no doubt, with FUNGOID, MAN OF MYCELIUM?
FUNGOID LOST... ...IN THE HELL VALLEY
I've seen the movie.
The movie plays FAST and LOOSE with the FUNGOID MYTHOLOGY!
It doesn't even have the TOADSTOOL FORCE in it!
IT'S GRAVY
Anyway, Fungoid is a superhero with a secret identity. Yes, a revolutionary notion.
WEBSITE CREATOR "SKIP" PERKINS
I believe that there was no "Night Hero", but instead a *crime-fighting duo!*
JULIAN - a doctor! Keeps weird hours! Perfect cover!
COLIN - master of the underground sewage network, can go ANYWHERE!

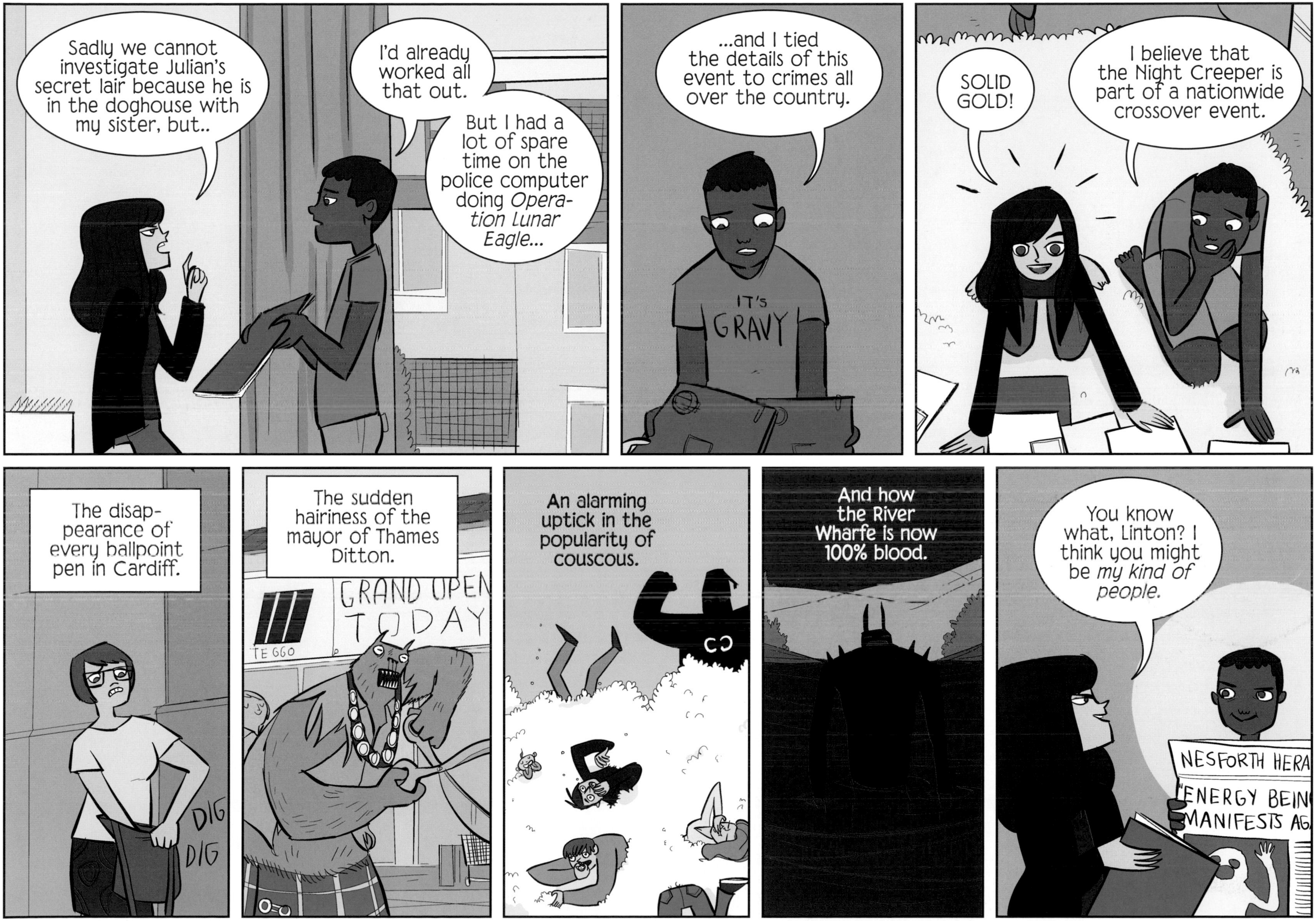
Sadly we cannot investigate Julian's secret lair because he is in the doghouse with my sister, but..
I'd already worked all that out.
But I had a lot of spare time on the police computer doing *Operation Lunar Eagle*...
...and I tied the details of this event to crimes all over the country.
IT'S GRAVY
SOLID GOLD!
I believe that the Night Creeper is part of a nationwide crossover event.
The disappearance of every ballpoint pen in Cardiff.
DIG DIG
The sudden hairiness of the mayor of Thames Ditton.
GRAND OPEN TODAY
TEGGO
An alarming uptick in the popularity of couscous.
And how the River Wharfe is now 100% blood.
You know what, Linton? I think you might be *my kind of people.*
NESFORTH HERA
"ENERGY BEIN
MANIFESTS AG

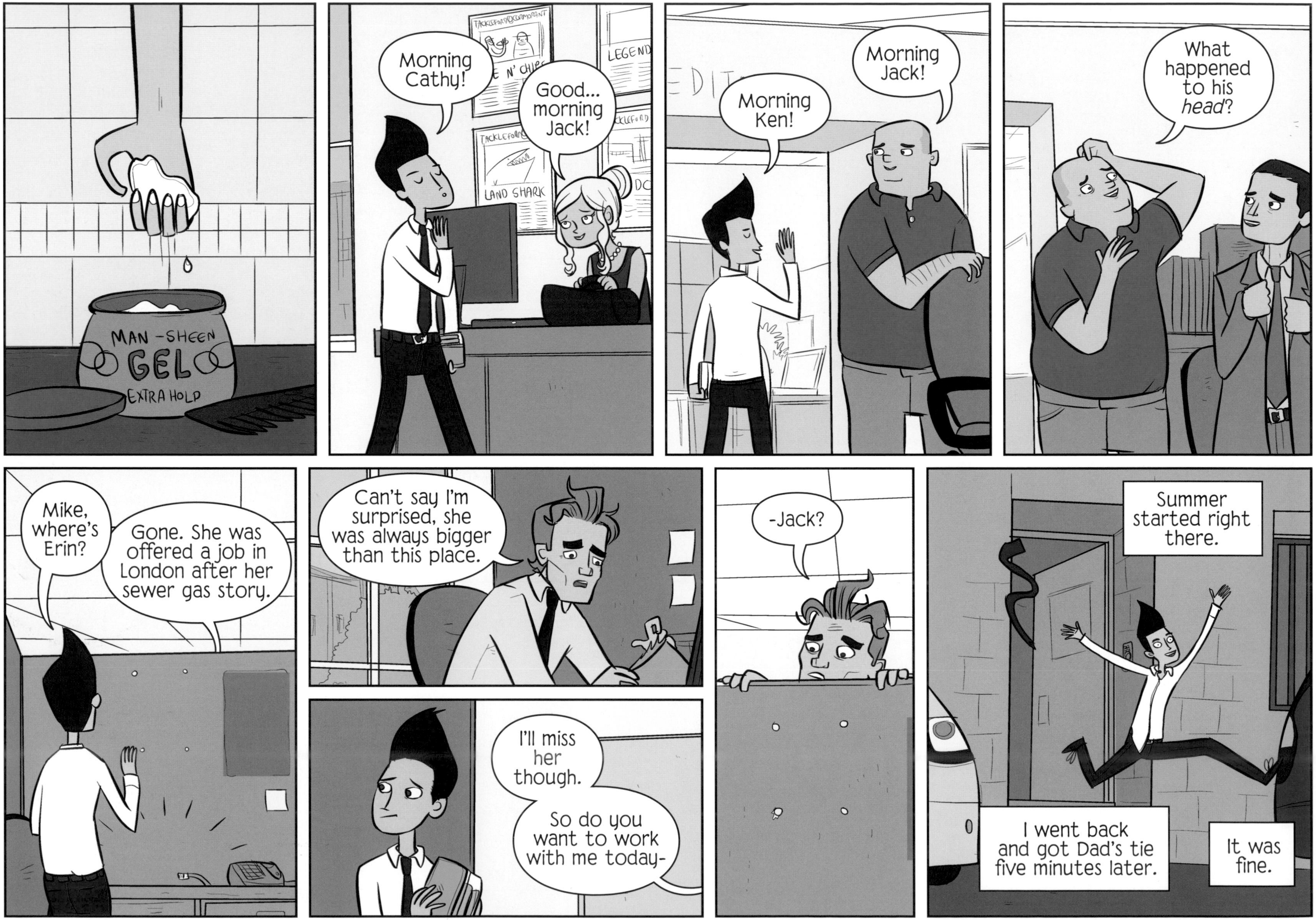
MAN-SHEEN
GEL
EXTRA HOLD
Morning Cathy!
Good... morning Jack!
LEGEND
LAND SHARK
Morning Ken!
Morning Jack!
What happened to his *head*?
Mike, where's Erin?
Gone. She was offered a job in London after her sewer gas story.
Can't say I'm surprised, she was always bigger than this place.
I'll miss her though.
So do you want to work with me today-
-Jack?
Summer started right there.
I went back and got Dad's tie five minutes later.
It was fine.

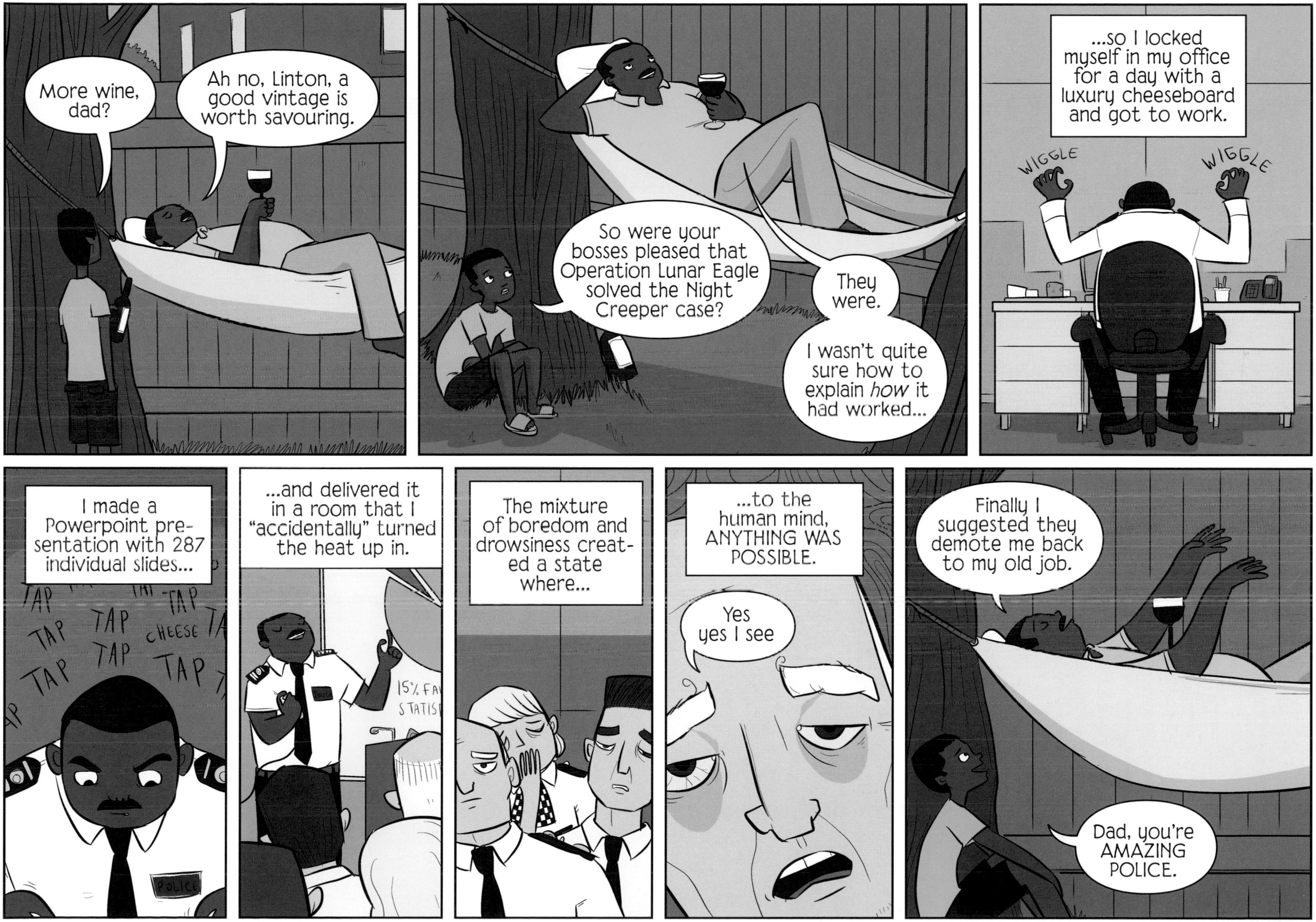
More wine, dad?
Ah no, Linton, a good vintage is worth savouring.
So were your bosses pleased that Operation Lunar Eagle solved the Night Creeper case?
They were.
I wasn't quite sure how to explain *how* it had worked...
...so I locked myself in my office for a day with a luxury cheeseboard and got to work.
WIGGLE
WIGGLE
I made a Powerpoint presentation with 287 individual slides...
TAP TAP TAP TAP TAP CHEESE TAP
...and delivered it in a room that I "accidentally" turned the heat up in.
The mixture of boredom and drowsiness created a state where...
...to the human mind, ANYTHING WAS POSSIBLE.
Yes yes I see
Finally I suggested they demote me back to my old job.
Dad, you're AMAZING POLICE.

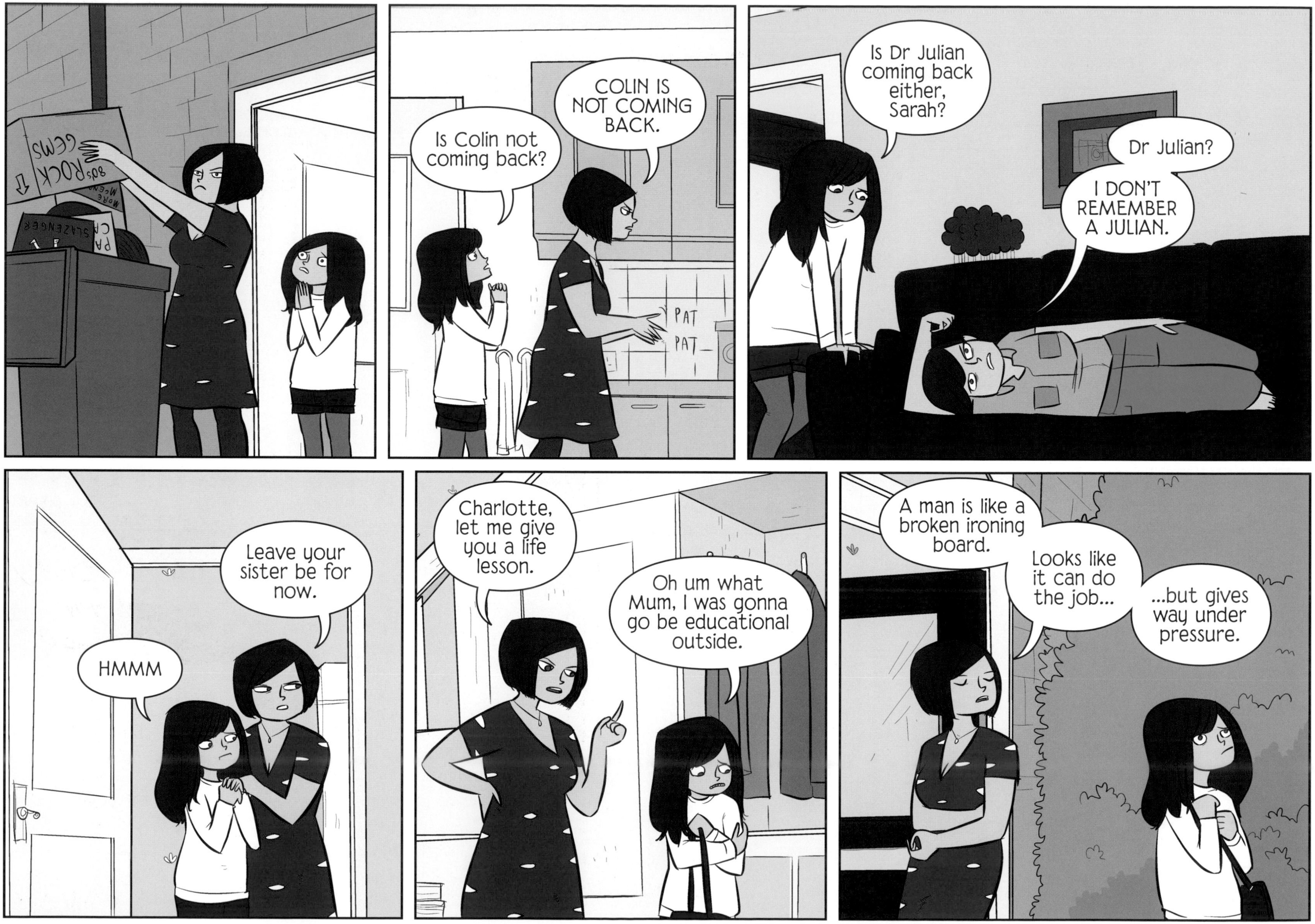
80s ROCK GEMS
MORE McENO
PAT CASH
SLAZENGER
Is Colin not coming back?
COLIN IS NOT COMING BACK.
PAT
PAT
Is Dr Julian coming back either, Sarah?
Dr Julian?
I DON'T REMEMBER A JULIAN.
Leave your sister be for now.
HMMM
Charlotte, let me give you a life lesson.
Oh um what Mum, I was gonna go be educational outside.
A man is like a broken ironing board.
Looks like it can do the job...
...but gives way under pressure.

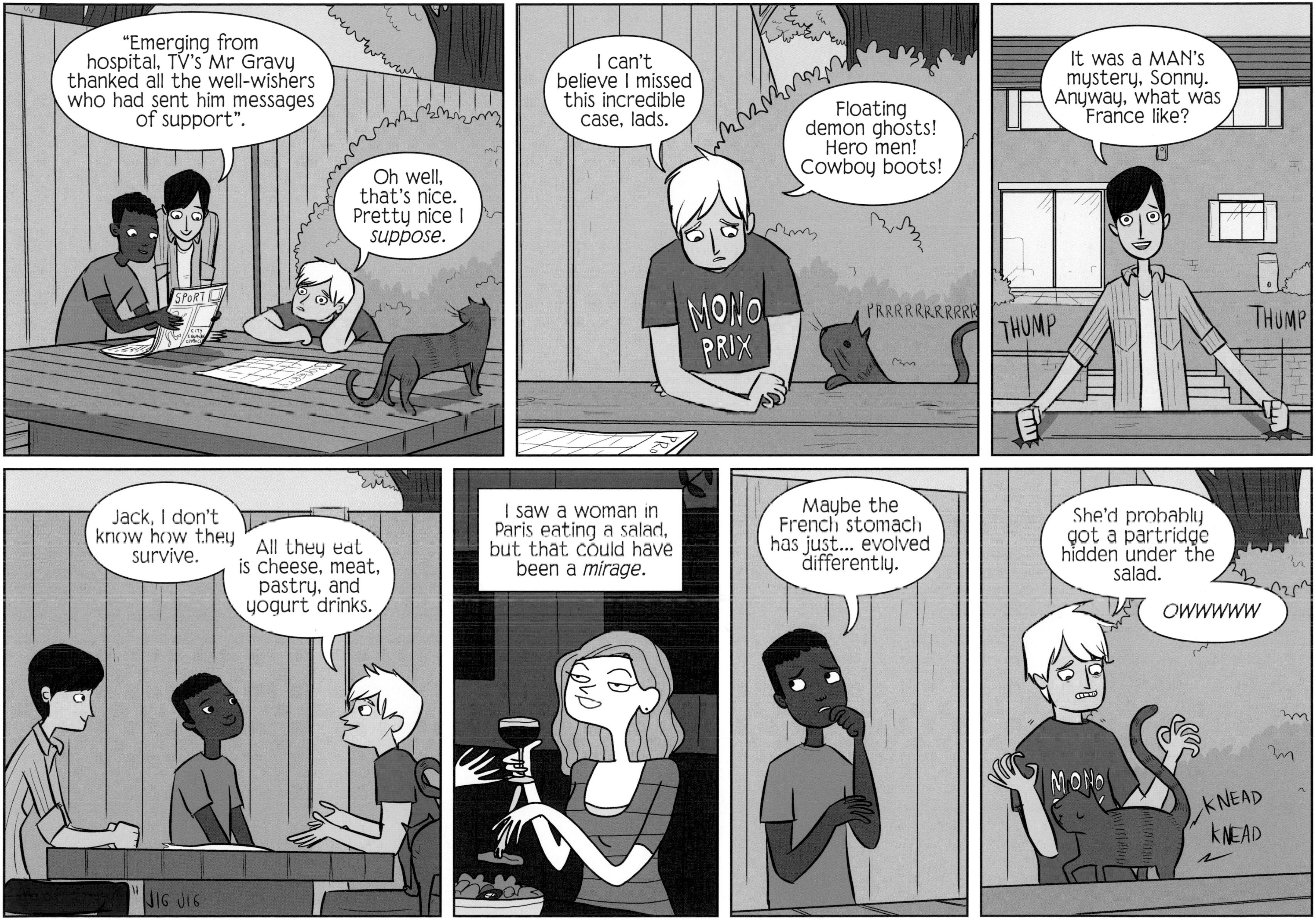
"Emerging from hospital, TV's Mr Gravy thanked all the well-wishers who had sent him messages of support".
SPORT
Oh well, that's nice. Pretty nice I *suppose*.
I can't believe I missed this incredible case, lads.
Floating demon ghosts! Hero men! Cowboy boots!
MONO PRIX
PRRRRRRRRRRR
It was a MAN's mystery, Sonny. Anyway, what was France like?
THUMP
THUMP
Jack, I don't know how they survive.
All they eat is cheese, meat, pastry, and yogurt drinks.
I saw a woman in Paris eating a salad, but that could have been a *mirage*.
Maybe the French stomach has just... evolved differently.
She'd probably got a partridge hidden under the salad.
OWWWWW
KNEAD
KNEAD

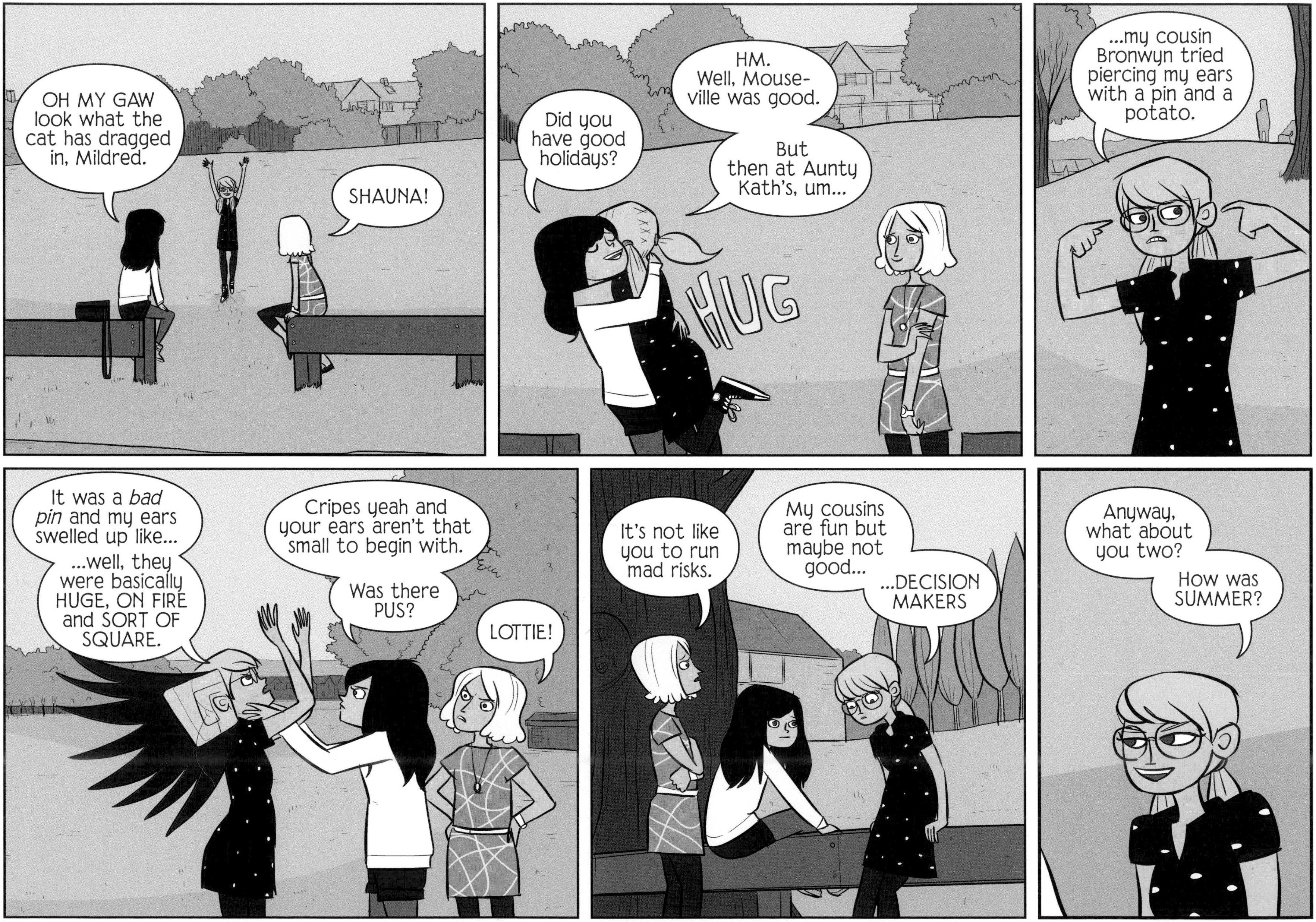
OH MY GAW look what the cat has dragged in, Mildred.
SHAUNA!
Did you have good holidays?
HM. Well, Mouse-ville was good.
But then at Aunty Kath's, um...
HUG
...my cousin Bronwyn tried piercing my ears with a pin and a potato.
It was a *bad pin* and my ears swelled up like...
...well, they were basically HUGE, ON FIRE and SORT OF SQUARE.
Cripes yeah and your ears aren't that small to begin with.
Was there PUS?
LOTTIE!
It's not like you to run mad risks.
My cousins are fun but maybe not good...
...DECISION MAKERS
Anyway, what about you two?
How was SUMMER?

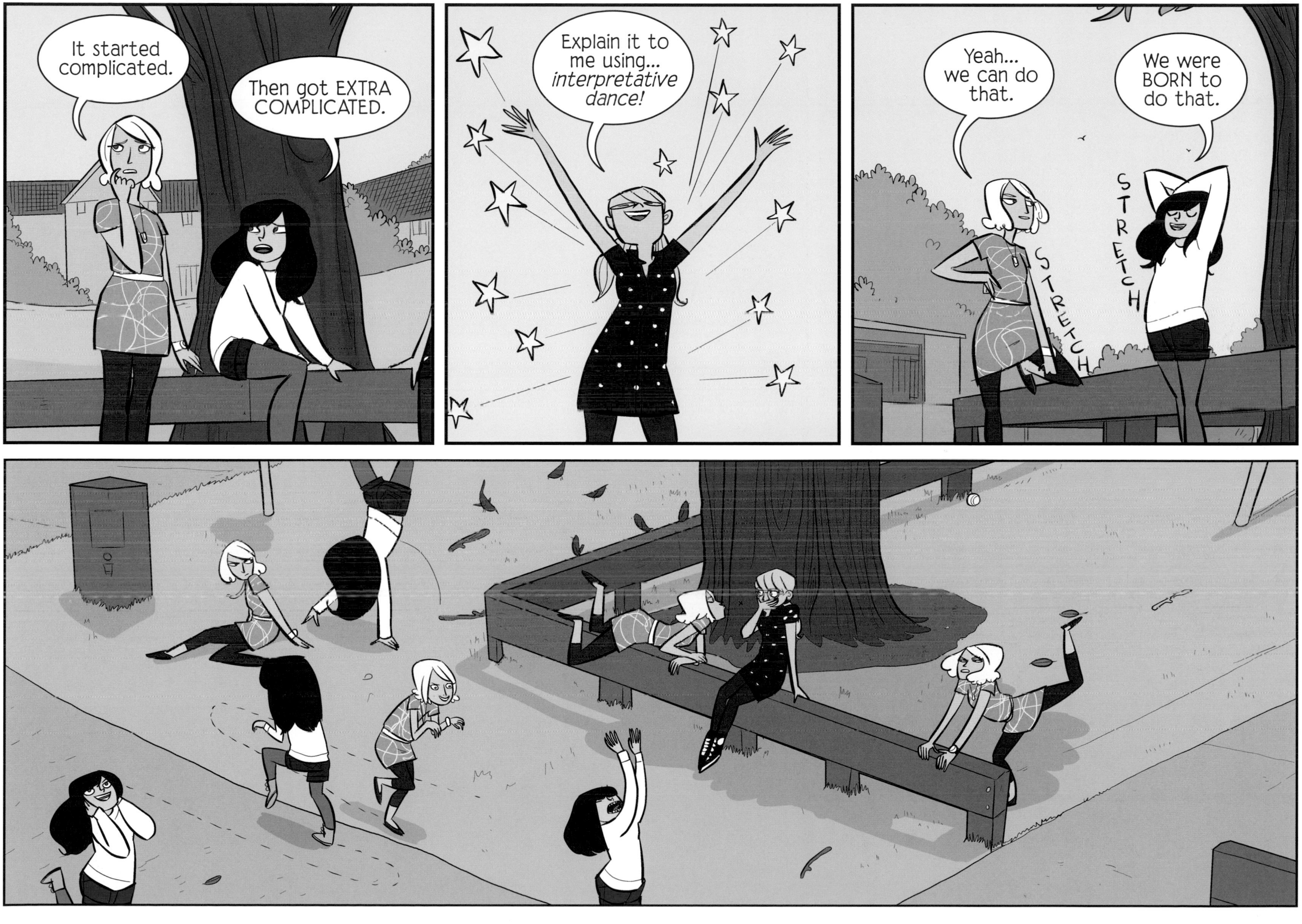
It started complicated.
Then got EXTRA COMPLICATED.
Explain it to me using... *interpretative dance!*
Yeah... we can do that.
We were BORN to do that.
STRETCH
STRETCH

FIN

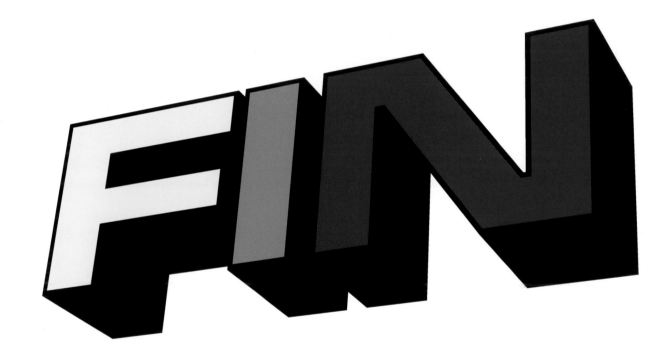

During a recent visit to local junk-hole "Help The Wretched", I was lucky enough to find a copy of Don Gravy's autobiography — SING SOFTLY TO ME, SWEET WIND. Oh, what a book. Don is lots of things in this book but modest is not one of them. Here are a selection of my favourite pages which will take you deep within the mind of one of Tackleford's most "beloved" entertainers.

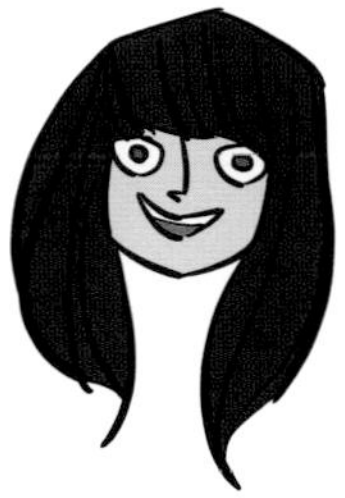

Charlotte Grote,
Keane End, Tackleford

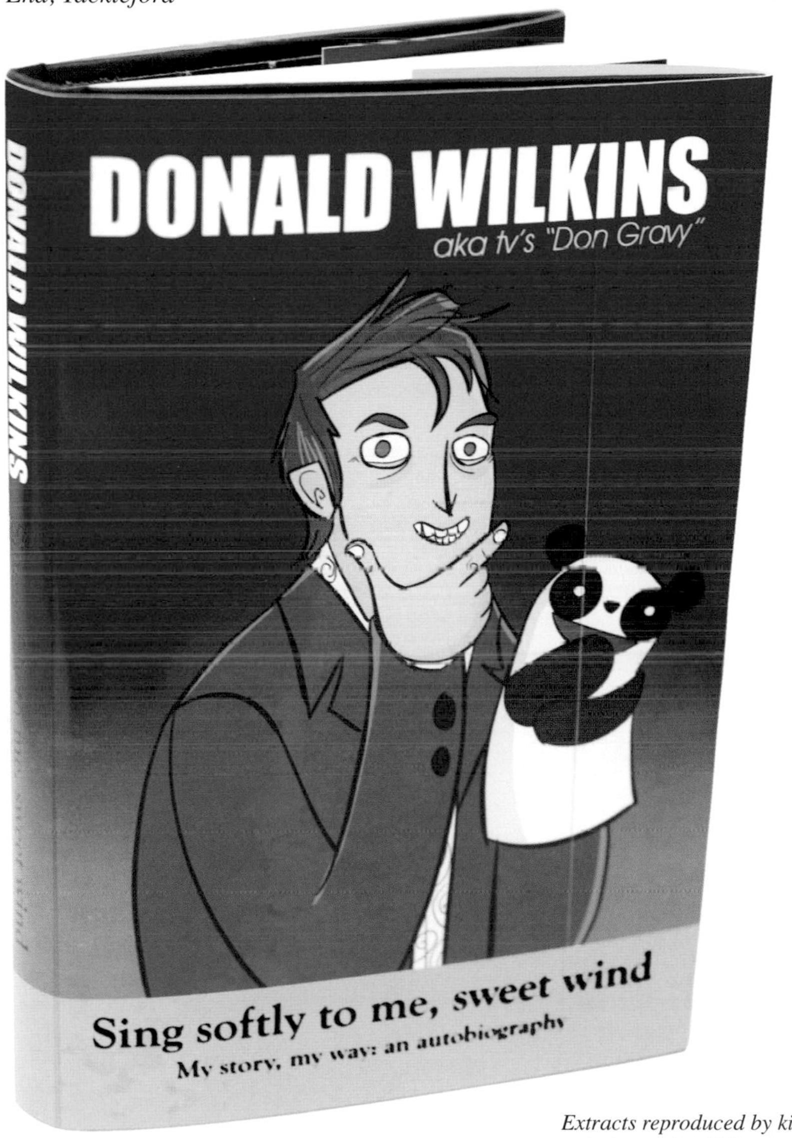
DONALD WILKINS
DONALD WILKINS
aka tv's "Don Gravy"
Sing softly to me, sweet wind
My story, my way: an autobiography

Extracts reproduced by kind permission of D. Wilkins Press

Like half of us, Don Gravy was once a boy. Things were well different back then.

SCHOOLDAYS

I suppose I was a happy child. I did the things other kids did - I ran around, I hid, I kicked a ball, I scuffed me knees. But England was very different in the Seventies. Nowadays, no one says boo to a kiddie without being hauled up before before the judge for cruelty. Back then, children were seen and not heard. We had corporal punishment, and we were glad of it. Some schools had the slipper, others the cane, some the belt. If you did something wrong, someone twice your size was going to whack you. It wasn't unusual for a lad to leave school at 18 with buttocks that resembled a transit map.

At Coward Cross Primary School however, our headmistress, Mrs Thomas, was "modern". She didn't believe in striking a child. I found out later it was because she had weak rotator cuffs in her shoulders, and couldn't achieve a decent blow without a 20-yard run-up, which the layout of her office prevented. At Cross Primary, we had "the desk".

School desks had, traditionally, been single-seat wooden tables with a compartment and a lid. But a new broom was sweeping though the school system, and these had been set aside for Formica-topped tables where we sat in groups. One old, wooden desk remained in each classroom however. And if you misbehaved, you went in it. I went in it almost every week. It wasn't that I was naughty, so much as I couldn't stop talking.

The desk was a wicked thing to do to a child. As a five year old, it was almost funny to be shut inside the wooden container for half an hour. At six, a little tighter. At seven, it took a real squeeze to get your knees in. At eight and nine, the heaviest member of the class might be invited to sit atop the desk lid to compress your straining form into the ink-stained void. By ten and eleven, most kids knew to keep their noses clean. But not me. I will never forget the afternoon when, after loudly announcing that I had not enjoyed my lunch that day (Spam fritters and cabbage), being stuffed into the desk, which was then lashed closed with bungee cords. The wood split, and I burst forth with an explosive fervour only aided by the cabbage-driven flatus of my dreadful dinner.

9

Don's schoolday anecdotes sound well spurious to me but who can tell?

SCHOOLDAYS

By fourteen I was done with school. I looked at the sad, tired faces of the teachers and knew I was best off out of there. I bunked off more than I showed up but, but by the time I was meant to be sitting exams at fifteen, they weren't sending anyone out to look for me any more. I spent my mornings down by the canal with my metal detector, and the afternoons in the pub, listening to the drunks tell their stories.

There was no way I was missing the last week of school, though. "Muck-up week" they called it. Every year, people would go crazy with pranks and jests on a grand scale. There were legendary tales of the Physics master who came out at the end of the day to find a live wolf in his car, the head of French, who went home for the summer unwittingly (and legally) married to the school ferret, and the time five enterprising youths managed to sneak a minky whale into the school pool. I just wrote the word "PLUMS" onto the canteen wall with purple spray paint. They never caught me.

Before we left on that final day, the Headmaster sat down those of us not going on to college for a "little chat". I'll never forget his words.

"Boys, not every one of us is meant to be something. Some are bound for greatness. Others are more like the polystyrene peanuts that provide ballast for a crystal vase in transit. There is nothing glamorous about the polystyrene peanut, but without it, the beautiful vase would arrive cracked."

"You're cracked, mate," I said, baring my bottom to general mirth.

As I walked free of the school gates one last time, I was full of dreams, big dreams. I wasn't going to work in a factory or apprentice as a plumber like the other lads leaving. I was going to be somebody. I knew I could make people laugh - that was my gift. People had been laughing at me since I was a boy. If they weren't laughing as I entered a room (and they often were), they were laughing as I left it. I had a destiny, and it didn't involve canning peas at H. Percy's Pulse Works.

Do factories still have radio stations? I suppose everyone just hums/whistles now.

PEAS FOR BREAKFAST, LUNCH AND TEA

The best thing about working at the pea and bean canning factory, or rather, "H. Percy's Pulse Works", was that there were a lot of places that you could have a nice sleep. It wasn't unusual to turn on the labelling machine in the morning to hear the sudden howl of a night shift worker who'd tucked himself in for a little shut-eye behind the main piston. I was a natural at the factory, much as I proved to be in everything else I've done in life. There were no awards for doing the job right, but it was clear from the silent respect of my colleagues on the canning line that I was a rising star in the field, and would probably have been running the factory by Christmas had fate not come calling.

In common with many British factories at the time, H. Percy had an in-house radio station, broadcasting to the workers to keep spirits up. They'd play top 40 hits, oldies, and take requests. Mornings were hosted by Big Marjorie Jackson, while afternoons were introduced by "Captain" Ken Mather. The night shift (or "quiet storm") was a smooth treat played in by Wendell Q. Christopher, dripping with white gold. This three had held sway over the radio station since 1973, and might have continued to do so had Ken and Wendell not come to blows over Big Marjorie's affections, following the disintegration of her marriage.

So it was, one fateful day, the factory's afternoon and midnight DJs grappled for Marjorie's love on a footbridge over the mushy pea vats. So it was, both tumbled into the green miasma and were swiftly consumed. So it was, Big Marjorie went into seclusion. And so it was that the factory, once filled with song, now lay silent, day and night.

Morale collapsed. Work accidents reached epidemic levels. There was a finger lost most days. Management was in crisis. But who would fill the DJ booth? The fateful seat was still warm, and few wanted to risk that cursed gig. I marched up to Hamilton Percy Sr's office, and knocked on his door.

"I'll play the records, Mr Percy," I said. "I have a good understanding of reggae, punk, new wave, soul, smooth jazz and skiffle, and I believe no further lives will be lost." He said yes.

Alison St Clair sounds like a right one! I shall purchase her greatest hits!!!

Kind words for Noel Edmonds here. By page 80 Don is calling him "a horrid little man"!

As Alison St Clair breezed into the studio, every head turned. 1987's biggest pop star, near enough for me to reach out and touch! To think that a year ago, I'd been spinning "Touch Me Somewhere Sentimental" by Grassy Knoll for the ladies on the factory floor, and now I was playing songs for the whole Tackleford and Wendlefield Valley on Puddle FM. Alison was gorgeous, dressed head to toe in leopardskin and polyurethane. Her perfume was like a drug. And by the time her top ten hit "Monkey Around" stopped playing, I was going to have to interview her, live on the air. Bright red and flustered, I tried to make small talk.

"Did you get the train here?" I asked, trying to get my notes in order.

"I take helicopters, darling," she said, her deep hazel eyes cutting into me. "Everywhere. I'm a *star*."

Well, I felt like a prize prat. A wally. Of course she took helicopters everywhere. As I tried to recover my train of thought, I head the last notes of "Monkey Around" fade out.

"Ladies and gentlemen, I'm here with Alison St Clair, and I have to say, she's lookin' gorgeous as ever. Alison's playing the Tackle Valley Stadium tonight, and I'm sure all your fans want to know, what will you be wearing?" My question hung in the air for a second. It didn't half sound stupid. Alison parted her cherry lips.

"Very little, darling. As ever." Well! If I'd been struggling before, I was a man lost at sea now. I stammered out a few more questions, before Ms St Clair placed a gloved hand on my arm.

"Don, I have something for you." She reached into the folds of her leopard cape, and produced a seven-inch single. "This is my new record. I cut it yesterday with Nigel Swann at Royal Records. It's called "Thigh Highs (All Night)". I'd like you to be the first person to play it."

Five minutes later, as Alison was being swept out of the room by her manager, my producer Felix dashed in, frantic.

"Don, mate, they cut to national transmission halfway through your interview. You've just been heard by 40 million people."

6

"Wilkins, thanks for coming in." Johnny Beerling, the controller of BBC Radio 1, cut an imposing figure, his hair like whipped ice cream atop a waffle-brown facial cone. He'd just returned from two weeks in Corfu. "I'm going to cut to the chase. We've offered Bates the breakfast show, and he said no. Doesn't want to give up the Golden Hour. So we'd like you to do it. What do you say?"

The Radio 1 Breakfast Show! The most listened-to radio programme in Britain! If you'd told the lad dreaming in his bedroom on a council terrace in Tackleford that in four years he'd be offered the top job on the nation's airwaves, well, I dare say he'd have fallen off that bed, perhaps awkwardly, maybe damaging his body in such a way that he would have been unable to have become one of the country's top disc jockeys.

Such are the perils and paradoxes of time travel, which sadly there is little scope to explore in this chapter. The greats that had filled the chair before me, great, unimpeachable men like Noel Edmonds, Mike Read and Mike Smith, booming voices that lifted the hearts of mums, dads and kids on the school run, lifted sleepy heads from the cereal bowl, playing the power hits that propelled lonely singletons from their beds to the workplace. To be such a vital cog in the national machine wasn't just an honour, it was a privilege. Beerling's breath was bated. He fingered his cravat impatiently. "Come on man. What do you say?"

"Radio's dead, Johnny," I sneered. "I've been asked to do telly. No one listens to the radio any more. Not interested."

Talkabout makes me wish I lived in a time when TV shows were still allowed to be boring.

The royal tittle-tattle on this page sounds EXTREMELY MADE UP.

As a junior presenter on BBC 2's "Talkabout", my duties were limited, but that suited me fine. A couple of man-on-the-street interviews per show, in-studio pieces when required, and occasional hosting duties when Carol Beffin or Lord Maudsley were away. I was busy with family duties. Marta and I had married after a whirlwind romance, and almost nine months to the day after our wedding, Hunter Hawksley Wilkins was born.

My son was, and is, everything to me. But the late nights were hell. Hunter would wake every twenty minutes, demanding to be fed or changed, and Marta insisted we use the Polish technique, where the father attends to all the child's needs after 6.30pm. As a result, I was surviving on around two hours' sleep a night. Some nights, the only thing that would pacify our sweet lad was his panda glove puppet, Simon. The only drawback to Simon was that he had to "hug" Hunter, which required my hand. As soon as my grip slackened, our son would begin to cry.

In mid-July 1989, I was scheduled to host Talkabout while Lord Maudsley went on a shooting holiday in Norfolk. But on that fateful day, I fell asleep giving my boy a "Simon hug", my arm stretched awkwardly into the crib for hours. Bleary and confused, I was woken mid-afternoon by the telephone.

"Don, where are you?" came our producer's voice. "You should have been in make-up fifteen minutes ago!" Fortunately, our home was a short run from BBC Broadcasting House, and I somehow managed to make it on air in time, in the clothes I had been wearing the previous day. I read the autocue. "Welcome to Talkbout, I'm Don Wilkins. On today's show, a consumer report on lethal black market skateboards, and more on the scandal of Britain's collapsing hospitals."

Every pair of eyes was trained on me. People seemed locked in a state midway between amusement and horror. Carol turned to me, ignoring the autocue. "Don, is there something you'd like to tell us?" She pointed at my hand. The panda was still on it. I was mortified. But with the composure that defines me as a person, I answered her. "This... is Simon. Say 'hello', Simon."

After a year of the "Don Gravy & Simon Show", things began to get a little out of hand - if you'll pardon my joke. We were on telly every week, in the gap between kiddies' TV and the news. Everyone saw it. There were only four TV channels back then, and two of them were terrible. Pretty girls would stop me in the street and give me their telephone numbers. Builders would shout "WHERE'S SIMON?" when I nipped out to the shop for a bag of crisps. I never had to buy a drink in a pub, never had to pay for a cab. The world stopped feeling real. For an appearance in Aldershot, a helicopter was chartered. I thought back to Alison St Clair... who's the big star now?

But I wasn't going to let it go to my head. You can take the lad out of Tackleford, but you can't take Tackleford out of the lad. I might have been getting my clothes made bespoke rather than off the peg, but that didn't make me fancy. I may have been dining at London's best restaurants and private clubs rather than eating a fish and chip supper from newspaper, but it's all just grub when it comes down to it. I may have had a cook, a cleaner, a maid and a driver, but I knew their names. You can't let that stuff go.

The peak of these crazy days came at the 1994 Royal Variety Performance. The Queen was there, and Prince Phillip, in the royal box, and I was booked to perform. Well, I put on quite the show. Simon had the kids in stitches, and the grown-ups too. Her Majesty was dabbing the corner of her eye and even Phil was smirking. After I performed, there was a knock on dressing room door. It was a royal footman, in full regalia - braid, medals, spurs and knee-boots. "Her Majesty Queen Elizabeth II requests the pleasure of your company at Buckingham Palace this evening." And so it was that a boy from the smoky streets of West Yorkshire found himself at a right royal lock-in with the Windsors - with the Queen Mother holding court - and the gin bottle - at a fully stocked wet bar. Modesty (not to mention the Official Secrets Act) does not permit me to recount the goings-on that night, but suffice to say that we were late to bed that night, with sore heads beneath the crown, the following morn.

Just one of many quite saucy pages, this was the only one not too rude to reproduce (oo-er).

They say it's a good life if you don't weaken, but alas, I've had a few slips along the way. My Dad, Paul, was a decent man, every day he left the house for Tackleford General Hospital, where he mopped floors, emptied bedpans, and kept his head down. It wasn't the sort of life you'd call glamorous. But in the pub at night, he shone. Paul could talk a blue streak and had charisma a mile wide. While Mum gave us kids our baths and our tea, he'd laugh the evening away over six or seven pints of heavy.

Now, Dad was kind, and we loved him. But we weren't the only ones. I remember the first time I saw my father with one of his "girlfriends". He was kissing Jacqueline Foster from the butchers, him with a leg of lamb under each arm, her still astride the shop bike. I saw him, he saw me, and I was red raw with rage. How could he step out on my beloved Mum? He ran after me and said words I'd never forget. "Son, your mother and me are solid as a rock. But I've got a lot of love to give, and it would be a crime not to share it." I nodded dumbly, and swore I would never be like him. Never would I cheat.

So why was I at Grimsby's leading French restaurant, The Kitty, with X, one of television's most recognisable beauties? Even in our secluded both, both of us knew we could be caught at any time - and her married to Y, her daytime sofa co host and notorious brawler. Both our hearts were beating like drums.

"You complete me, Don," she said breathlessly, unloading an oyster into her Cupid's Bow mouth. "I've never felt more alive, being here with you now."

"And you I, X", I replied, "no woman has ever filled me with such divine fire." Her diamond necklace glittered in the candlelight, scattering her bosom with a thousand points of light. I knew that what I was doing was wrong, that Marta was at home in our Mayfair home while I played it fast and loose in "the Monte Carlo of East Yorkshire." But as it turned out, I was my father's son. And I never understood Paul Wilkins better than at the moment X took my hand and led me from the restaurant into the fishy night air. Oh X. Oh *Grimsby.*

I think Marta is meant to be the villain here but she sounds like a 100% human hero.

As the third dinner plate shattered around my ears, I realised that Marta and I had problems that a £5 bunch of flowers and a box of Terry's All Gold wouldn't solve. And there it was on the cover of today's News Of The World, in glorious black and white. "SHARON: TV LOVE RAT DON GRAVY ROMPED WITH ME WHILE HIS WIFE HAD SHINGLES".

"It's a misunderstanding!" I shouted, dodging shards of exploding porcelain. "We didn't really romp! There was a little light horseplay that got out of hand, a moment of weakness, maybe some shennanigans!" Marta didn't seem interested in the semantics of the matter. And who was I trying to kid? I'd got sloppy. There was a void at the centre of myself that I tried to fill with showgirls, luxury desserts, and sweet champagne wine. My chickens had come home to roost, and by the end of the night, this old fox was out of the henhouse.

What had first drawn me to Marta? As a judge on the Miss Rutland Competition panel I'd watched her parade, of course, but she wasn't a piece of meat to me, a trophy. I loved her mind. And what a mind. Unfortunately, that ingenuity was now put to work as she systematically destroyed every single one of my possessions in an orchestrated chain reaction that most closely resembled a Domino Rally.

As my 1971 MGB sports car careened into my collection of Fabergé eggs, the wreckage of which she then swept into to swimming pool, before setting the curtains on fire, I was struck dumb with the same admiration that had always been the foundation stone of our union. Sadly that speechlessness left me unable to intervene when she drove our spotless vintage Land Rover into our garden gazebo, which she'd filled with all my golf equipment, my awards, and the certificates for my shares, stocks and bonds. The car's engine exploded. The fire brigade were called. Marta turned to me, triumphant. "I am now going to my mother's. She is, coincidentally, an excellent divorce lawyer."

At that moment, the telephone rang. It was my agent, Suzanne. "Don, the BBC want to see you," she said. "They're... not happy."

I couldn't even find Lord Montague on Wikipedia, I'm not sure this happened at all. [NOTE: Stride FM is now "Tackleford Power Hits 94.9 - Music As Individual As You Are"]

12

They say that in showbusiness you should be nice to people on the way up, because that way they'll be nice to you on the way down. Now, I wasn't always an angel backstage. I worked hard, and expected the people around me to work hard too. So I made a few make-up girls cry. So I fired a few managers. So I spread the odd rumour about fellow presenters that might seen them swiftly removed. Of course I did. It was the Nineties, everyone was at it. I gave the little people jobs, the least they could have done was to be grateful.

So when Lord Montague called me into his grand office at the BBC, I expected a ticking off over the newspaper stories. A slap on the wrist. I'd given them ratings. I'd given them *magic*. They gave me my cards. The Mr Gravy And Simon show was cancelled.

"You can keep your stinking job," I told Montague. "I'll take Simon to ITV. That's where the real money is anyway." Then I bared my bottom to him, before taking my leave. Sometimes the old ways are the best.

Well, as it turned out, ITV *was* where the real money was. And they were keeping hold of it. No one wanted a kids' TV presenter who cheats on his wife and leaves his children without a father. I went to Channel 4. They offered me a late night slot. I told them, stick your graveyard shift, I'm going to satellite TV. Well, I did. And they told me that no one wanted a "puppet act" any more, television had moved on. It was all about "youth" and "edge", and I had neither. I was 41 years old, and I was on the scrapheap.

It turned out that no-one wanted TV's Mr Gravy. I couldn't go back to radio with Simon - he didn't speak! I just waggled his hands about and made him nod. After a humiliating meeting at Puddle FM (now re-branded as "Stride - News, Sport & Talk"), I realised that it was all over.

So I walked down to the river with Simon. Simon, who had taken me to my fortune. I placed the puppet over my hand, as I had done so many times before. Sweet Simon, who had never let me down. His sightless black plastic eyes stared up at me as if to say, "what now Don? What now?" And I could take it no more. I rained blows down upon that panda, cursing him, cursing fate. Every blow, a strike against my own right hand. When I could take it no more, I cast Simon into the water and watched his furry body sink into the murk. It was my lowest moment. My right hand, now bare, was black and blue.

I must have walked along the river bank for miles, plagued with the most desperate thoughts. Should I throw myself into the deep? Go up into the hills and live as a hermit? Or retrain as a chartered accountant and open up a high-street storefront, eventually building up a healthy clientele? All of these prospects seemed so bleak that I could not, would not countenance them.

And then I started up the hill back to Keane End, and the old Peas And Beans sign caught my eye. If there was one thing I knew how to do, it was can peas. Of course, there would be a healthy helping of humble pie to swallow, but nothing goes better with pie than peas. I knew that much.

I reached the old factory gates, and watched the day shift leave and the night shift roll in. This wouldn't be forever. Just a stop along the way, before I got back on top. I walked in. The smell was the same as it ever was. I walked up the steps, past the pea vats, to the foreman's office, and knocked on the door. A kid answered, barely 21, bum-fluff on his chin.

"Have you got anything going?" I asked. The lad looked me up and down with disbelief. "Aren't you Don Gravy?"

"I used to be," I said. "I used to be."

I think Don had a contractual obligation to write more book. This chapter is 115 pages long.

You can tell he is weakening by this point.

ON MUSIC

Music nowaways is rubbish. It's all just shouting. People say to me that "hip-hop" is poetry. It's not. It's just shouting over a beat. My son tries to tell me that "indie music" is wonderful. The lad's cracked. It's just shouting over guitars. There's not been a decent note of music played since 1987 when Steve 'Silk' Hurley's "Jack Your Body" went to Number 1 in the charts. It was all over. Mike Smith and I went to Beachy Head that Sunday night and threw all our LPs and cassettes into the sea. Not a word was spoken. We knew it was over. I listen to audio books now.

ON CRIME AND PUNISHMENT

These days we're too easy on criminals. Bring back hanging, I say. Bring back the guillotine. Bring back the firing squad. Bring back nailing criminals to a piece of hardboard, covering them in jam, and letting wasps sting them to death. It was good enough for my Grandfather's generation.

ON POLITICS

Back in 1995, before the scandal, I was approached by Peter Mandelson about running for the Labour Party in a marginal seat. Now I'd always been interested in politics, but I told Mandelson "no". I was too busy with my career. It turned out later that he'd mistaken me for another Donald Wilkins, a gentleman who I believe ran a chain of key-cutting shops in the Northampton area. Still, I wish I'd said yes. I'd probably be Prime Minister now. Then we'd see change.

ON LORD SUNDERLAND

Lord Sunderland is Britain's greatest hero. Without him, I doubt we'd have fought back the Swiss in '54. A legend.

ON THE A71(M) TACKLEFORD RING ROAD

Oh the ring road! Don't get me started! Try getting past Junction 7 (for Coward Cross) between 8 and 8.30. You can't. Static. So here's my idea. Three lanes in either direction are simply not enough. I propose that the A71(M) should operate as an orbital one-way system, thereby increasing capacity to six-lanes.

Obviously, this puts drivers only wishing to travel a short distance against flow of traffic at a disadvantage, as one might have to undertake a 35-mile journey to reach the nearest junction. So on Mondays, Wednesdays and Fridays, the road will run anticlockwise. On Tuesdays and Thursdays, the road will run clockwise. At the weekends, two-way flow is restored. In this way, few are seriously disadvantaged.

Despite a dozen letters to the Departments of Transport of consecutive governments, this proposal has been criminally ignored. This country!

ON HRH PRINCE PHILLIP

Phil's a good lad. He's a mate. Even when things went south for me, he'd still call up for a chat. He's much more down to earth than you'd think. For a long time he was obsessed with Laser Tag, always tapping me up for strategies.

ON FOOD

Beef's the best meat. It just is. The cow's the only beast you'd have in your house. A chicken would be running all over the place. A pig lives in filth. A sheep... don't get me started on sheep! And as for the rest, a zoo, a bloody zoo. But cows... good people. I love eating them.

The best vegetable to eat with beef? I think I'd say the potato. Controversial nowadays, what with the popularity of rice, but I still think the potato is best. Pasta? Forget about it.

ALSO FROM JOHN ALLISON & ONI PRESS

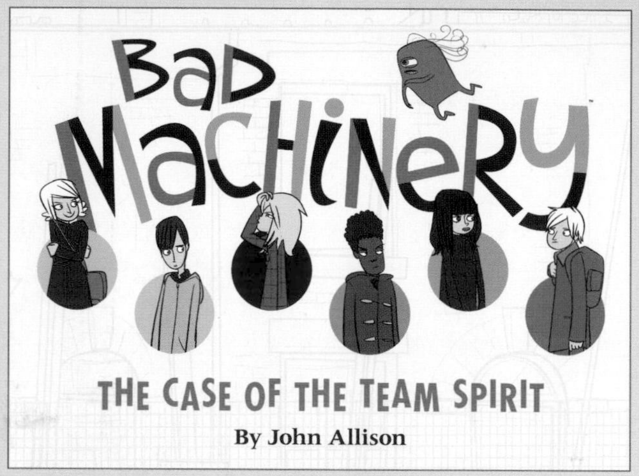

Bad Machinery
THE CASE OF THE TEAM SPIRIT
By John Allison

BAD MACHINERY, VOLUME 1:
THE CASE OF THE TEAM SPIRIT
By John Allison
136 pages, softcover, full color
ISBN 978-1-62010-084-4

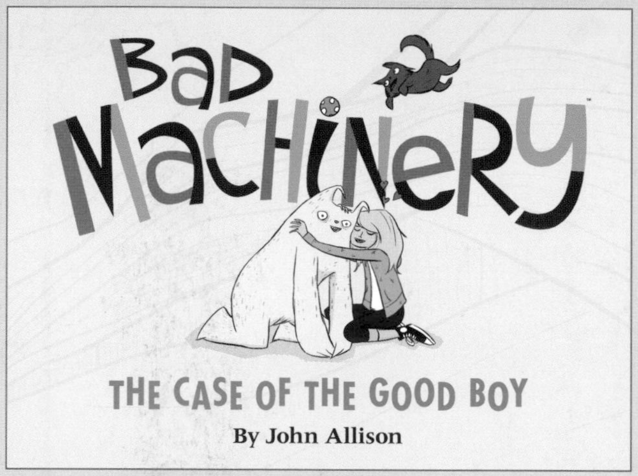

Bad Machinery
THE CASE OF THE GOOD BOY
By John Allison

BAD MACHINERY, VOLUME 2:
THE CASE OF THE GOOD BOY
By John Allison
144 pages, softcover, full color
ISBN 978-1-62010-114-8

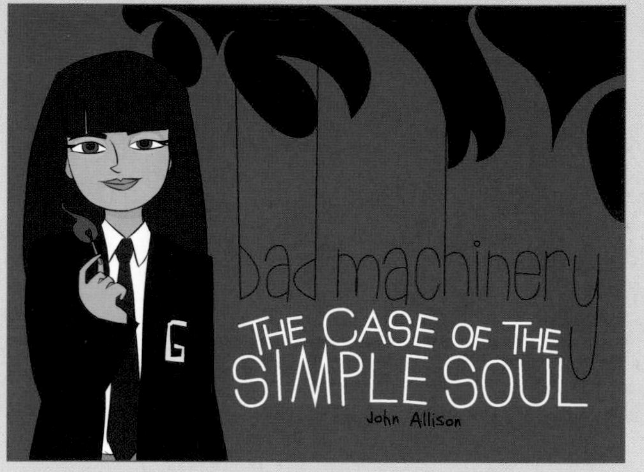

G
bad machinery
THE CASE OF THE
SIMPLE SOUL
John Allison

BAD MACHINERY, VOLUME 3:
THE CASE OF THE SIMPLE SOUL
By John Allison
136 pages, softcover, full color
ISBN 978-1-62010-193-3

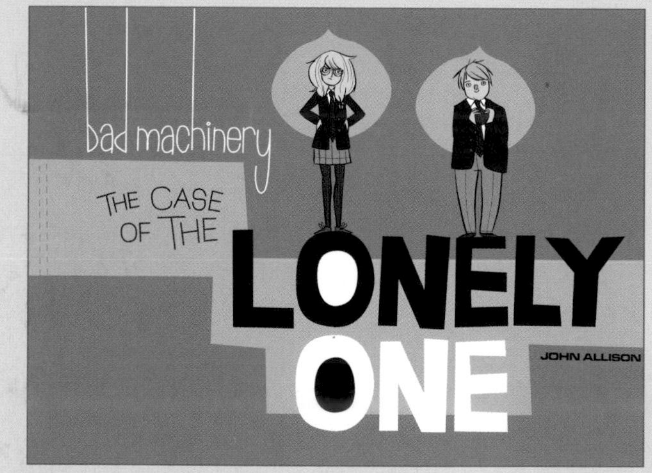

bad machinery
THE CASE OF THE
LONELY
ONE
JOHN ALLISON

BAD MACHINERY, VOLUME 4:
THE CASE OF THE LONELY ONE
By John Allison
136 pages, softcover, full color
ISBN 978-1-62010-212-1

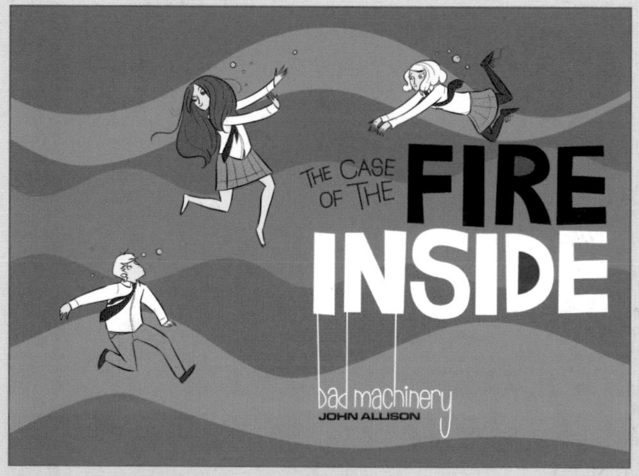

THE CASE OF THE
FIRE
INSIDE
bad machinery
JOHN ALLISON

BAD MACHINERY, VOLUME 5:
THE CASE OF THE FIRE INSIDE
By John Allison
128 pages, softcover, full color

ISBN 978-1-62010-297-8

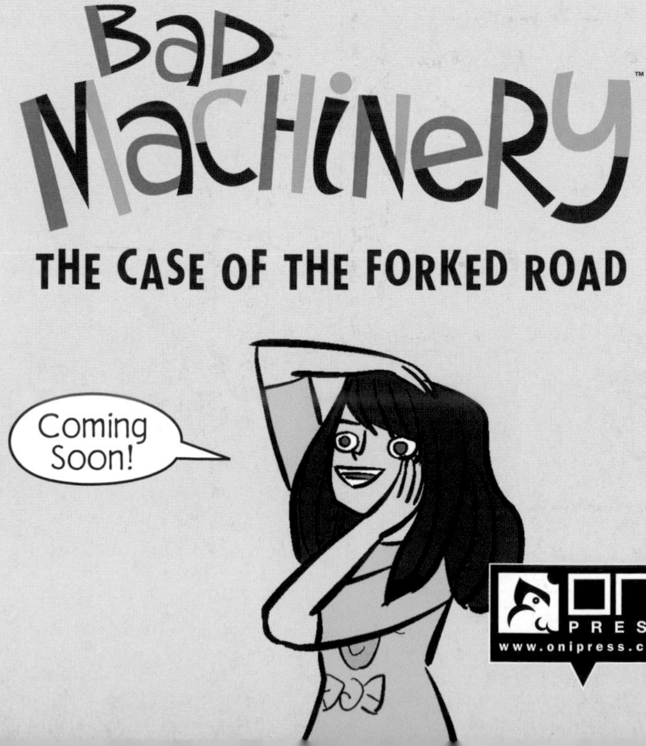

Bad Machinery
THE CASE OF THE FORKED ROAD
Coming Soon!
ONI PRESS
www.onipress.com